FRANCIS FRITH'S

VILLAGES OF KENT PHOTOGRAPHIC MEMORIES

THE FRANCIS FRITH COLLECTION

www.francisfrith.com

Francis Frith's

Villages of Kent

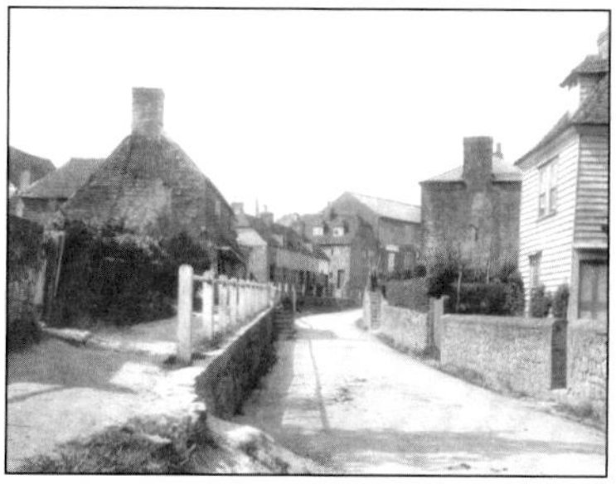

Photographic Memories

Francis Frith's
Villages of Kent

Paul Harris

THE FRANCIS FRITH COLLECTION®

First published in the United Kingdom in 2001 by
The Francis Frith Collection®
Hardback Edition 2001
ISBN 1-85937-445-X

Paperback Edition 2001
ISBN 1-85937-294-5

Reprinted in Paperback 2003, 2006

British Library Cataloguing in Publication Data

Villages of Kent Photographic Memories
Paul Harris

The Francis Frith Collection
Frith's Barn, Teffont,
Salisbury, Wiltshire SP3 5QP
Tel: +44 (0) 1722 716 376
Email: info@francisfrith.co.uk
www.francisfrith.com

Printed and bound in Great Britain

Front Cover: **Chilham, The Post Office 1913** 65335t

Frontispiece: **Wrotham, St Mary's Road 1903** 51026

The colour-tinting is for illustrative purposes only, and is not intended to be historically accurate

AS WITH ANY HISTORICAL DATABASE THE FRITH ARCHIVE IS CONSTANTLY BEING CORRECTED AND IMPROVED AND THE PUBLISHERS WOULD WELCOME INFORMATION ON OMISSIONS OR INACCURACIES

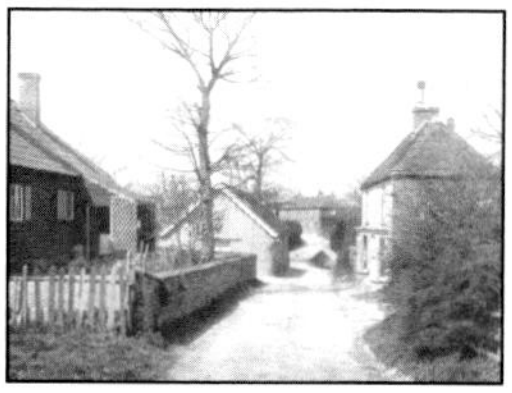

Contents

Francis Frith: *Victorian Pioneer*

Francis Frith, Victorian founder of the world-famous photographic archive, was a complex and multi-talented man. A devout Quaker and a highly successful Victorian businessman, he was both philosophic by nature and pioneering in outlook.

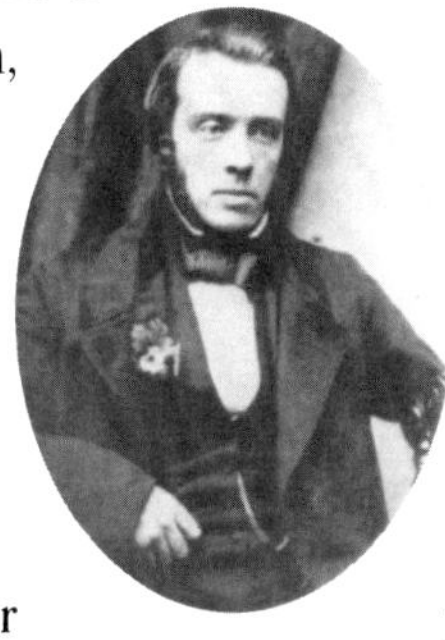

By 1855 Francis Frith had already established a wholesale grocery business in Liverpool, and sold it for the astonishing sum of £200,000, which is the equivalent today of over £15,000,000. Now a very rich man, he was able to indulge his passion for travel. As a child he had pored over travel books written by early explorers, and his fancy and imagination had been stirred by family holidays to the sublime mountain regions of Wales and Scotland. 'What lands of spirit-stirring and enriching scenes and places!' he had written. He was to return to these scenes of grandeur in later years to 'recapture the thousands of vivid and tender memories', but with a different purpose. Now in his thirties, and captivated by the new science of photography, Frith set out on a series of pioneering journeys to the Nile regions that occupied him from 1856 until 1860.

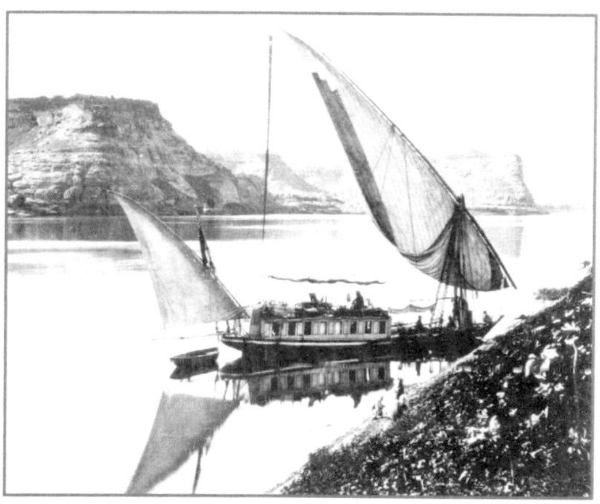

Intrigue and Adventure

He took with him on his travels a specially-designed wicker carriage that acted as both dark-room and sleeping chamber. These far-flung journeys were packed with intrigue and adventure. In his life story, written when he was sixty-three, Frith tells of being held captive by bandits, and of fighting 'an awful midnight battle to the very point of surrender with a deadly pack of hungry, wild dogs'. Sporting flowing Arab costume, Frith arrived at Akaba by camel sixty years before Lawrence, where he encountered 'desert princes and rival sheikhs, blazing with jewel-hilted swords'.

During these extraordinary adventures he was assiduously exploring the desert regions bordering the Nile and patiently recording the antiquities and peoples with his camera. He was the first photographer to venture beyond the sixth cataract. Africa was still the mysterious 'Dark Continent', and Stanley and Livingstone's historic meeting was a decade into the future. The conditions for picture taking confound belief. He laboured for hours in his wicker dark-room in the sweltering heat of the desert, while the volatile chemicals fizzed dangerously in their trays. Often he was forced to work in remote tombs and caves where conditions were cooler. Back in London he exhibited his photographs and was 'rapturously cheered' by members of the Royal Society. His reputation as a photographer was made overnight. An eminent modern historian has likened their impact on the population of the time to that on our own generation of the first photographs taken on the surface of the moon.

Venture of a Life-Time

Characteristically, Frith quickly spotted the opportunity to create a new business as a specialist publisher of photographs. He lived in an era of immense and sometimes violent change. For the poor in the early part of Victoria's reign work was a drudge and the hours long, and people had precious little free time to enjoy themselves. Most had no transport other than a cart or gig at their disposal, and had not travelled far beyond the boundaries of their own town or village. However, by the 1870s, the railways had threaded their way across the country, and Bank Holidays and half-day Saturdays had been made obligatory by Act of Parliament. All of a sudden the ordinary working man and his family were able to enjoy days out and see a little more of the world.

With characteristic business acumen, Francis Frith foresaw that these new tourists would enjoy having souvenirs to commemorate their days out. In 1860 he married Mary Ann Rosling and set out with the intention of photographing every city, town and village in Britain. For the next thirty years he travelled the country by train and by pony and trap, producing fine photographs of seaside resorts and beauty spots that were keenly bought by millions of Victorians. These prints were painstakingly pasted into family albums and pored over during the dark nights of winter, rekindling precious memories of summer excursions.

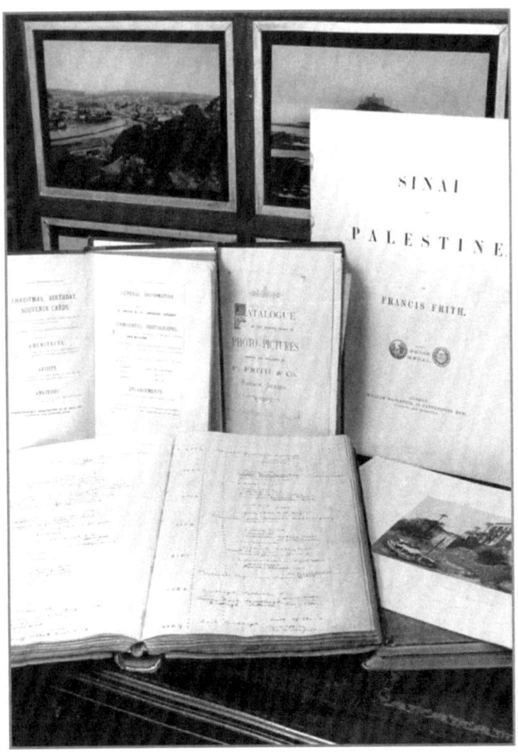

The Rise of Frith & Co

Frith's studio was soon supplying retail shops all over the country. To meet the demand he gathered about him a small team of photographers, and published the work of independent artist-photographers of the calibre of Roger Fenton and Francis Bedford. In order to gain some understanding of the scale of Frith's business one only has to look at the catalogue issued by Frith & Co in 1886: it runs to some 670 pages, listing not only many thousands of views of the British Isles but also many photographs of most European countries, and China, Japan, the USA and Canada – note the sample page shown on page 9 from the hand-written *Frith & Co* ledgers detailing pictures taken. By 1890 Frith had created the greatest specialist photographic publishing company in the

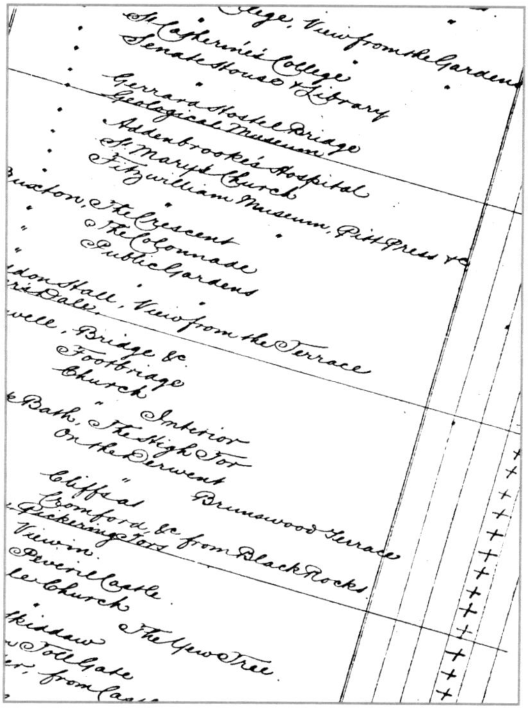
St Catherine's College
Senate House & Library
Gerrard Hostel Bridge
Geological Museum
Addenbrooke's Hospital
St Mary's Church
Fitzwilliam Museum, Pitt Press &c
The Crescent
The Colonnade
Public Gardens
Hall, View from the Terrace
Bridge &c
Footbridge
Church
Interior
The High Tor
On the Derwent
Cliffs at
Brunswood Terrace
Cromford, &c from Black Rocks
View in
Peveril Castle
Church
The Yew Tree
Toll Gate

world, with over 2,000 outlets – more than the combined number that Boots and W H Smith have today! The picture on the right shows the *Frith & Co* display board at Ingleton in the Yorkshire Dales (left of window). Beautifully constructed with a mahogany frame and gilt inserts, it could display up to a dozen local scenes.

Postcard Bonanza

The ever-popular holiday postcard we know today took many years to develop. In 1870 the Post Office issued the first plain cards, with a pre-printed stamp on one face. In 1894 they allowed other publishers' cards to be sent through the mail with an attached adhesive halfpenny stamp. Demand grew rapidly, and in 1895 a new size of postcard was permitted called the court card, but there was little room for illustration. In 1899, a year after Frith's death, a new card measuring 5.5 x 3.5 inches became the standard format, but it was not until 1902 that the divided back came into being, with address and message on one face and a full-size illustration on the other. *Frith & Co* were in the vanguard of postcard development, and Frith's sons Eustace and Cyril continued their father's monumental task, expanding the number of views offered to the public and recording more and more places in Britain, as the coasts and countryside were opened up to mass travel.

Francis Frith died in 1898 at his villa in Cannes, his great project still growing. The archive he created continued in business for another seventy years. By 1970 it contained over a third of a million pictures of 7,000 cities, towns and villages. The massive photographic record Frith has left to us stands as a living monument to a special and very remarkable man.

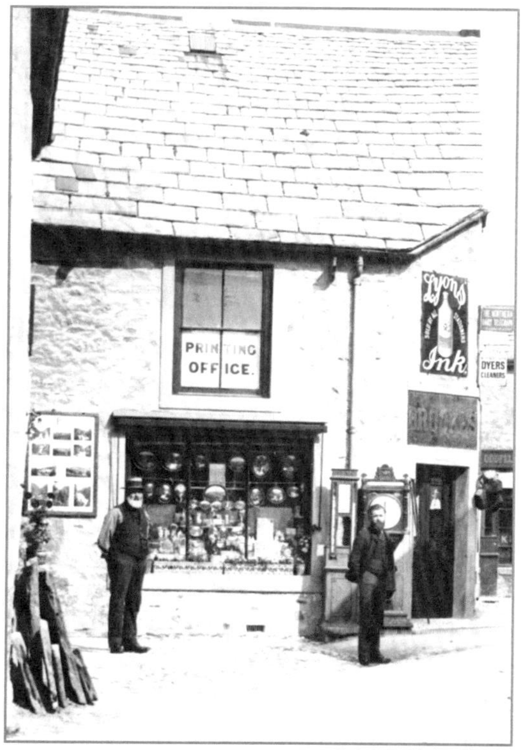

Frith's Archive: *A Unique Legacy*

Francis Frith's legacy to us today is of immense significance and value, for the magnificent archive of evocative photographs he created provides a unique record of change in 7,000 cities, towns and villages throughout Britain over a century and more. Frith and his fellow studio photographers revisited locations many times down the years to update their views, compiling for us an enthralling and colourful pageant of British life and character.

We tend to think of Frith's sepia views of Britain as nostalgic, for most of us use them to conjure up memories of places in our own lives with which we have family associations. It often makes us forget that to Francis Frith they were records of daily life as it was actually being lived in the cities, towns and villages of his day. The Victorian age was one of great and often bewildering change for ordinary people, and though the pictures evoke an impression of slower times, life was as busy and hectic as it is today.

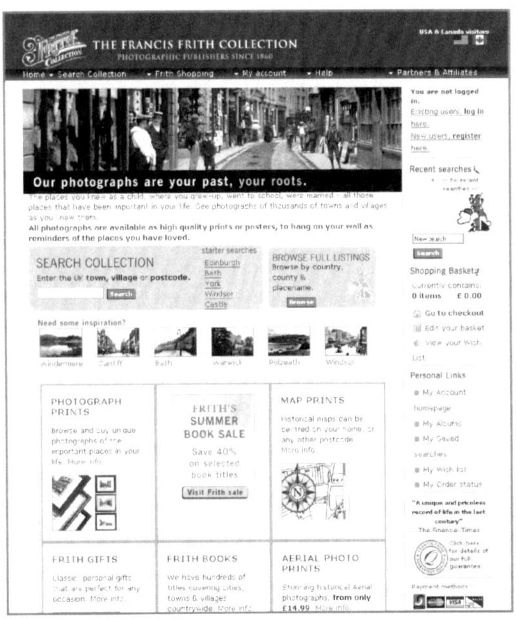

See Frith at www.francisfrith.com

We are fortunate that Frith was a photographer of the people, dedicated to recording the minutiae of everyday life. For it is this sheer wealth of visual data, the painstaking chronicle of changes in dress, transport, street layouts, buildings, housing, engineering and landscape that captivates us so much today. His remarkable images offer us a powerful link with the past and with the lives of our ancestors.

Today's Technology

Computers have now made it possible for Frith's many thousands of images to be accessed almost instantly. In the Frith archive today, each photograph is carefully 'digitised' then stored on a CD Rom. Frith archivists can locate a single photograph amongst thousands within seconds. Views can be catalogued and sorted under a variety of categories of place and content to the immediate benefit of researchers.

Inexpensive reference prints can be created for them at the touch of a mouse button, and a wide range of books and other printed materials assembled and published for a wider, more general readership. The day-to-day workings of the archive are very different from how they were in Francis Frith's time: imagine the herculean task of sorting through eleven tons of glass negatives as Frith had to do to locate a particular sequence of pictures! Yet the archive still prides itself on maintaining the same high standards of excellence laid down by Francis Frith, including the painstaking cataloguing and indexing of every view.

It is curious to reflect on how the internet now allows researchers in America and elsewhere greater instant access to the archive than Frith himself ever enjoyed. Many thousands of individual views can be called up on screen within seconds on one of the Frith internet sites, enabling people living continents away to revisit the streets of their ancestral home town, or view places in Britain where they have enjoyed holidays. Many overseas researchers welcome the chance to view special theme selections, such as transport, sports, costume and ancient monuments.

We are certain that Francis Frith would have heartily approved of these modern developments in imaging techniques, for he himself was always working at the very limits of Victorian photographic technology.

The Value of the Archive Today

Because of the benefits brought by the computer, Frith's images are increasingly studied by social historians, by researchers into genealogy and ancestory, by architects, town planners, and by teachers and schoolchildren involved in local history projects.

In addition, the archive offers every one of us an opportunity to examine the places where we and our families have lived and worked down the years. Highly successful in Frith's own era, the archive is now, a century and more on, entering a new phase of popularity.

The Past in Tune with the Future

Historians consider the Francis Frith Collection to be of prime national importance. It is the only archive of its kind remaining in private ownership and has been valued at a million pounds. However, this figure is now rapidly increasing as digital technology enables more and more people around the world to enjoy its benefits.

Francis Frith's archive is now housed in an historic timber barn in the beautiful village of Teffont in Wiltshire. Its founder would not recognize the archive office as it is today. In place of the many thousands of dusty boxes containing glass plate negatives and an all-pervading odour of photographic chemicals, there are now ranks of computer screens. He would be amazed to watch his images travelling round the world at unimaginable speeds through network and internet lines.

The archive's future is both bright and exciting. Francis Frith, with his unshakeable belief in making photographs available to the greatest number of people, would undoubtedly approve of what is being done today with his lifetime's work. His photographs, depicting our shared past, are now bringing pleasure and enlightenment to millions around the world a century and more after his death.

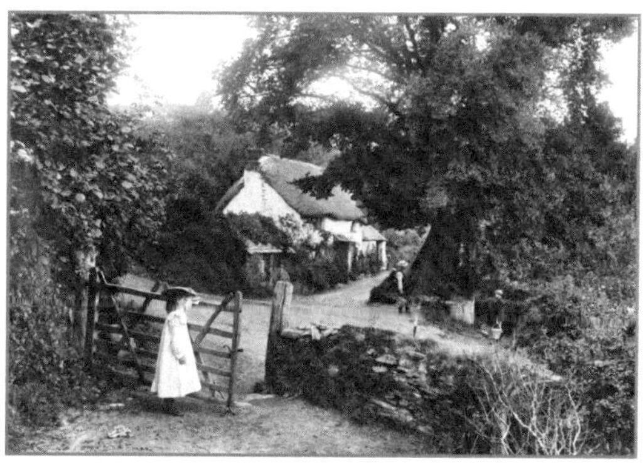

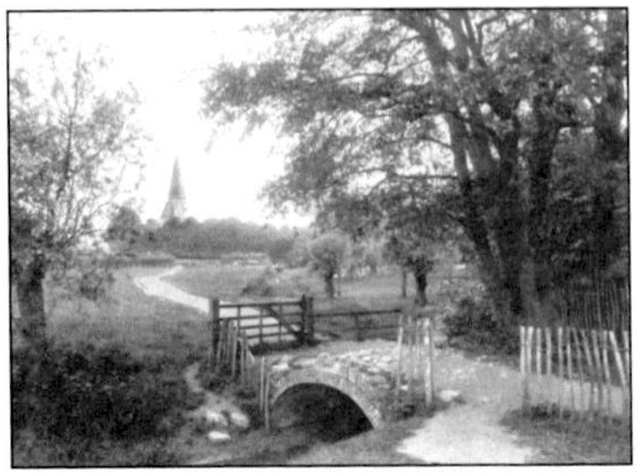

Villages of Kent - *An Introduction*

It has been estimated that Kent contains as many as 300 villages. Although I have not counted them personally, looking at the map convinces me there are at least that number, and possibly more. Not all Kent's villages were photographed by Francis Frith and his successors, so you will not see each and every one featured in the pages of this book. What is pictured, however, is a good representation of villages and village life in the 'Garden of England' from around the end of the 19th century up to about 40 years ago. Of course, much has changed, even since the 1960s, and major commercial and residential developments have transformed the face of the county beyond recognition in some places. The coming of the motorways, out of town shopping and the Channel Tunnel have also wrought many changes to the rural scene, though this has not necessarily always been for the worse.

Scenically, Kent is an interestingly diverse county, which divides readily into areas with distinct characteristics. For the purpose of this book, I have defined them as firstly, the area between the Medway and Thames rivers, largely in the north and west of the county; secondly, west Kent and the Weald, which stretches almost down to the edge of Romney Marsh, and borders on Sussex; thirdly, the North Downs from between Ashford and Maidstone down towards and including Romney Marsh; and finally, east Kent from the North Sea to the Channel Coast near Dover.

Between the Thames and Medway, despite modern development, there are still oases of rural

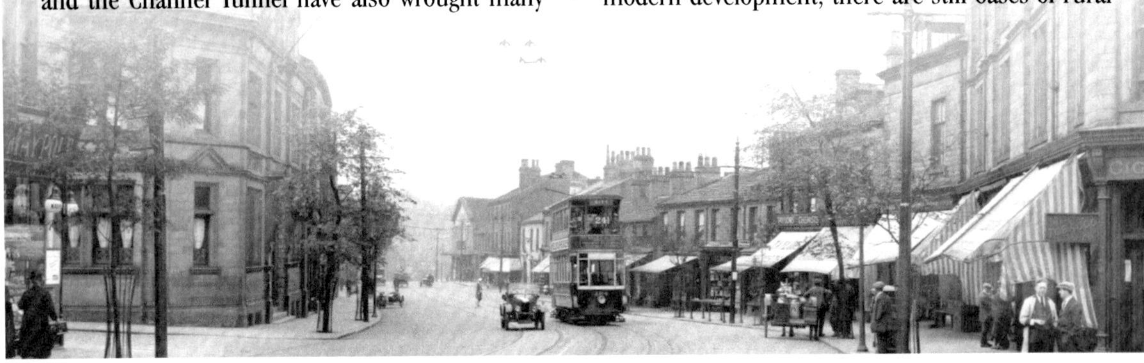

calm to be found, which are sometimes in dramatic contrast to their surroundings. For instance, the much-photographed village of Aylesford, said to be one of England's oldest, sits almost next to an extensive industrial estate, whilst prehistoric megalithic structures overlook it from the hills above. Similarly, Charles Dickens's landscape of the Isle of Grain is within sight of a massive power station and the passing traffic of the Thames. In the western part of this area, some of the villages are said to be the most attractive in Kent.

The river Medway is responsible for that well-known but mysterious division of Kent into two halves. To the east and south of the river the inhabitants are known as 'Men of Kent', whilst to the north and west they are known as 'Kentishmen'. Some date this division to a battle fought in the year 455AD between the Jutes or Saxons under Hengist and the Britons under Vortigern. This supposedly took place on the Medway, and led to the partition of the kingdom. Others point to the probable creation of two Romano-British administrative units during the 5th century, the distinctions long outliving the memory of these kingdoms. We shall probably never know the real reason.

West Kent and what is known as the Weald present an entirely different prospect. Here the oast houses and attractive white weatherboarded cottages sit amidst woodland and pasture, conveying a more traditional countryside image to the visitor. This is an area of villages with wide thoroughfares, of warm beer and cricket on the green. Here the landscape includes large country houses, for instance those of the authors Sir Arthur Conan Doyle and Vita Sackville West, and the 'secret garden' of Frances Hodgson Burnett. Here we are on the border of the neighbouring county; as someone once said, on warm summer evenings 'a dog barking in Sussex can be heard in Kent'.

Different again is the area from the North Downs south to Romney Marsh. Within a stone's throw of Ashford, the 'haunted' village of Pluckley and its neighbour Smarden were the inspiration for H E Bates's popular 'The Darling Buds of May', which has been made into a television production in recent years.

Further south, down on Romney Marsh, we enter a world of medieval churches, smugglers and morning mists that linger over the water-filled dykes. Here the empty expanses echo to the croak of marsh frogs and the plaintive call of wading birds. This isolation has over the years been much sought after by those of an artistic or literary inclination. During the 20th century the area was home and inspiration to Edith Nesbit, Russell Thorndike, Noel Coward, H G Wells and Joseph Conrad, among others.

The expansion of Ashford in recent years, and the siting of two nuclear power stations at Dungeness and the coming of the M20 and the Channel Tunnel, although causing a major impact, have still left much rural beauty unaffected. Many

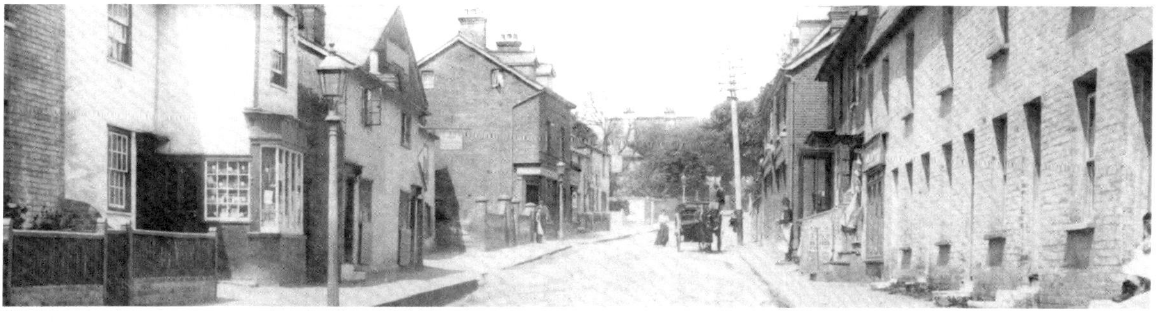

of the scenes depicted in this book are little changed today, and in some cases new bypasses have restored the tranquillity of earlier years to some Kentish villages.

East Kent is bordered on two sides by sea, the North Sea and the Channel. Between the two lie marshland, downs, hops, blossom and apple orchards, estuary and cliff. To this landscape have come invading Celts, Romans, Saxons, and Vikings. Napoleon and Hitler would have liked to have done the same - and modern tourists still do in their thousands. This is Kent's much fortified 'bulwark shore'. The history of this part of Kent is to a large extent the history of England itself, a heritage that can be seen and sensed in the ancient settlements to be found in this evocative part of the Kentish countryside.

Not all here is to do with war and invasion, though. This fertile ground has given rise to innovation of one sort or another down through the years. East Kent, after all, gave us the Church of England, James Bond, the humble sandwich and Viagra! The landscape abounds in legend and mystery. It is said that Hengist and Horsa arrived at Pegwell Bay in three keels to become the leaders of the first Saxon settlers in Kent. Here, too, it is said, came Saint Augustine in the year 597 to bring Roman Christianity to the Saxon inhabitants of Kent. Also, according to the medieval historian Geoffrey of Monmouth, King Arthur fought his adversary Modred at nearby Richborough when returning from wars in Gaul. Some of the villages in this vicinity are rumoured to be the final resting place of a solid gold treasure, a buried 'golden man', which awaits discovery by a lucky archaeologist or treasure-seeker. Perhaps the labyrinth of tunnels carved out of the chalk beneath the village of Eastry was the result of an attempt to find the treasure. These caves have been claimed to be the secret hiding place of Thomas Becket whilst escaping the wrath of his adversaries in the 1170s.

Kent is fertile ground indeed: its history, folklore and traditions are still preserved in the many and interesting villages and hamlets that lie scattered amongst its hills and valleys and along its coasts.

I have dealt with each area in a sort of broad geographical sequence in this book. Therefore, although the photographs are not put in exact order of a 'tour', the locations follow a coherent direction, so that those appearing next to one another in the text are likely to be near in geographical terms also. In 'Between the Thames and Medway' I have started at the westerly end of the area and moved steadily eastwards to end on the Isle of Grain. I have explored 'The Weald of Kent' by starting in the Tunbridge Wells area and moving south-eastwards through the Weald to the borders of Romney Marsh. 'The North Downs to the Marsh' is more or less as the chapter title says, starting at Lenham and moving southwards to Romney Marsh and then eastwards along the coast. 'Coast to Coast' starts on the remote and sometimes lonely Isle of Sheppey next to the

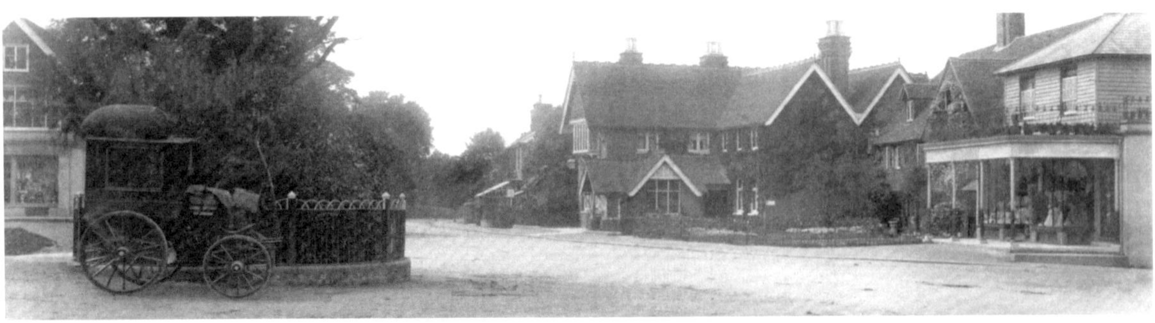

North Sea, and progresses across the county to the area between Canterbury and the coast at Pegwell Bay; thence it goes southwards to St Margaret's at Cliffe, the picturesque village that has been the starting point for many a Channel swimmer, and is England's nearest point to continental Europe.

I hope you enjoy this collection of fine quality photographs from the Frith archives of some of the villages of Kent, and the people and activities that were found within them. In these fast-changing times, it can be helpful to understand and appreciate the past in order to put our own lives, times and concerns into broader context. I hope this book will be of some assistance in this appreciation.

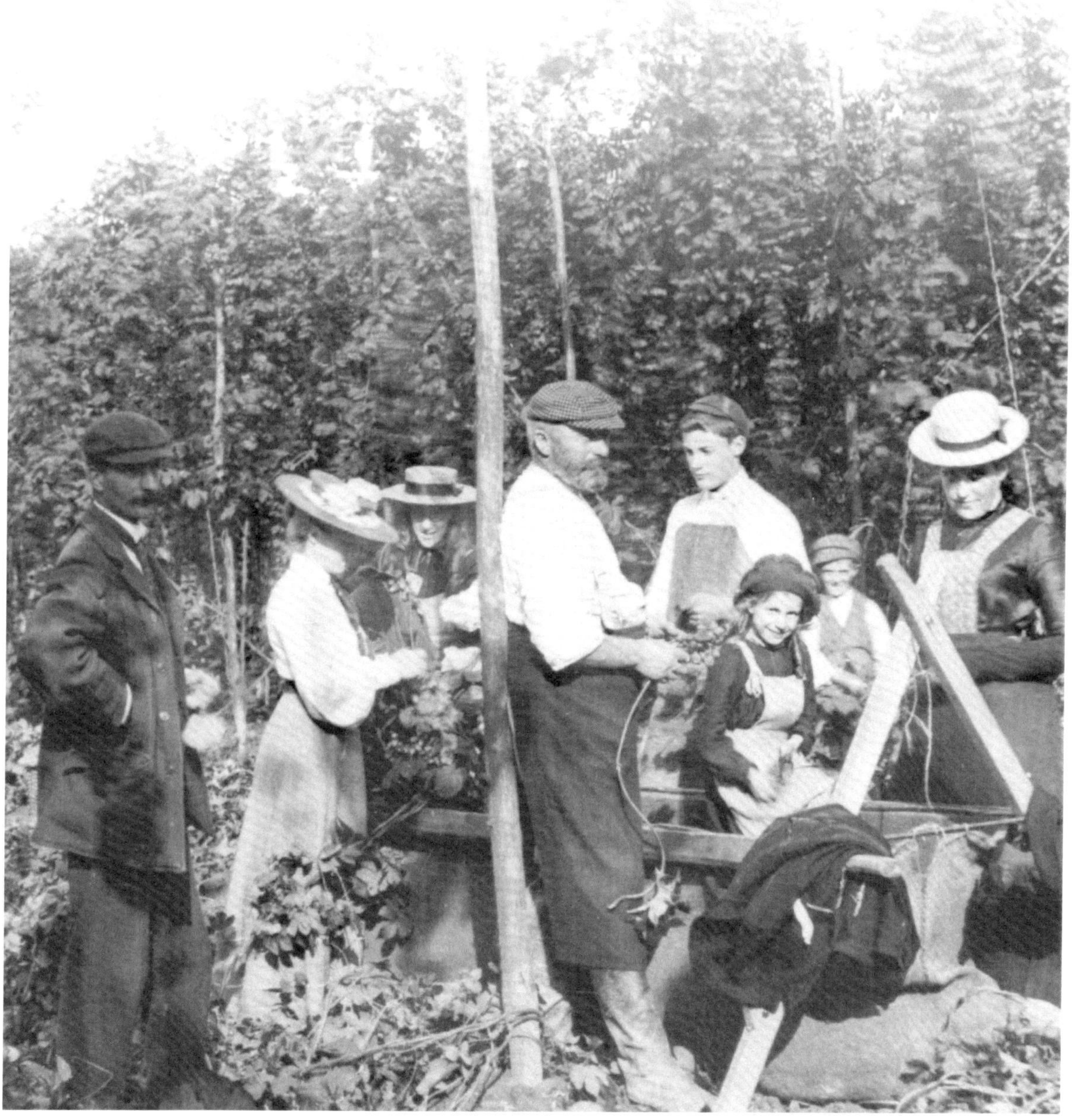

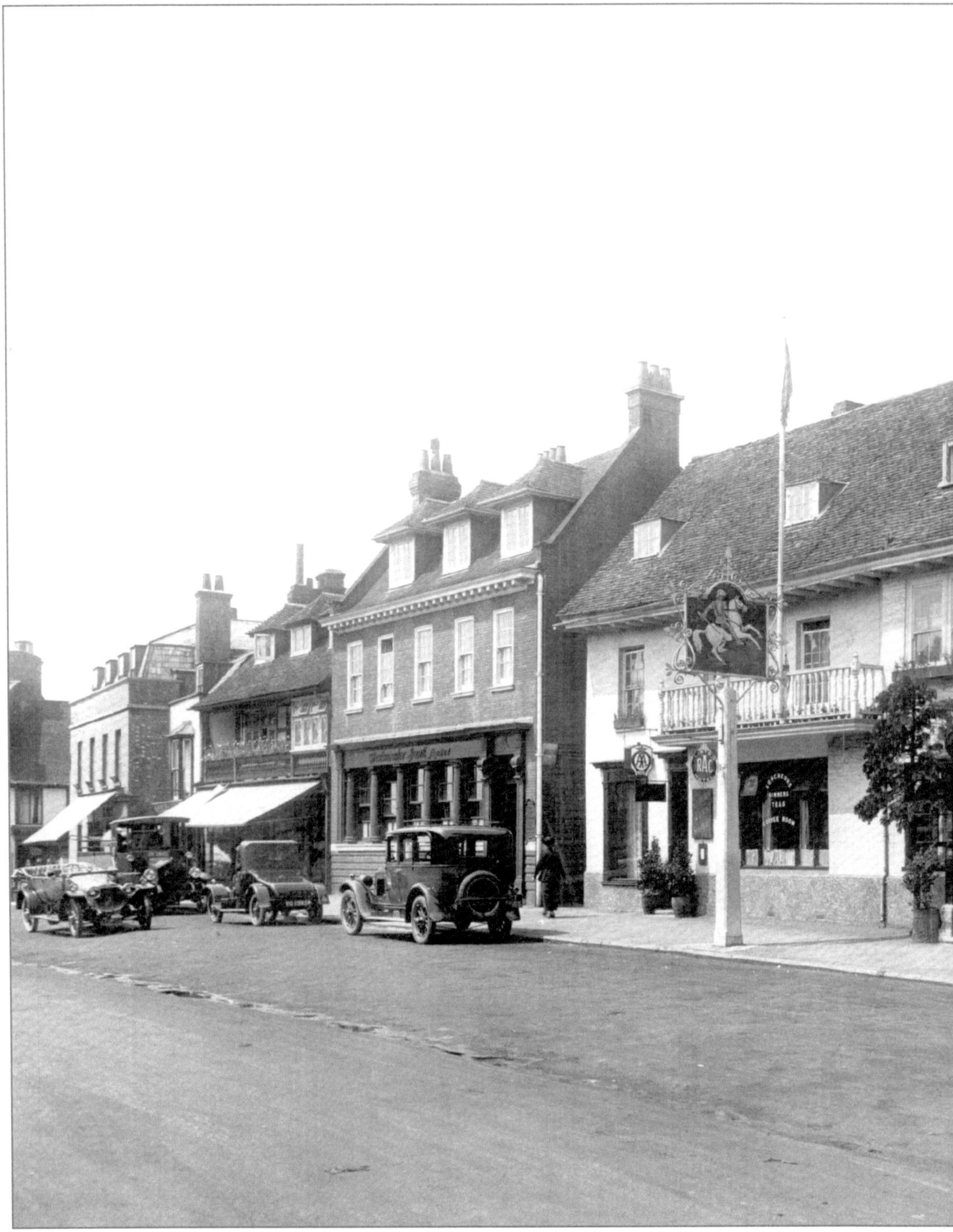
RAC
DINNERS
TEAS

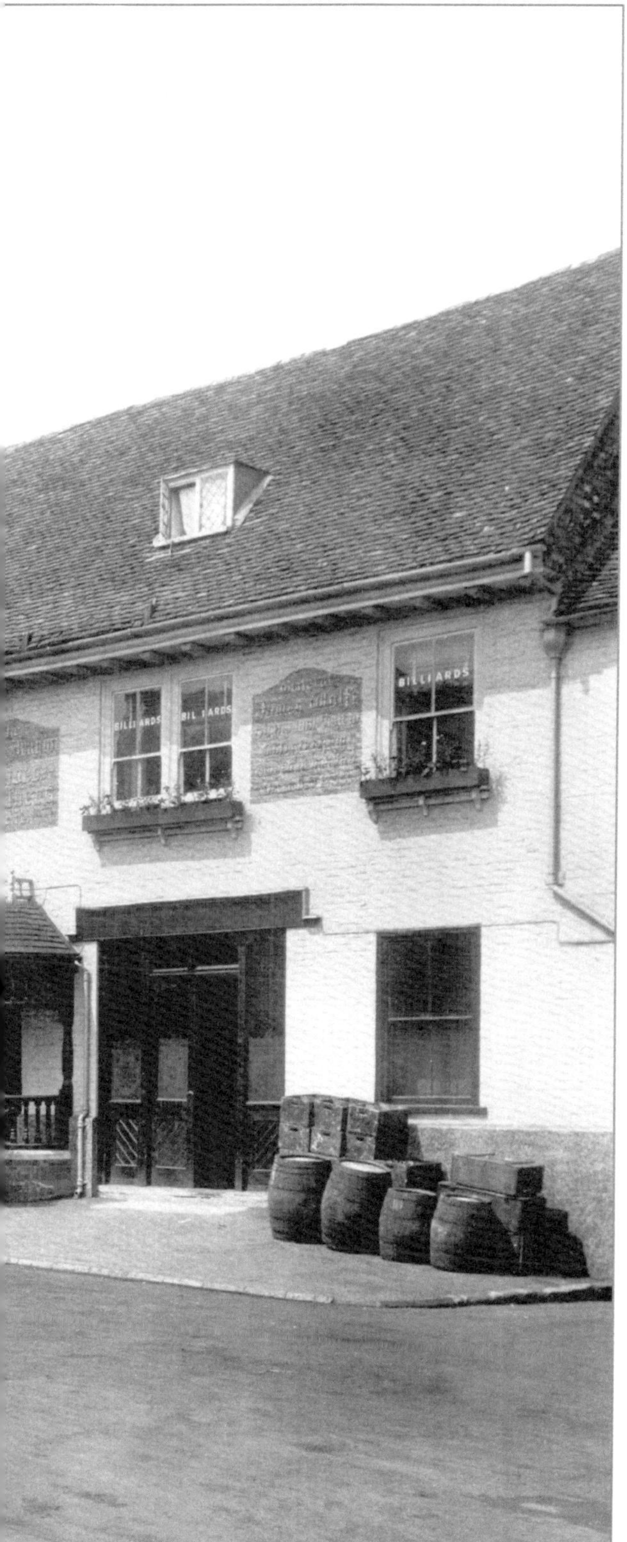

Between the Thames and the Medway

Westerham, The Village 1925 78191
It is a quiet morning in this pleasant small town, situated on a gentle hill a few miles west of Sevenoaks. General Wolfe spent his childhood in Quebec House and is said to have passed his last night in his beloved town at the George and Dragon, shown here in the foreground. The Westminster Bank (third building in from either side of the picture) seems busy enough, judging by the cars parked outside.

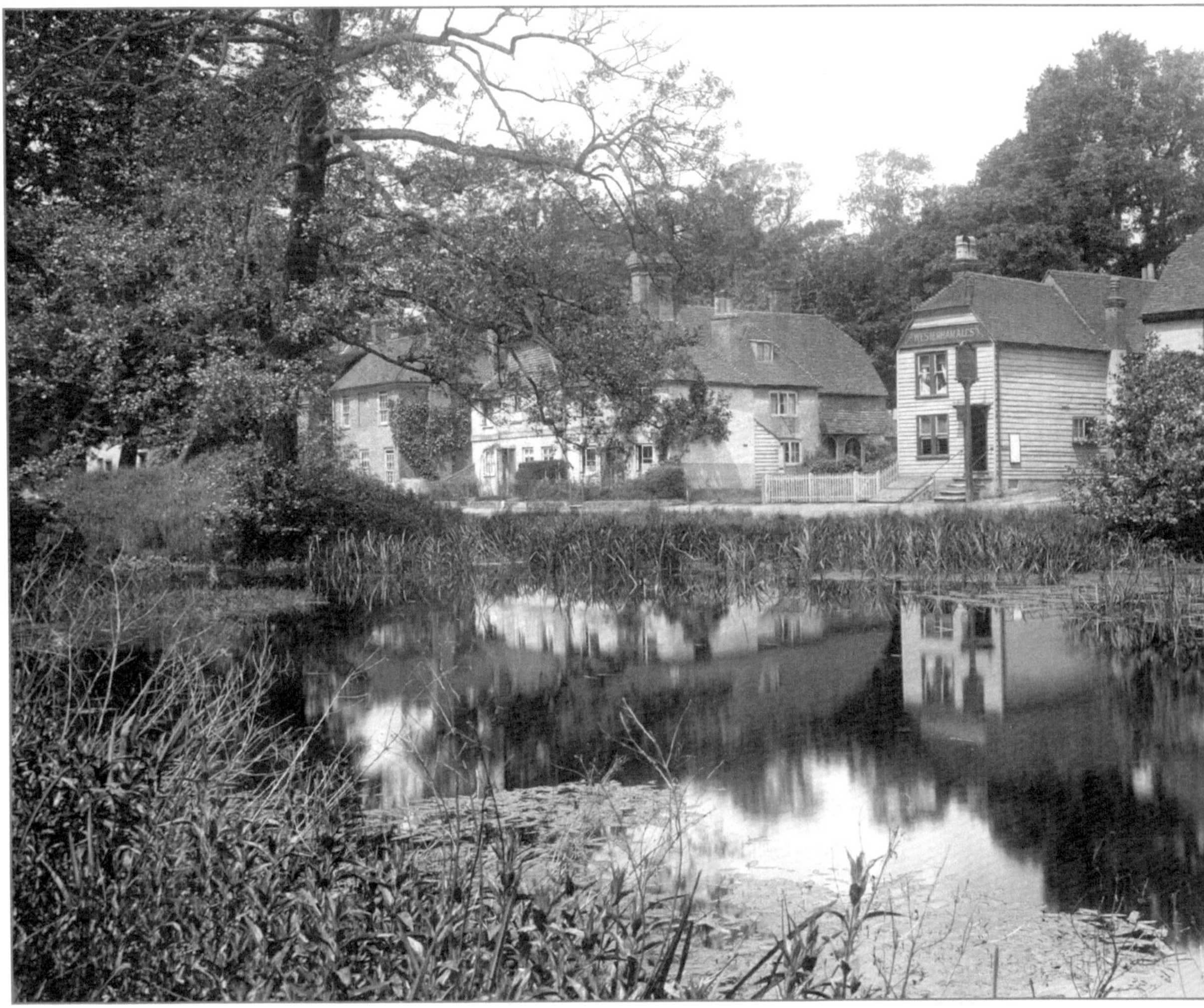

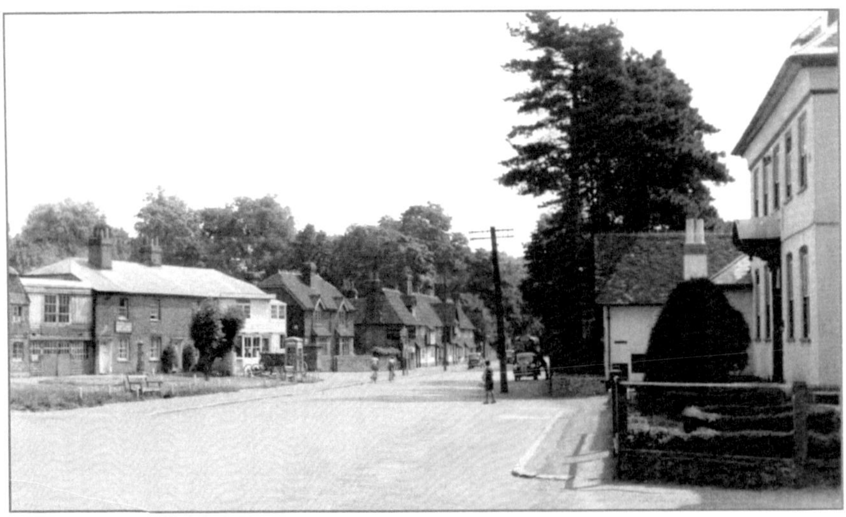

Brasted, The Village c1955 B580006
Brasted stands on the river Darent, four miles west of Sevenoaks. Its broad, spacious street is fringed with brick and weatherboarded cottages in the Wealden style.

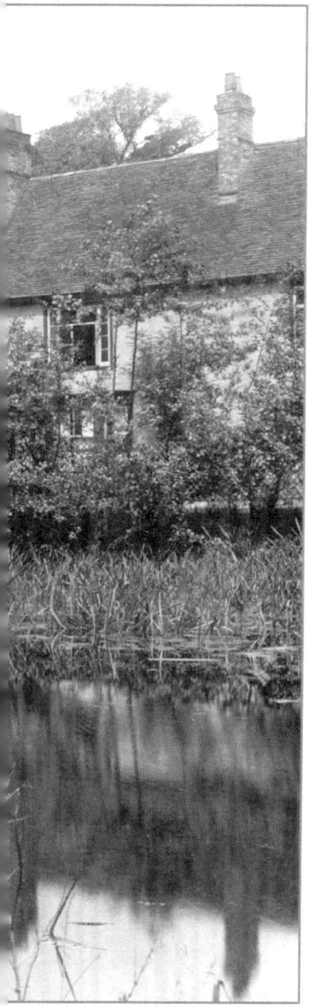

◄ **Westerham**
The Village 1922

78191A

A beautifully tranquil scene is created by the water in the foreground. The simple weatherboarded house with the half-hipped roof in the middle of the line of buildings is a public house. It is selling Westerham-brewed ales, though its sign is, unfortunately, illegible.

▼ **Brasted, The Village c1955**

B580033

This is a quiet residential road in a village of fine buildings. The most impressive is probably Brasted Place, built by Robert Adam in local stone for the court physician of George III, John Turton, for services rendered. Brasted Place was the seat iof the Tipping family, and once the retreat of the ousted monarch Louis Napoleon, who could be seen walking the streets with his tame eagle.

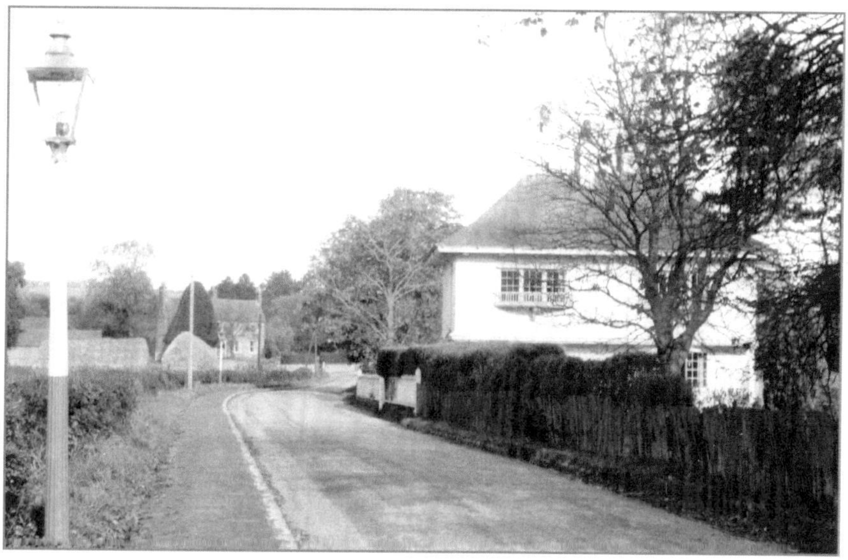

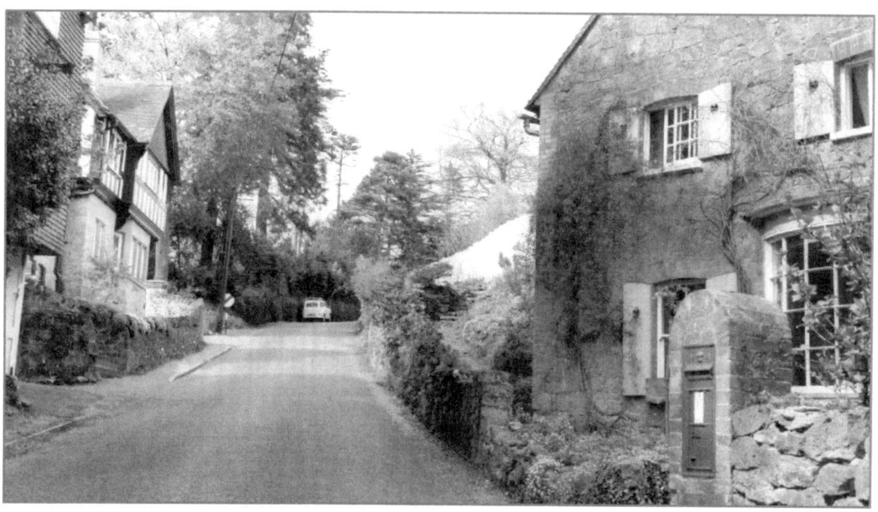

◄ **Crockham Hill**
The Village c1955

C467029

This lovely village is said to command one of the finest views in Kent across the Weald towards Ashdown Forest. It sits alongside the Surrey boundary, two miles north of Edenbridge. Octavia Hill, one of the pioneering founders of the National Trust, is buried in the churchyard.

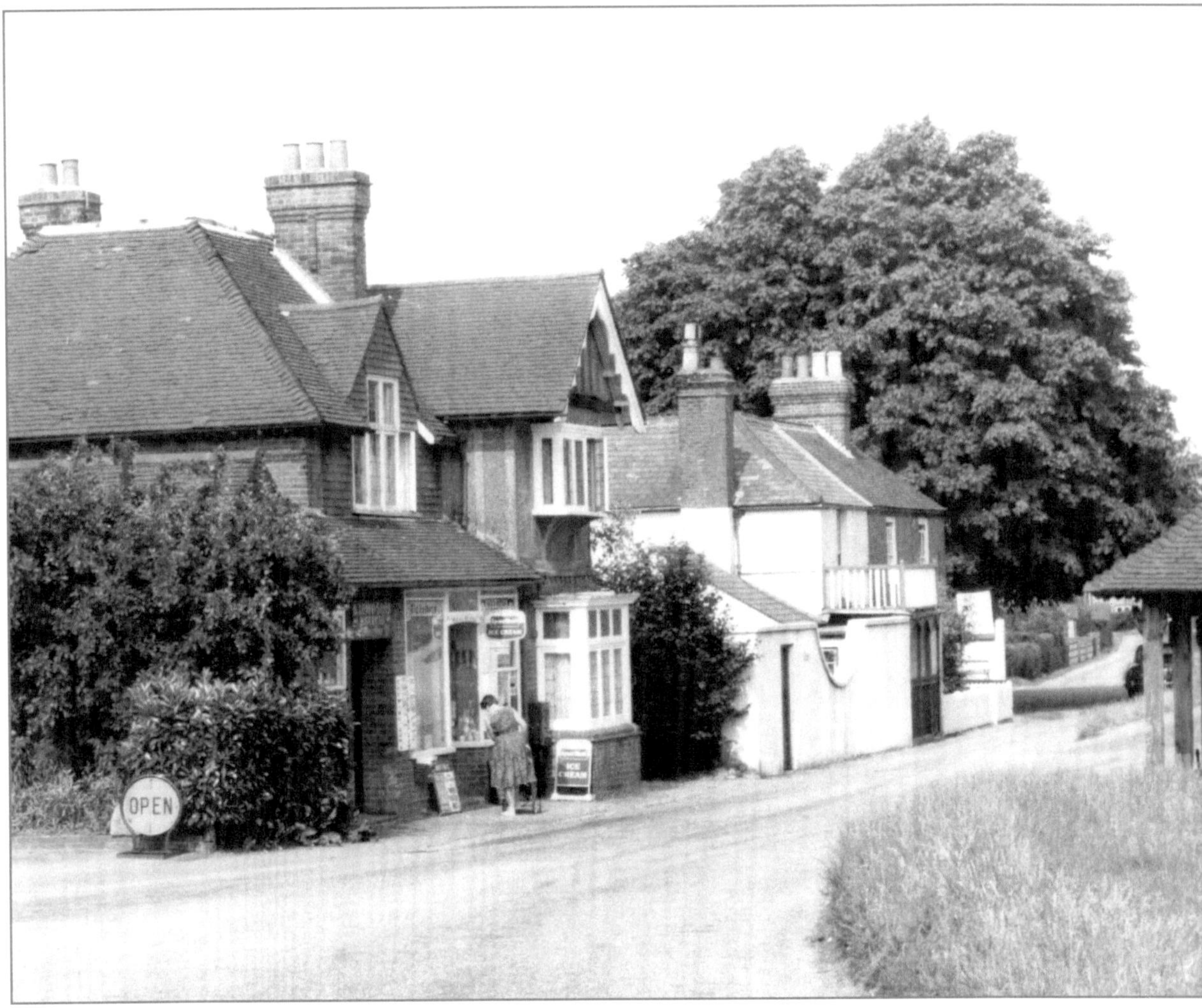

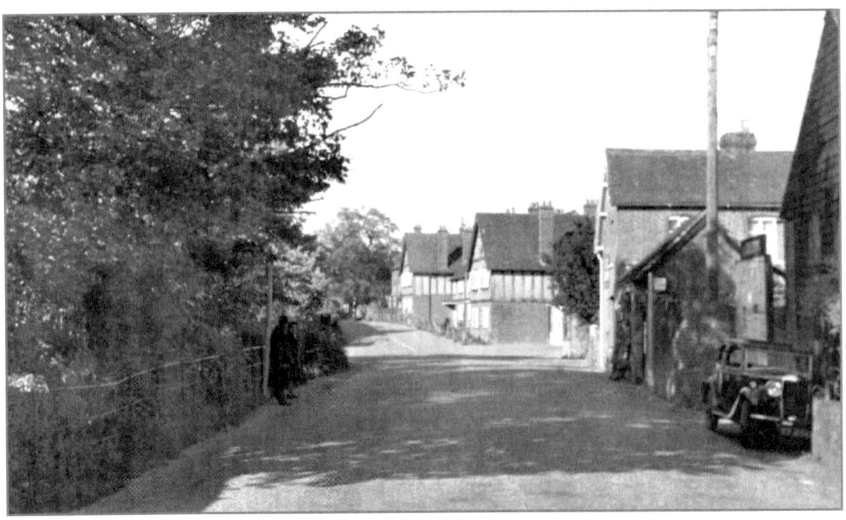

◄ **Four Elms**
The Village c1950
F156005
Four miles south-east of Westerham, Four Elms has developed in recent years, as a result of the spread of the railways into rural Kent and the growth of commuter travel.

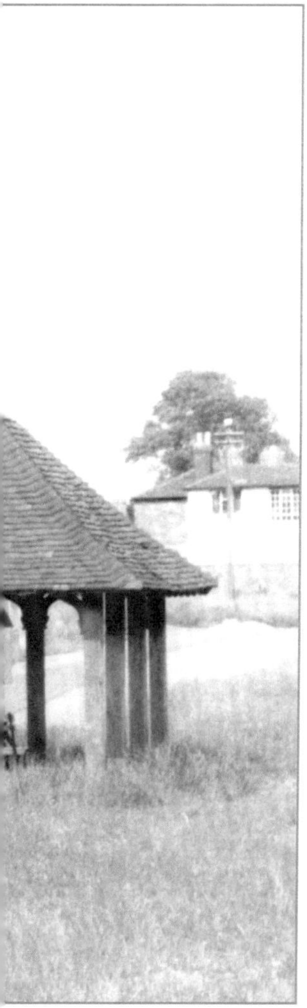

Ide Hill, The Village c1960 149036
Ide Hill is little more than a hamlet, but it is an attractively-situated one. Like Crockham Hill, it is well-placed on the greensand ridge overlooking the Weald and its woodlands. Ide Hill sits on one of the highest points in Kent, and was one of the first acquisitions of the National Trust.

Hever, The Church 1906 53552
This view of the village was taken in the days before its castle, once the home of Anne Boleyn, became internationally famous and attracted hordes of visitors. The splendid 14th-century tower and wood-shingled spire of the parish church rise over the cottage roofs. Inside there is a fine old barrel roof and Jacobean pulpit. On the right, sitting down amongst his wares, we can just see a basket-maker at work.

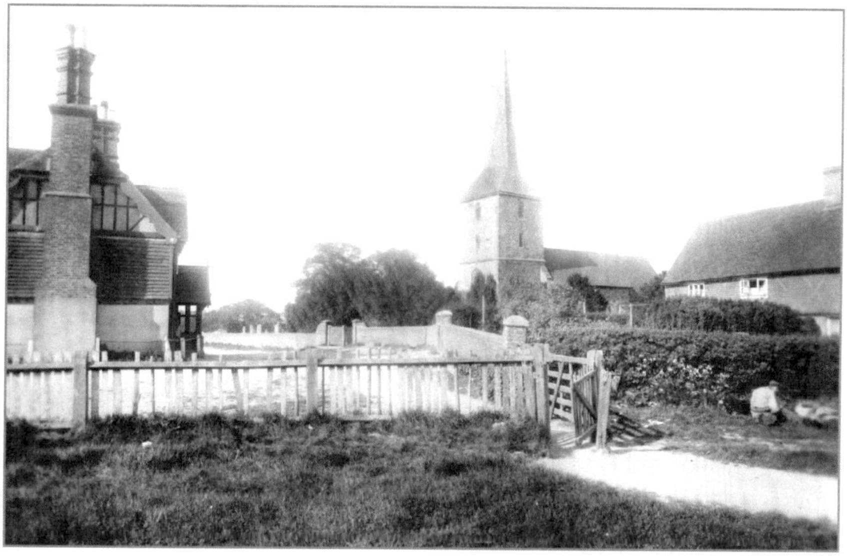

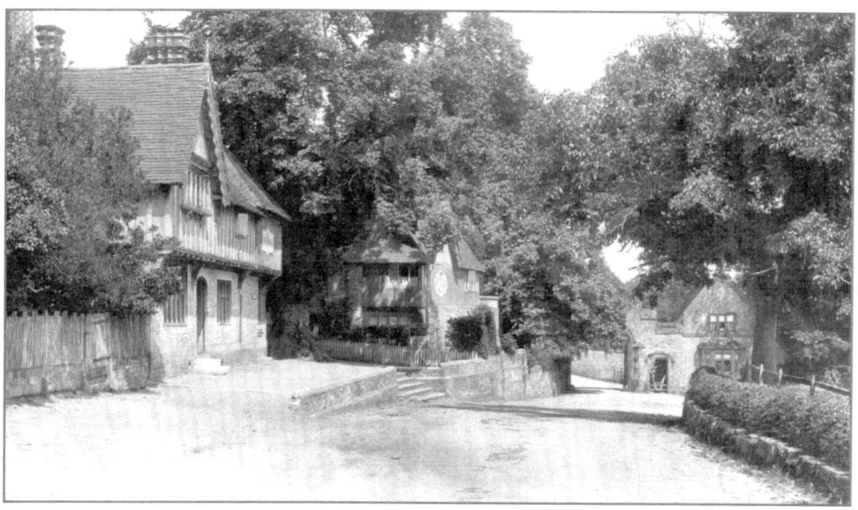

Penshurst, The Village 1891 29388
The village is more well-known for its much-visited stately home, Penshurst Place - its entrance arch can be seen at the bottom of the lane. However, it is delightfully attractive in its own right, as we can see from this view, which shows late 15th-century timber-framed buildings close by the church. The village stands at the confluence of the rivers Eden and Medway and was originally known as Penchester.

▼ **Chiddingstone, The Church and Cottages c1955** C86013

This little cluster of 16th- and 17th-century gabled timbered cottages, along with the pub (not visible in the photograph), was acquired in its entirety by the National Trust in 1939. The church is 14th-century in the main. Chiddingstone is often claimed to be the most attractive village in Kent. Wild boar once roamed the surrounding countryside, and are commemorated here in the names of Boar Place and Boreshill.

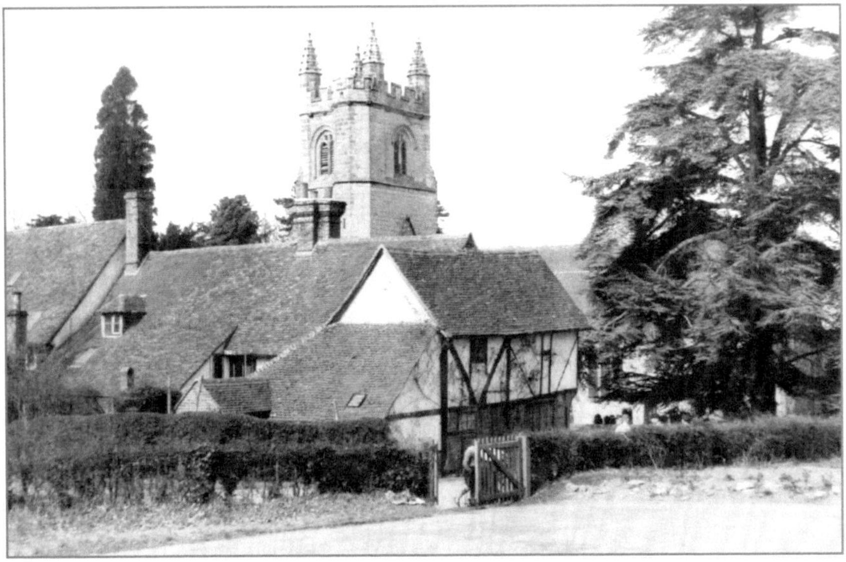

▼ **Leigh, The Old Oak Tree and the Green c1960** L539009

Leigh stands near the River Medway, and is another contender for the 'most attractive village in Kent' title. Certainly it seems very well planned around its spacious central green with its mature chestnut trees. Note the beautiful weatherboarded house surrounded by the picket fence on the right. Locals sometimes call the village Lye or West Leigh. The village boasted a mineral spring of similar quality to those in Tunbridge Wells.

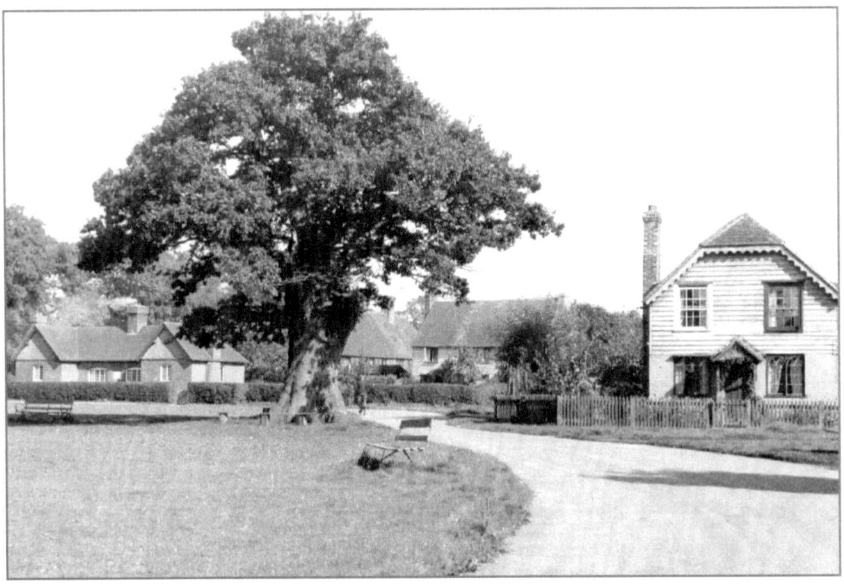

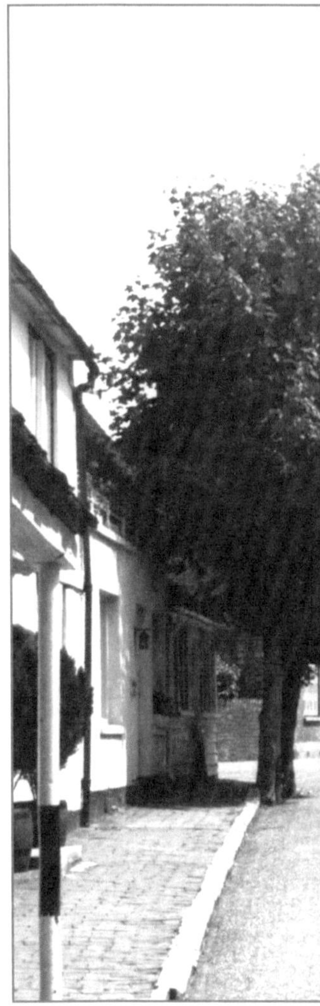

▲ **Cowden, The Village c1965** C225032

This beautiful village is situated on the Sussex border on a headstream of the Medway river. The village contains a number of fine weatherboarded houses and a school with Tudor timbering. Note that on the left-hand side of the road the old trees are now obliged to sink their roots in tarmac. The village seems so much at peace that it is hard to believe there was once a thriving iron foundry close by at Furnace Mill.

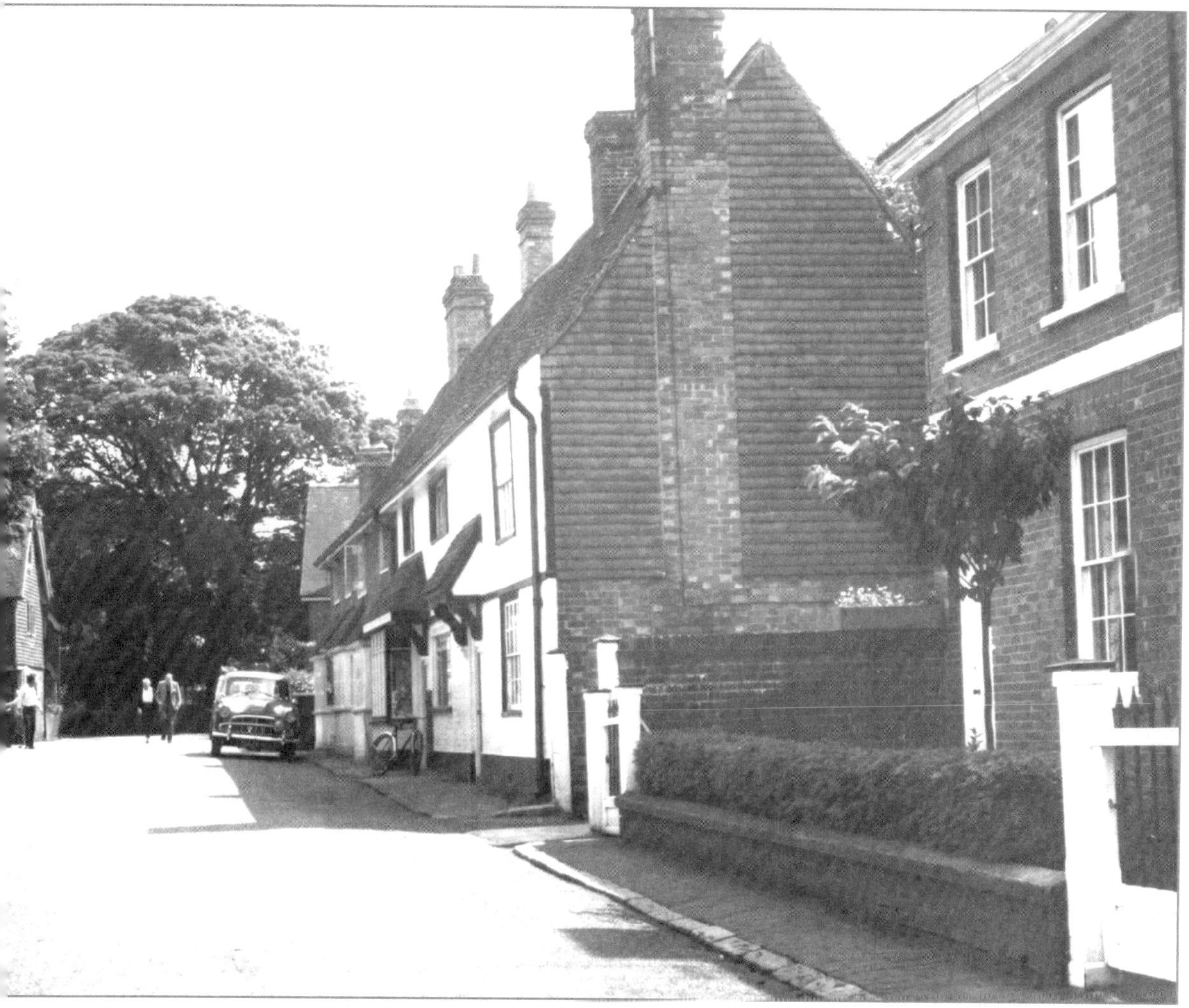

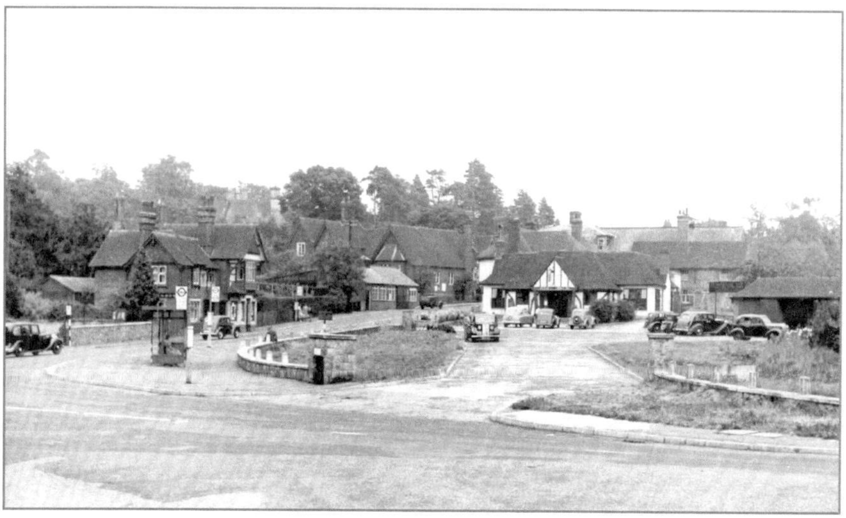

Riverhead, The Square c1950 R319005
This comparatively busy scene for the 1950s suggests that we are near a more substantial settlement here - Riverhead has now been absorbed by the sprawl of Sevenoaks. However, there are still some splendid Georgian houses. The church, with its small spire, was built in the Decorated style in 1831. Montreal Park, the seat of Earl Amherst, stands close by in fine grounds.

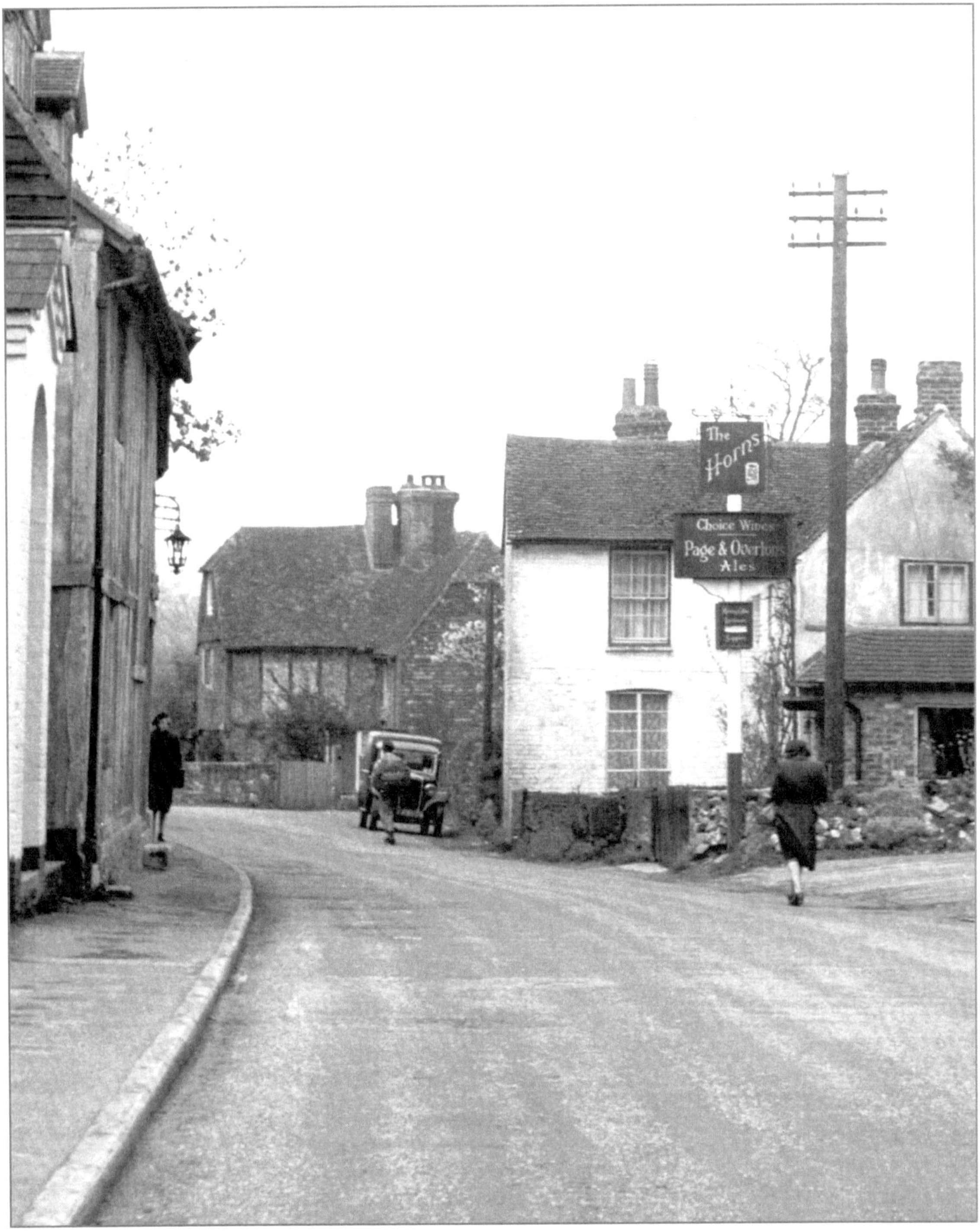

Otford, High Street c1950 087005
Otford is on the main Sevenoaks to Dartford road, alongside the River Darent; it has become something of a commuter village today. New road developments have done away with the village green, but were obliged to skirt the village pond - it now sits in the middle of a roundabout. It is said to be the only pond designated as a listed building! This wonderfully nostalgic scene reminds us of quieter days.

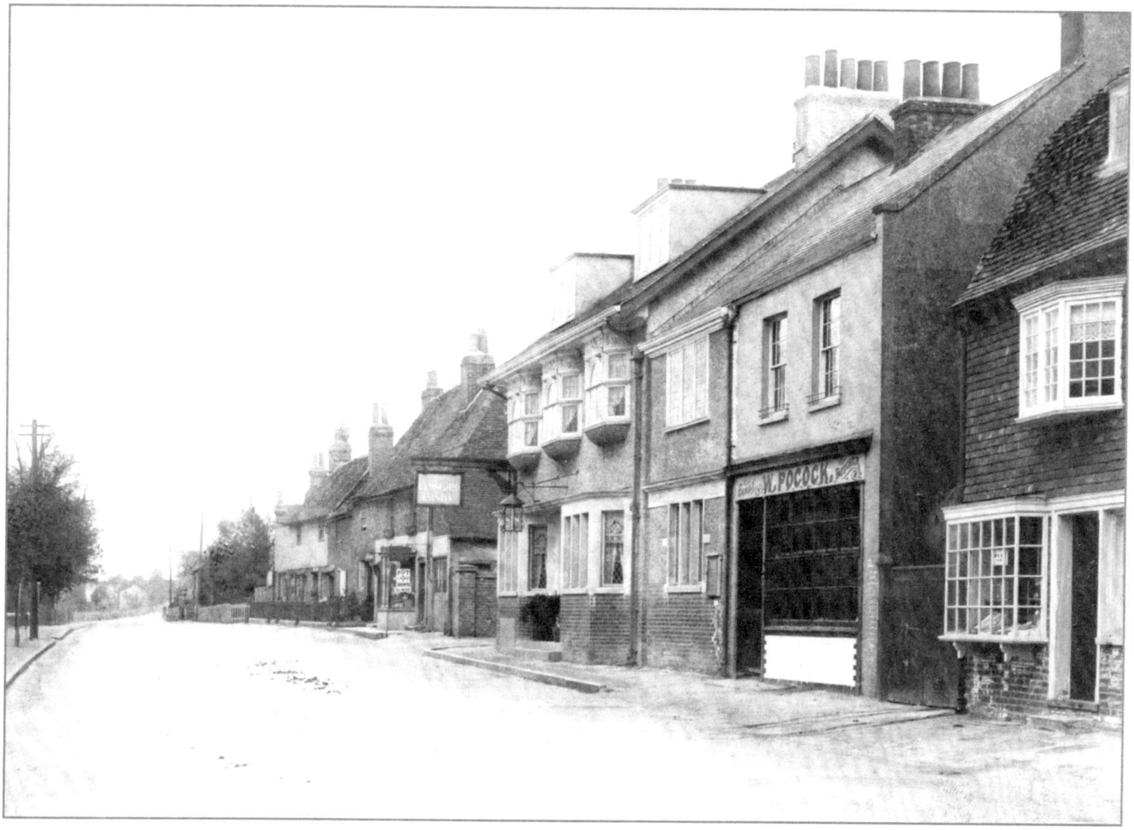

Eynsford, The Village 1905 53250

This attractive village stands in the beautiful valley of the River Darent north of Sevenoaks. Here we see an empty street scene before motor traffic was commonplace. W Pocock, on the right, is a butcher's shop. Next door is the Eynsford Castle public house, so-called because it stood opposite the entrance to the ruin of a Norman castle. Eynsford's most famous son was Leslie Hore-Belisha, who introduced the Belisha beacon in 1934 whilst he was Minister of Transport. John Wesley once preached here to assembled villagers.

Eynsford, The Bridge c1955 E55001

The river flowing beneath the 15th-century bridge is the Darent, which rises near the county boundary with Surrey near Westerham and runs through a myriad of Kent villages to the Thames near Long-reach. The riverside site at Eynsford has been occupied since at least Roman times - a short distance away is the well-preserved Roman villa of Lullingstone.

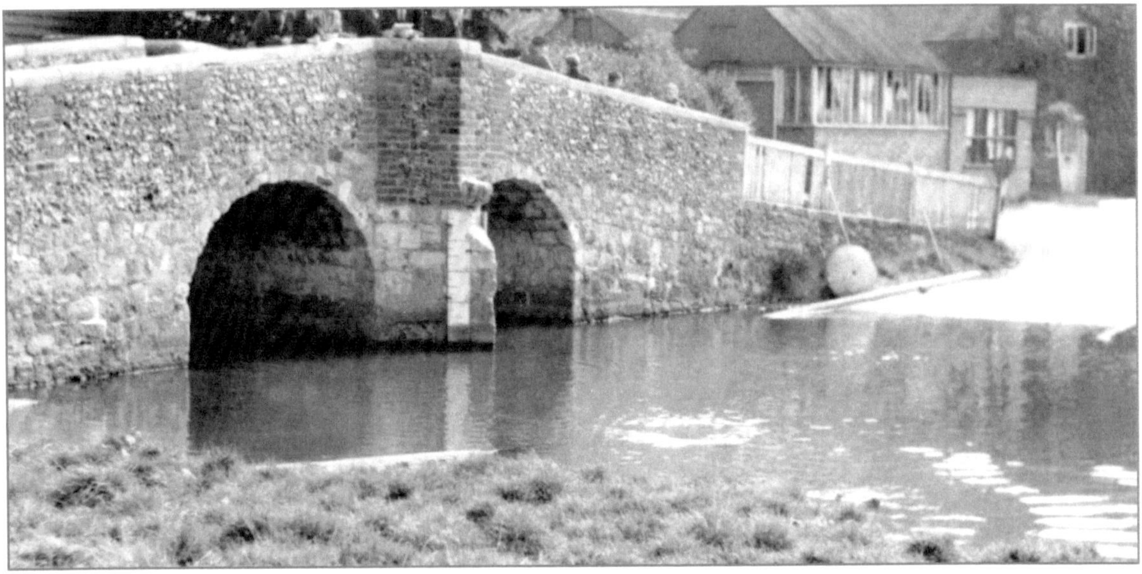

Farningham, The Bridge and the Lion Hotel c1955 F154005

Farningham is just a short distance from Eynsford, set at another pretty crossing of the Darent between ridges of chalk hills. Known at the time of Domesday as Ferlingeham, it was once a significant market centre, and in later centuries had important paper mills. During the 18th century the Lion Hotel was a stagecoach stop on the way to and from London. Since the 1920s, the village has been bypassed by the A20.

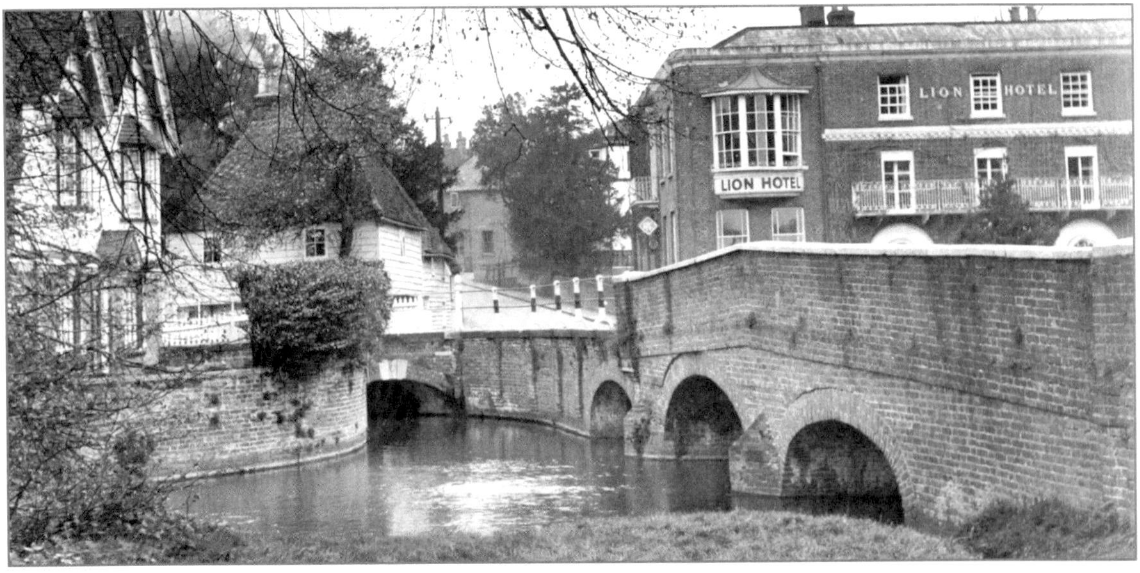

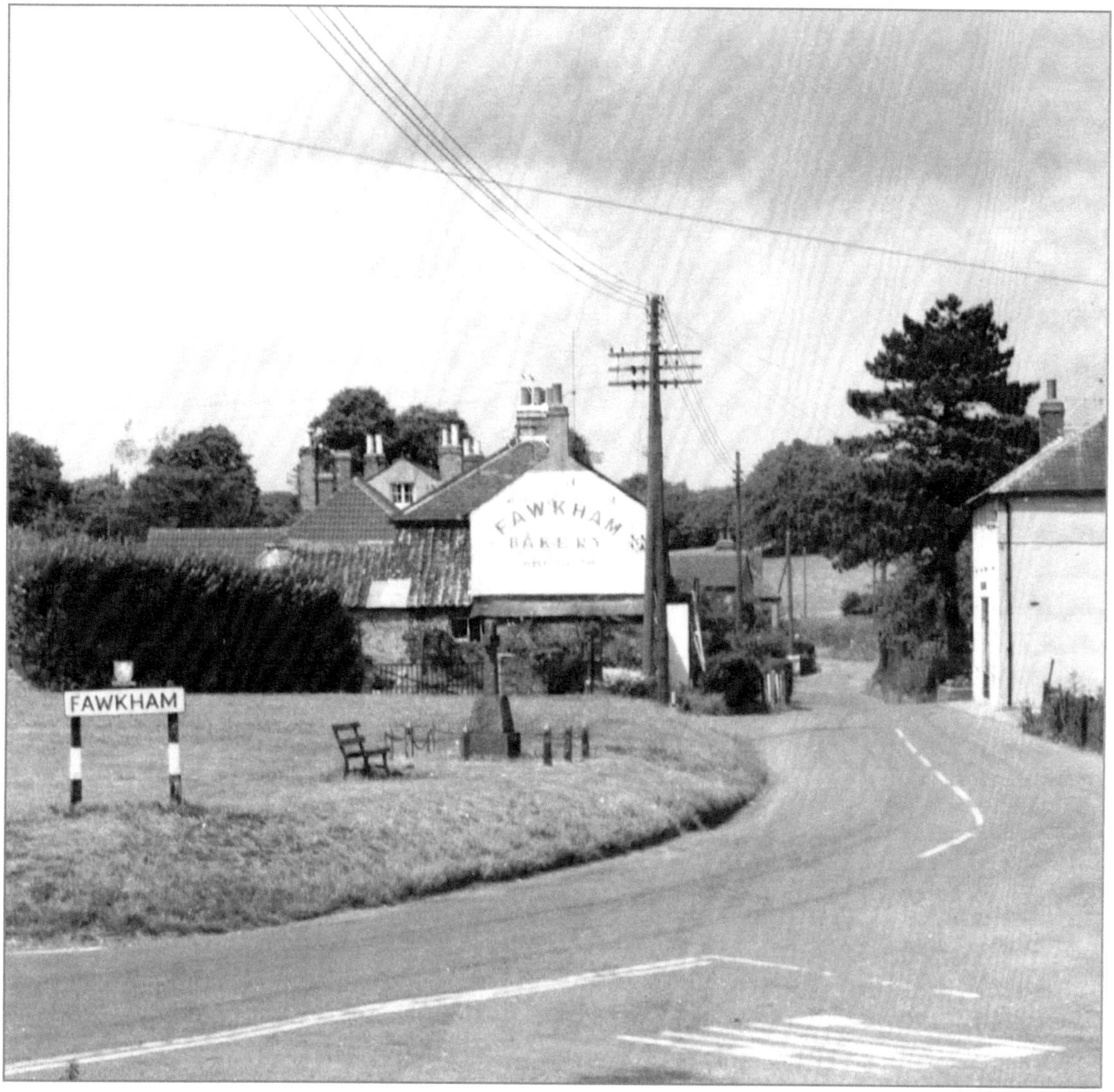

Fawkham Green, The Village c1960 F155020
Though Fawkham was given a station on the LC & DR railway in the late 19th century it has retained its unspoilt charm and tranquillity. Beyond the village green is the Fawkham Bakery, its painted sign smothering the broad gable. Fawkham's church, repaired and reseated by the Victorians, has a wooden tower and Norman windows.

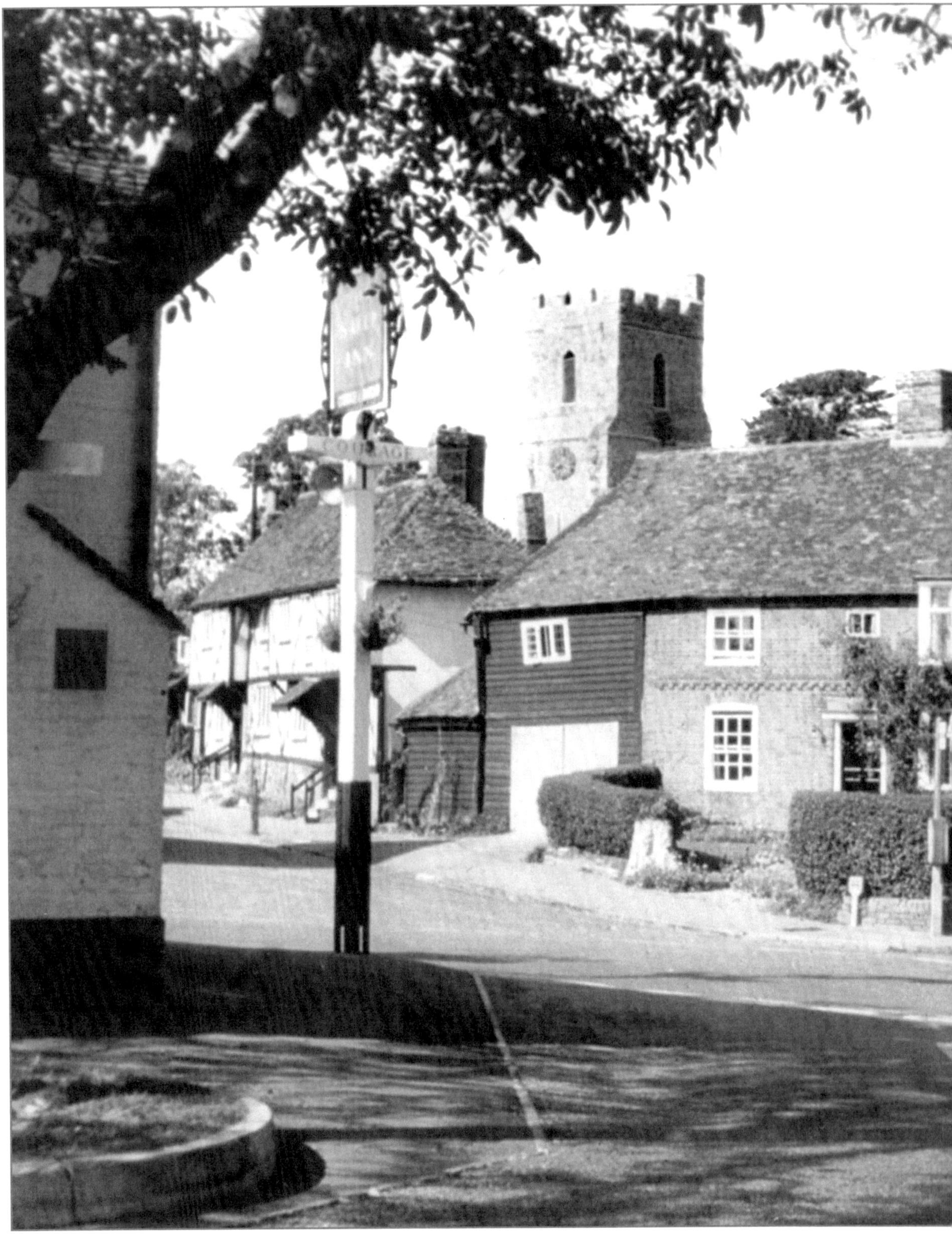

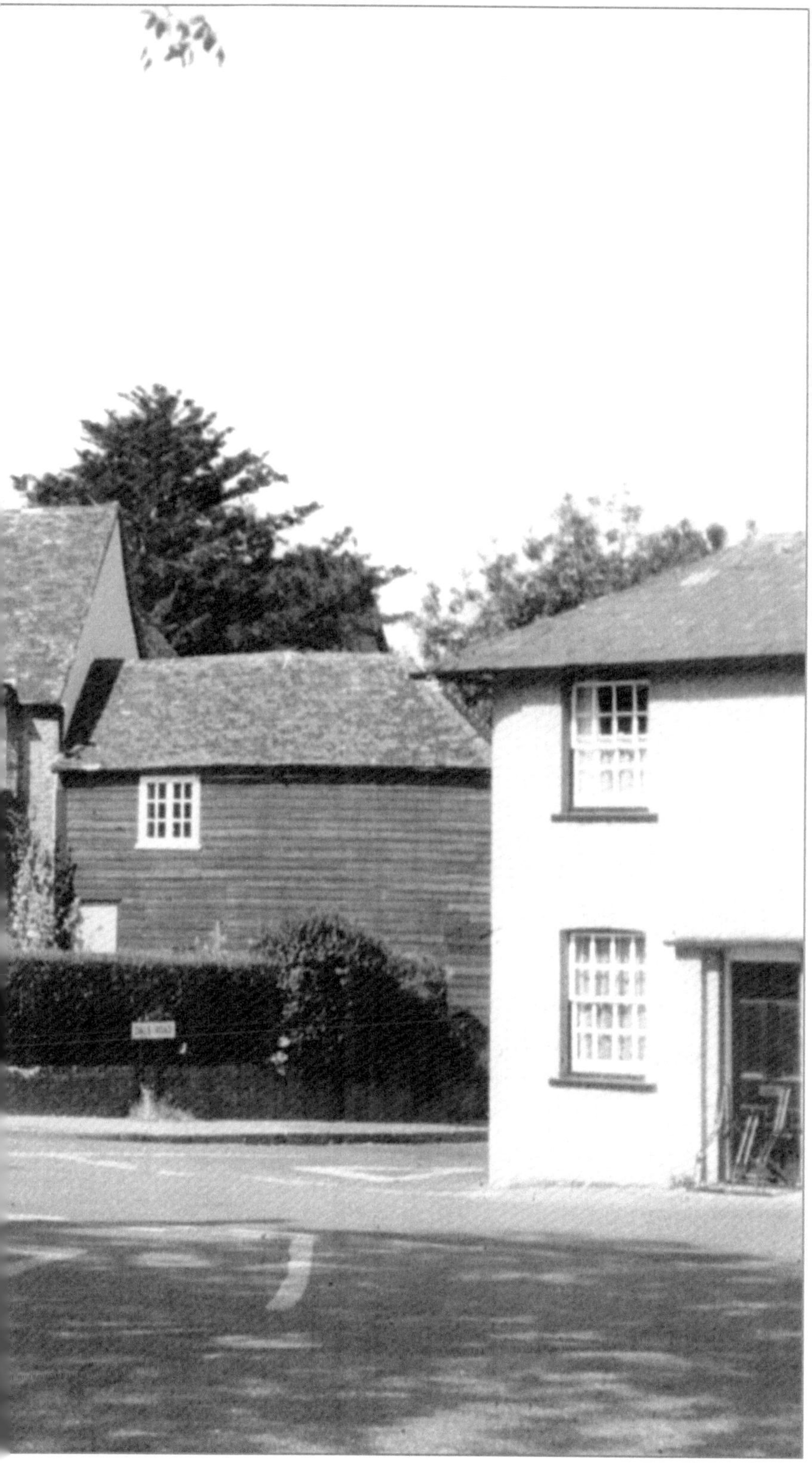

South Fleet
The Village c1960
S536501
This village stands near Watling Street, three miles south-west of Gravesend. It gained its name from a river passage that once reached it from the Thames at Northfleet. The attractive 14th-century church here is worth a visit for the octagonal font inscribed with the signs of the zodiac. The timber-framed house in front of the church is 16th-century. On the left, in the foreground, is the Ship Inn. The gardens at Spring Head gained a reputation for watercress growing.

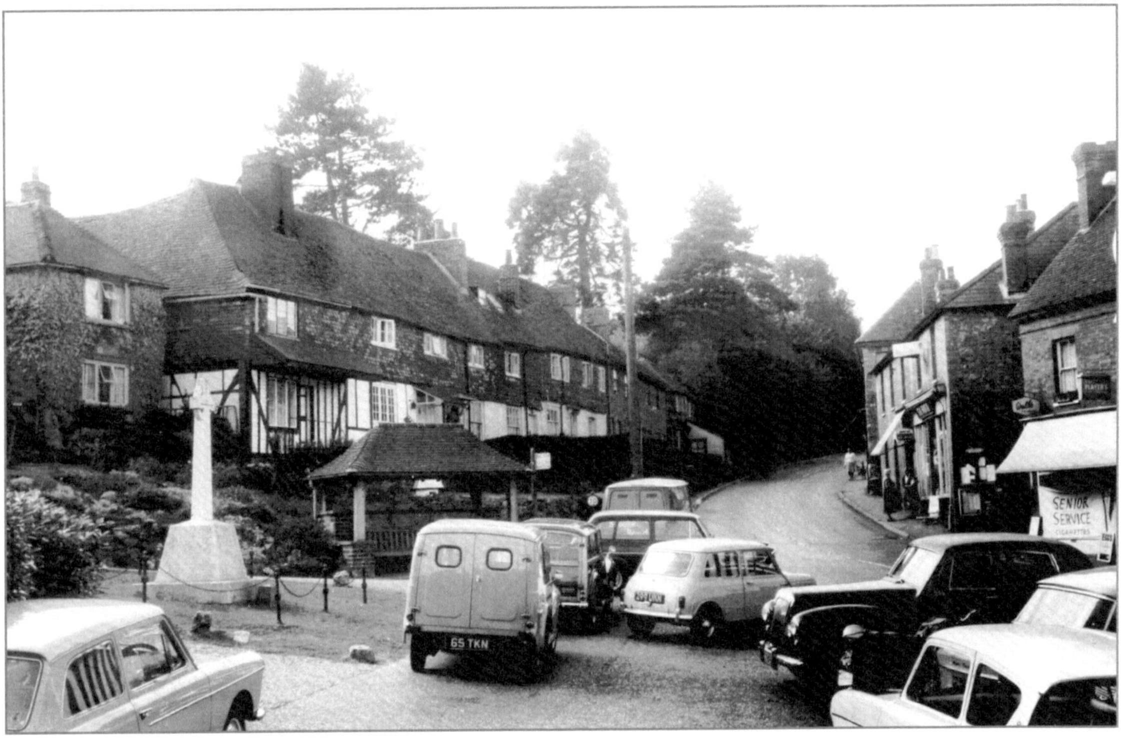

Ightham, The Village and the Memorial Cross c1960 14052
This village was anciently known as Eightham, and was once a market town, with a Whit-Wednesday fair called Cockscomb Fair. At Ightham Mote, which stands in a ravine in the Weald, is a celebrated fortified mansion, with a moat refreshed by natural springs. Here we see the village square, surrounded with black and white houses and clogged with randomly-parked cars.

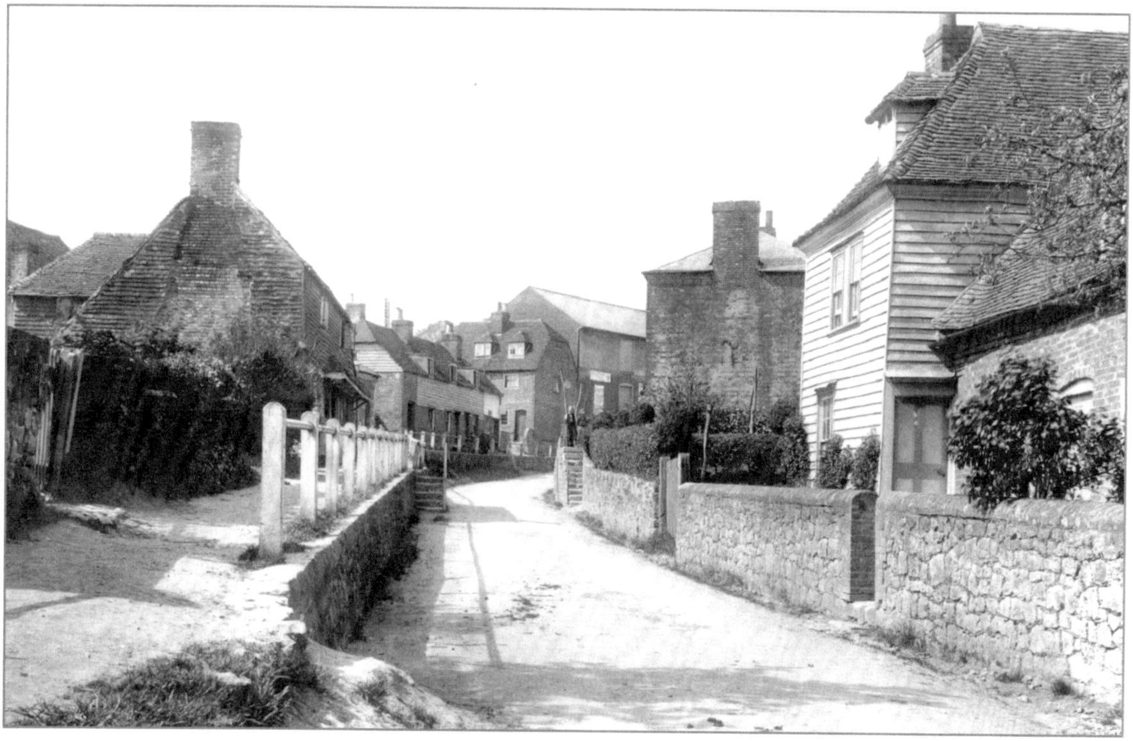

Wrotham, St Mary's Road 1903 51026
Wrotham stands at the foot of chalk hills alongside the Pilgrim's Way, and was once a substantial market centre. Its long street winds between brick, tile- and timber-clad cottages with their pleasing confusion of rooflines. Note the safe walkways above the road. Today the village remains unspoiled, despite substantial road development nearby.

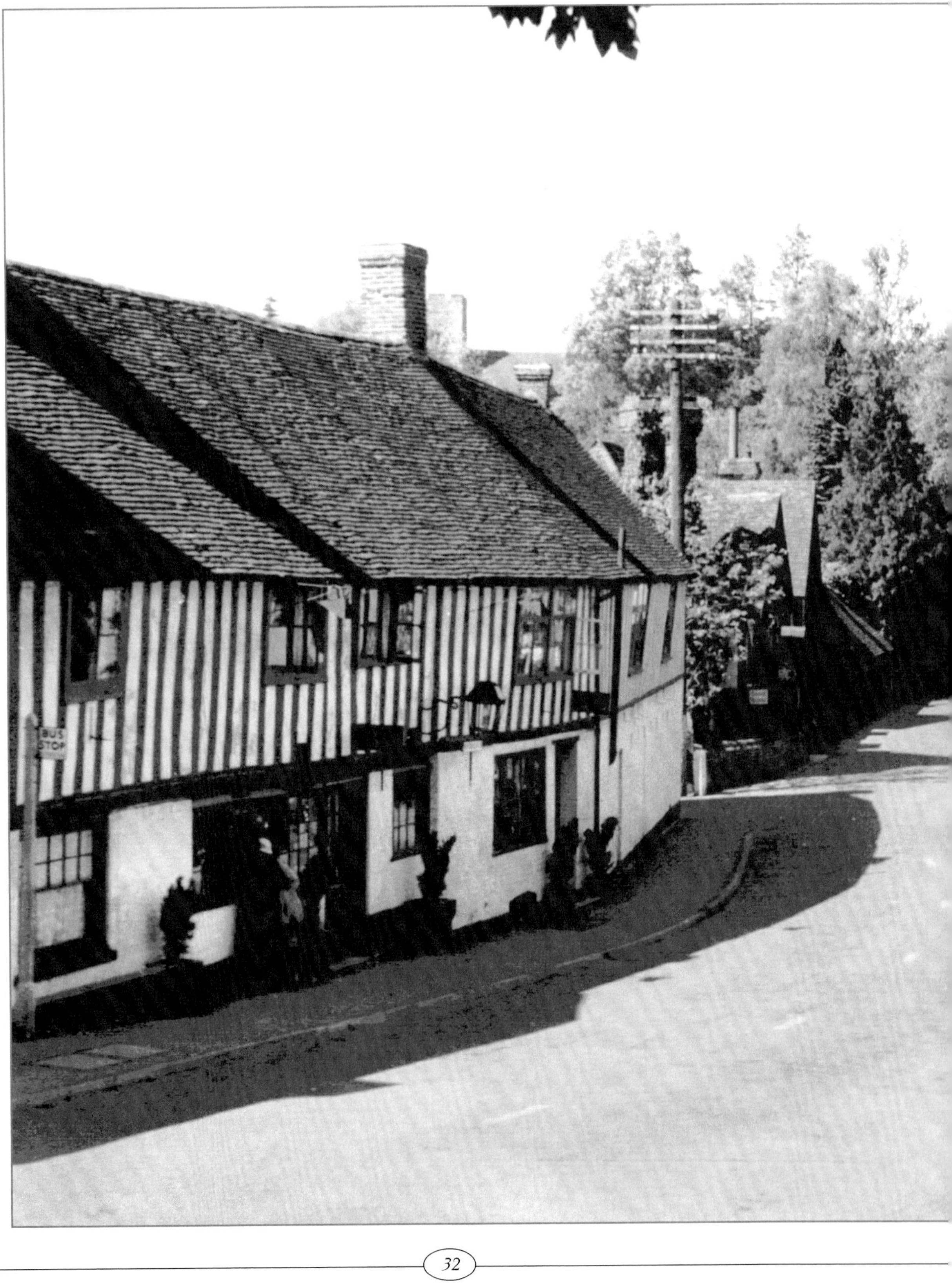
BUS STOP

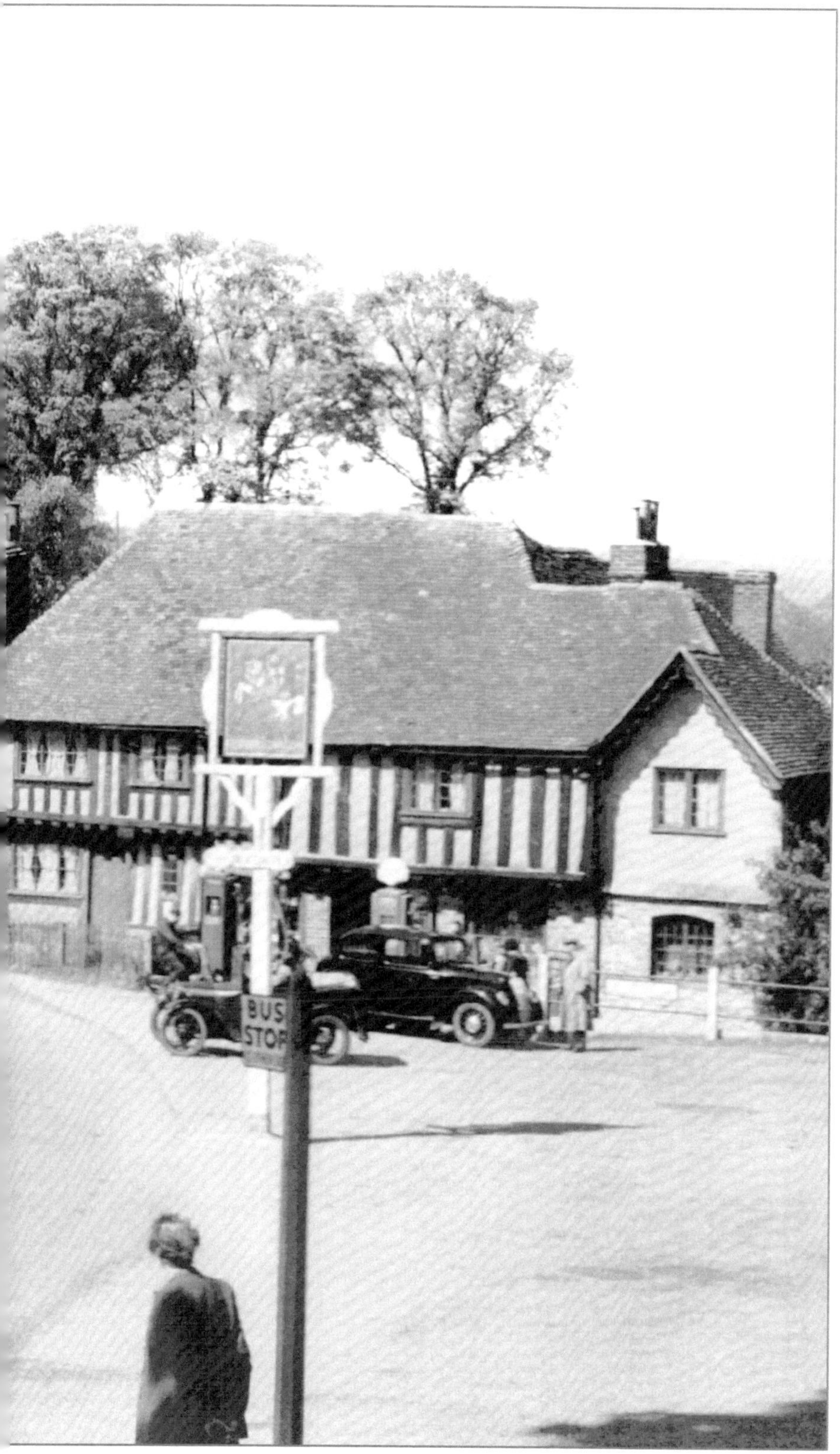

Ightham, The Square c1950 14006

This beautiful collection of 15th- and 16th-century half-timbered houses includes the hotel and public house the George and Dragon, shown on the right, a fine example of Tudor architecture in an historic village setting. Local legend has it that the Duke of Northumberland was imprisoned here after the discovery of the Gunpowder Plot. It is also believed that Guy Fawkes stayed here the night before the attempted plot was carried out.

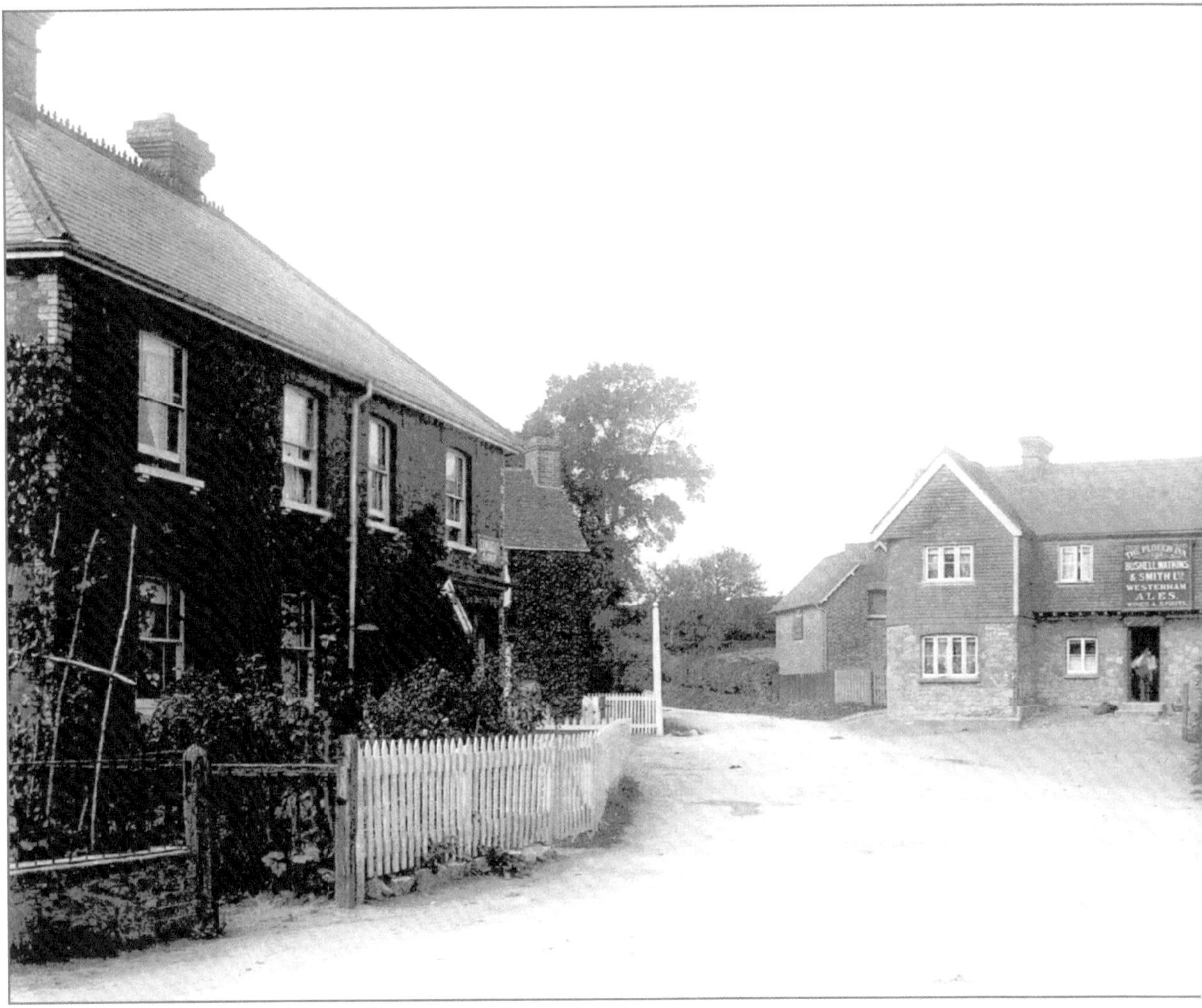

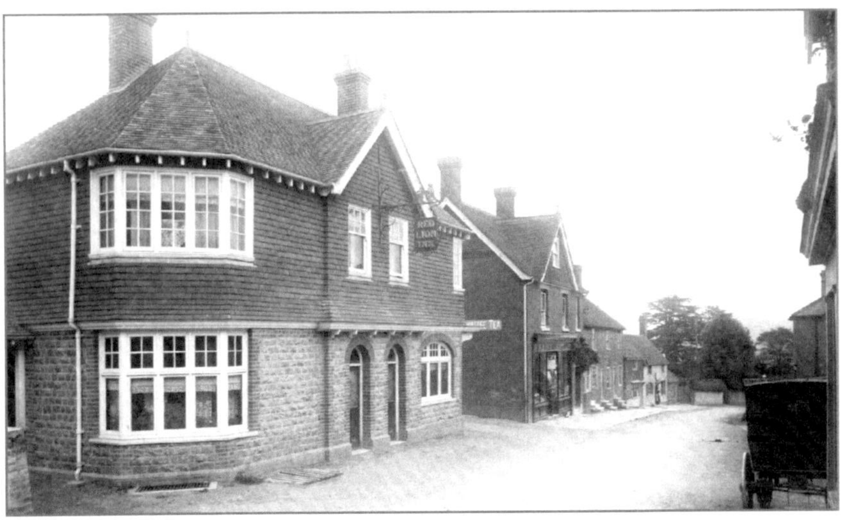

◄ **Plaxtol, The Village 1901** 47600

A lone carriage is parked on the other side of the street from the newly-built Red Lion Inn. Just beyond, down the road, is J J Bacon's Stores. The village has a wealth of old houses, including a row of Kentish weatherboard cottages flanking the side of the parish church. To the east of the village is Old Soar Manor, a manor house built in the 13th century.

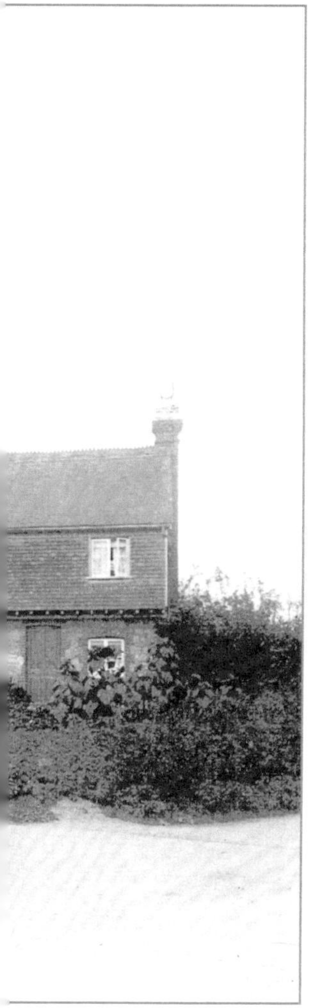

◄ **Ivy Hatch, The Village 1901** 47617

This hamlet contains little more than we can see here. The public house is the Plough Inn, offering clientele Bushell, Watkins and Smith's local Westerham ales. On the left, behind the white picket fence, is a small shop advertising Sunlight soap. Auction posters are wrapped round the wooden village signpost.

▼ **Plaxtol, The Rectory 1901** 46413

Before its restoration, Plaxtol's church was an almost complete 17th-century creation, with a fine hammerbeam roof and an ancient reredos. The old rectory, of warm red brick, with its tall chimneys and light-gathering broad bay windows has creeper running rampant all over it.

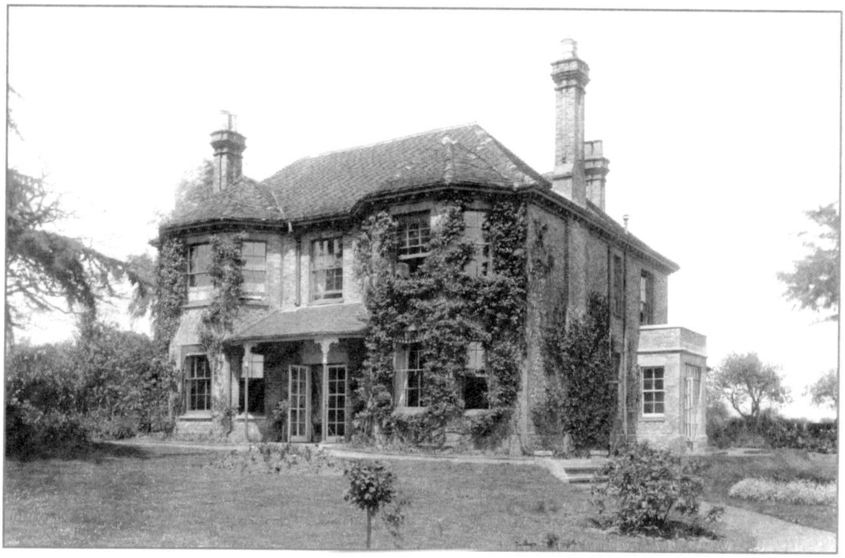

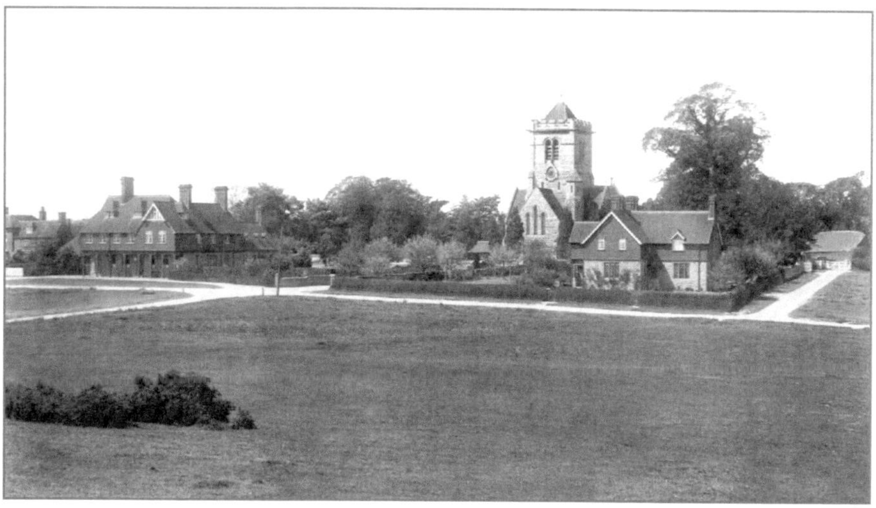

◄ **Shipbourne The Village 1901** 46419

This was once a place where sheep were washed in a stream (bourne), hence the name. Shipbourne is a very attractive open village with a large green. The compact church is Victorian, and was built in 1881 in the Early English style. Christopher Smart, the translator of Horace, was a native of Shipbourne. In Victorian times there was a working men's institute here.

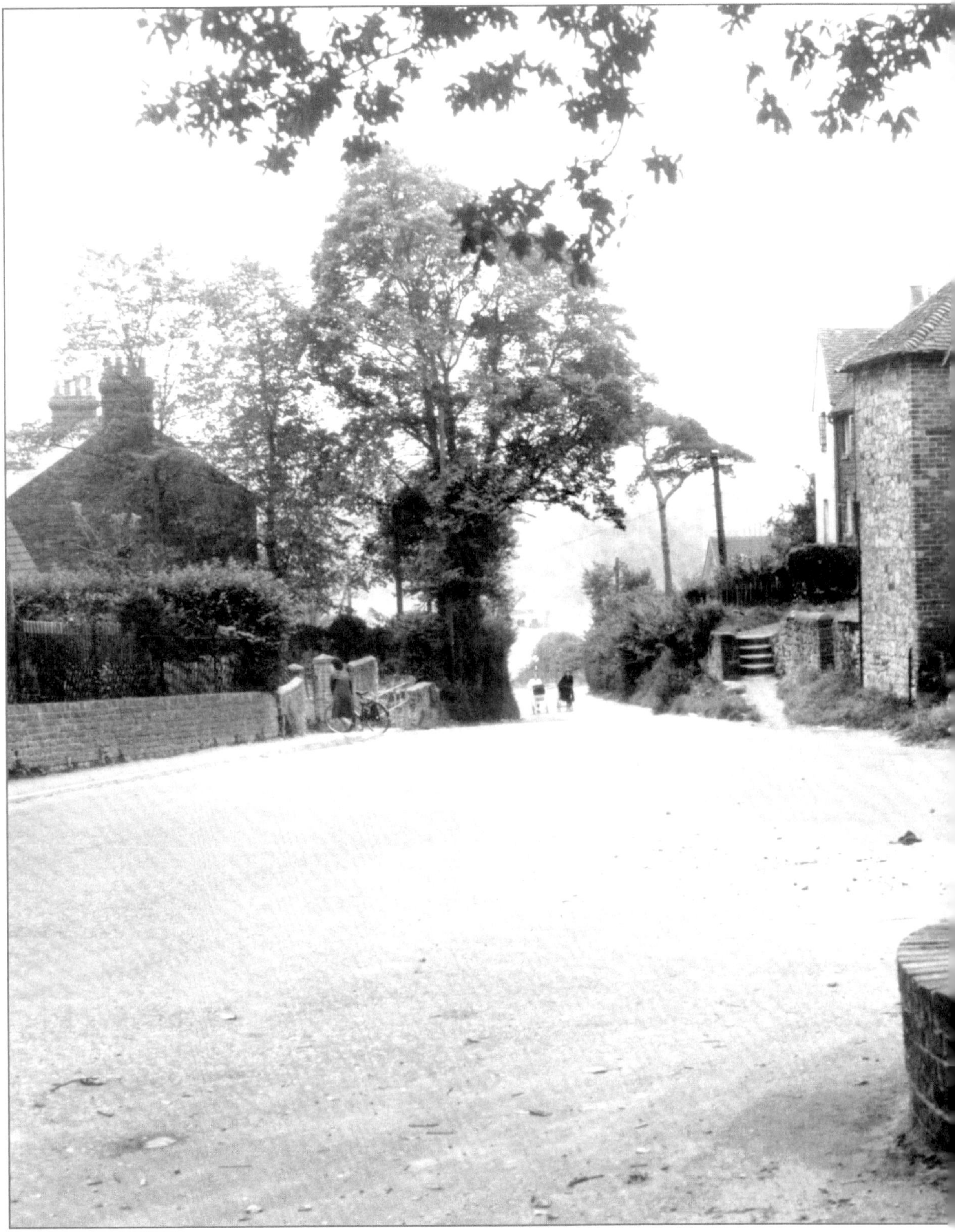

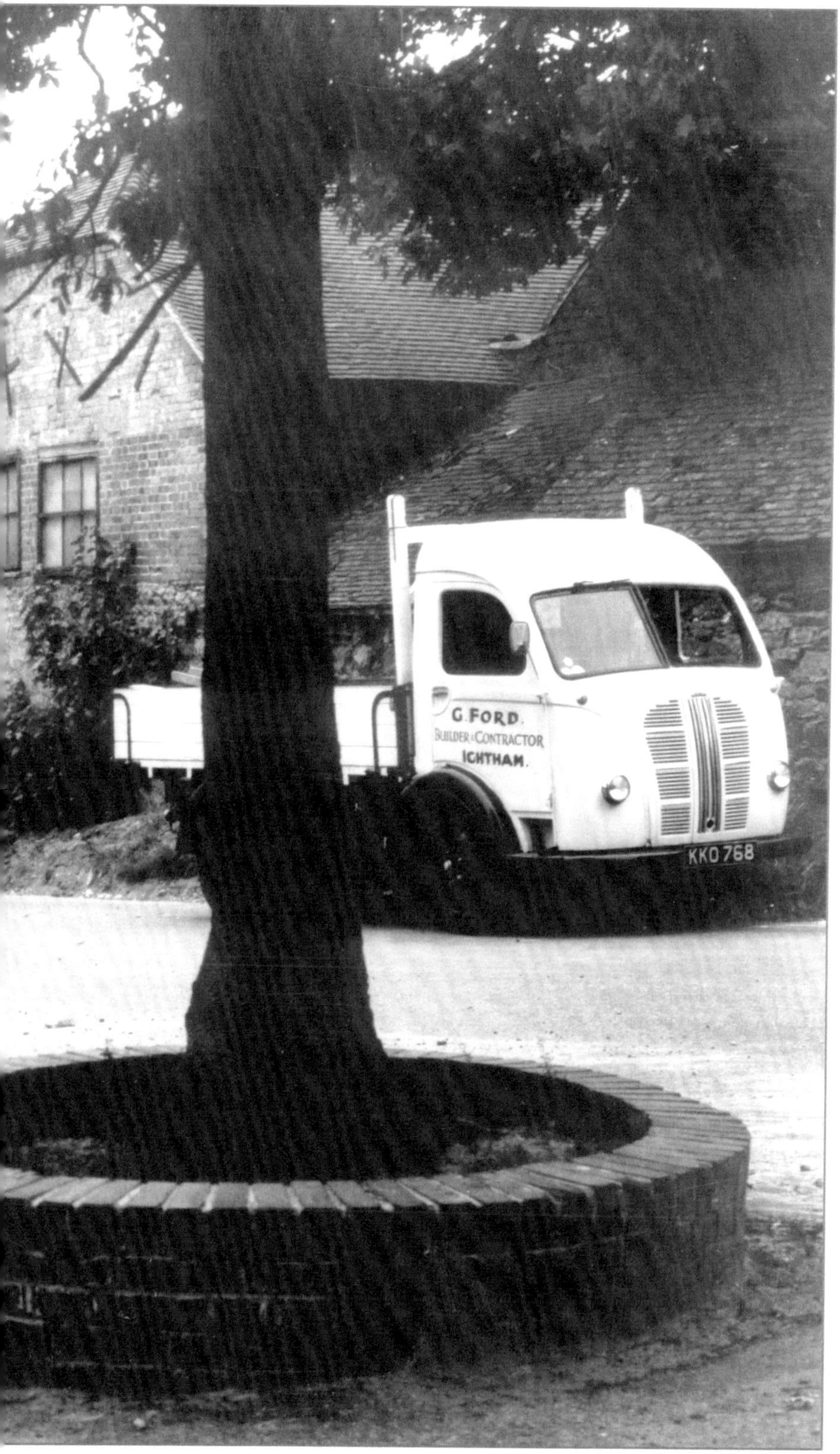

Borough Green Quarry Hill c1955

B145012

Borough Green was once a hamlet in Ightham and Wrotham parishes, six miles to the east of Sevenoaks. The two old houses in the centre show how piecemeal were the alterations carried out by various owners down the centuries: below each has a wall of stone rubble, and above at least two courses of brick, laid at different times. Tie-bars draw together the various layers of the structures. The neat white pickup truck belongs to G Ford, Builder Contractor, of Ightham.

▼ **West Peckham, The Village and Stores c1960** W403001

This village seems archetypal: it has a village green, a local store and a red telephone box; surrounded by fields and oasthouses it retains a deep rural tranquillity. On a nearby hill is an old cottage, once the abode of the notorious highwayman Jack Diamond, who is said still to haunt the area in ghostly form.

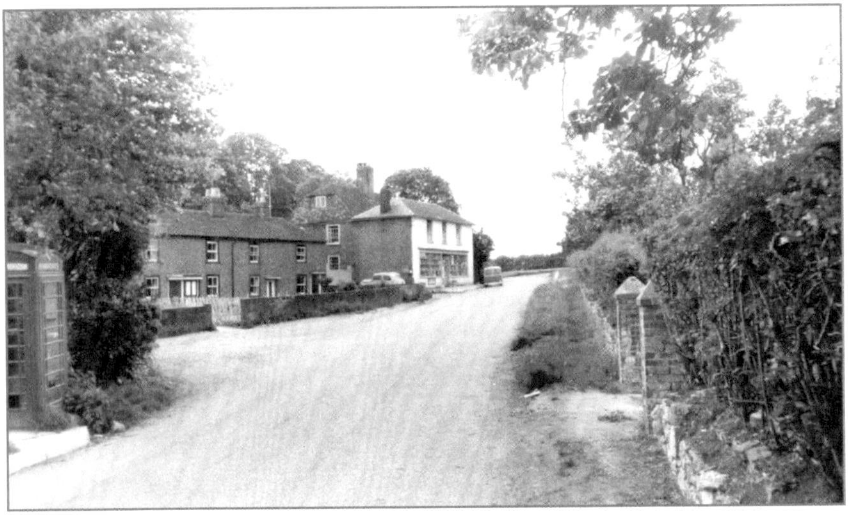

▼ **Hadlow, The King's Head c1950** H461006

Hadlow lies in the Medway valley close to Tonbridge. A car is turning by the King's Head, with the eccentric Hadlow tower looming over the roofs in the background. This was constructed in the early 19th century by Walter May so that he could enjoy a prospect of the sea; however, the South Downs prevented his dream from being realised. In 1823, William Cobbett on one of his 'Rural Rides' was much impressed by the tower, calling it 'the most singular thing I have ever seen'. It is now protected by a preservation order.

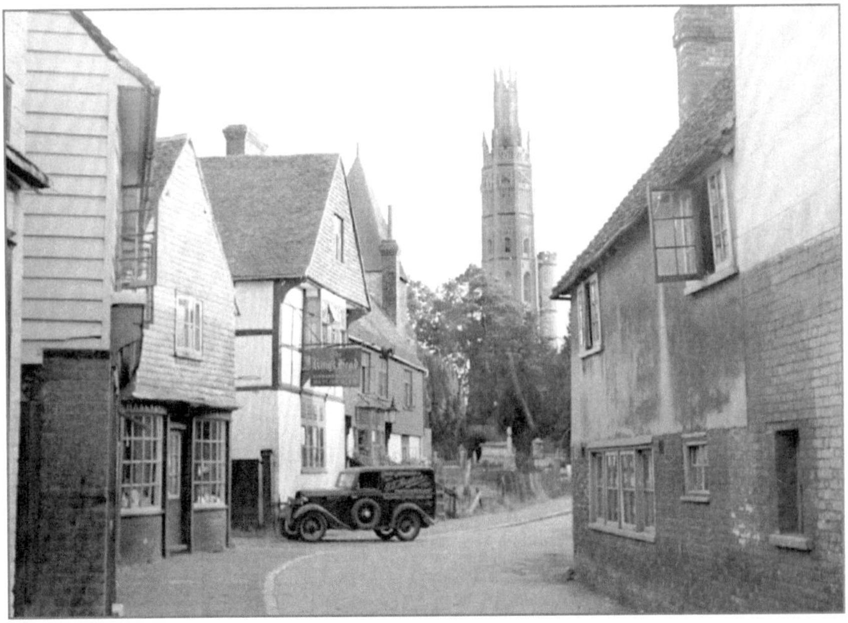

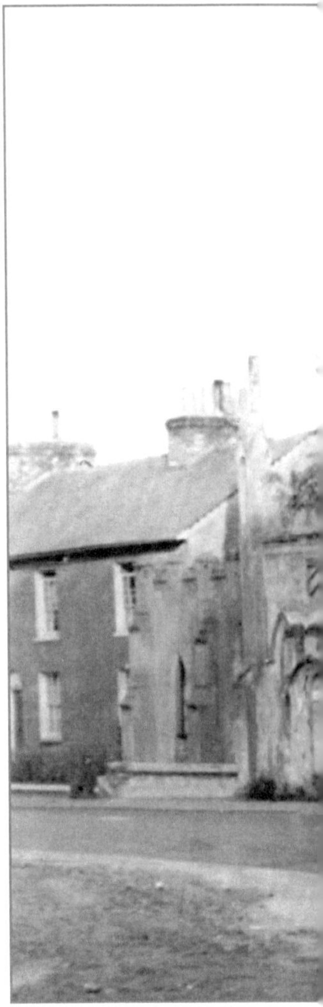

▲ **Hadlow, The Castle Entrance c1950** H461002

These attractive ivy-clad ruins are not as ancient as they look: they are part of the castle constructed as a folly by Walter May along with his 170 foot high tower. Such Gothick confections were very popular with more eccentric landowners at the end of the 18th century. Demolition was begun in 1951, but was almost immediately stopped following protests by the local artist Bernard Hailstone.

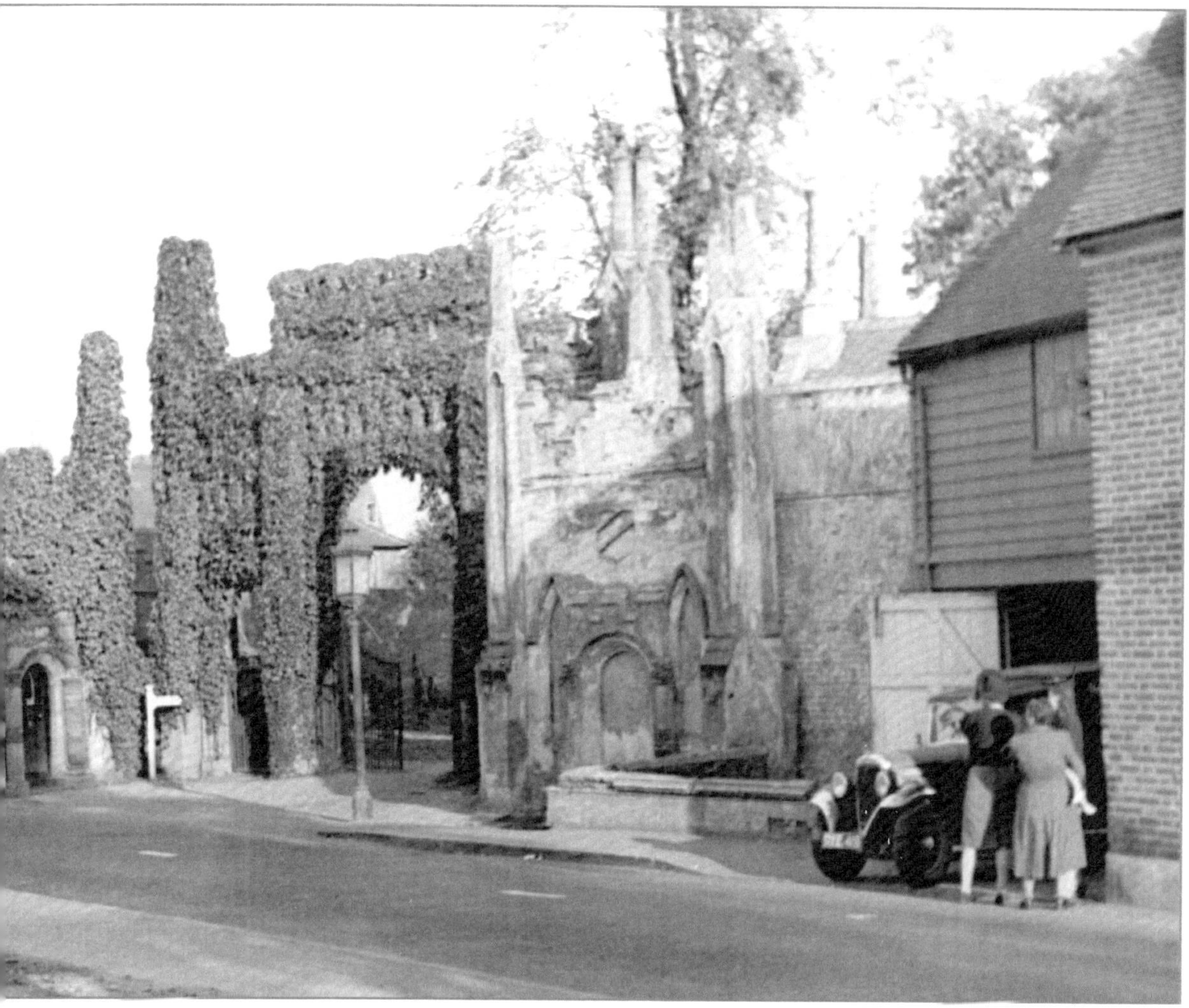

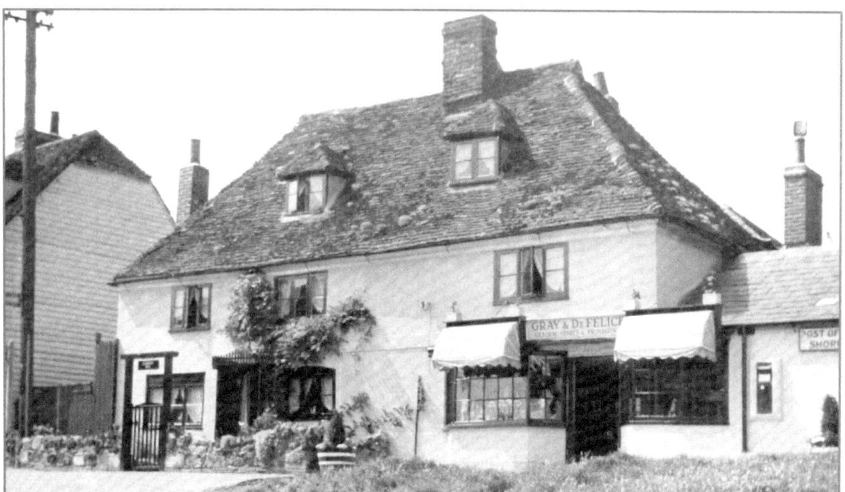

Shorne, The Post Office c1955 S530010

Here is the local post office in more rural days; it also served as a general stores. In 1895 the village had the benefit of a post and money order office, supervised from Gravesend. There is a story that when Charles Dickens lived at nearby Gadshill, he had a tunnel constructed that led under the main road and came up in his garden on the other side in the parish of Shorne; here he would do his writing.

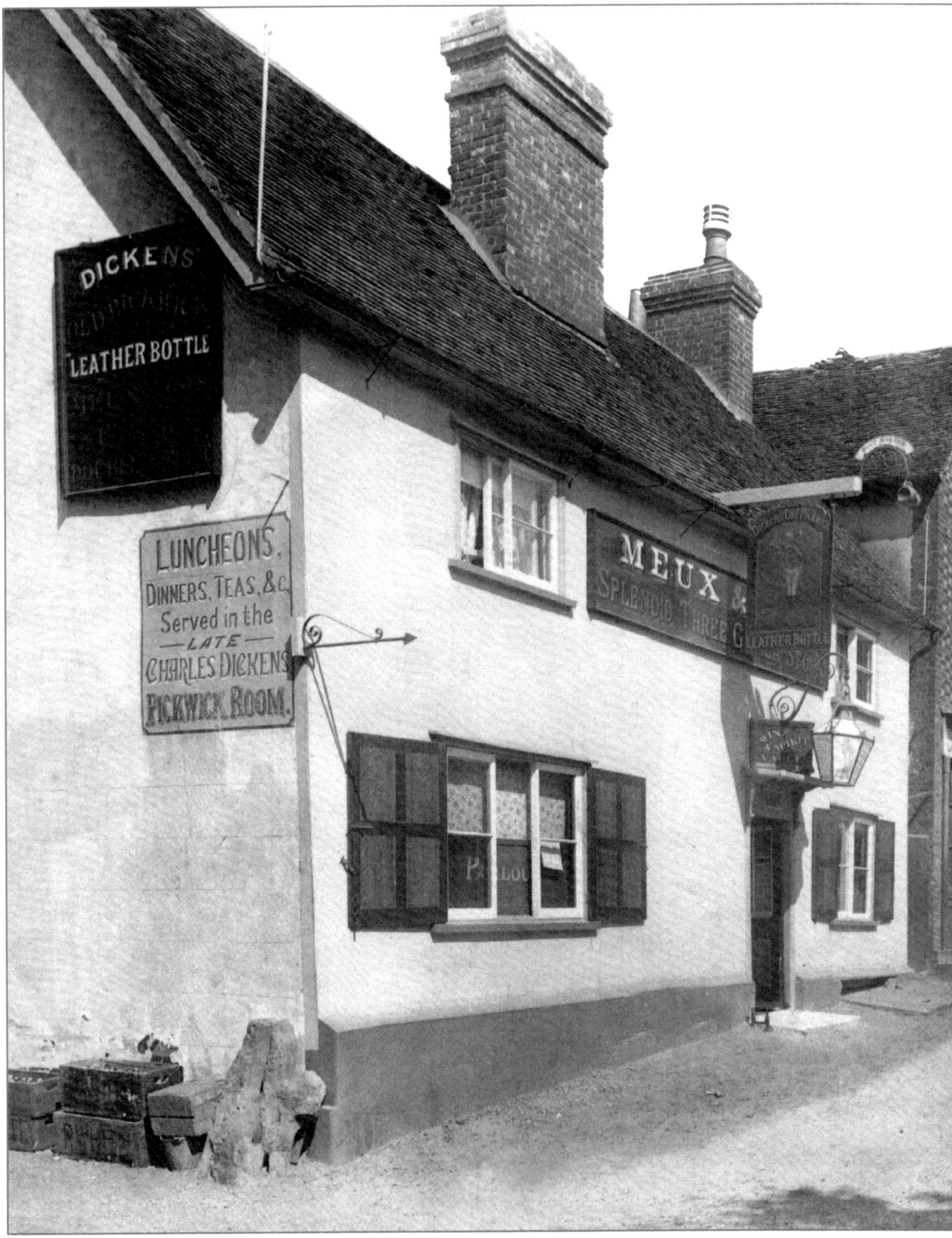
DICKENS
LEATHER BOTTLE
LUNCHEONS,
DINNERS, TEAS, &c.
Served in the
LATE
CHARLES DICKENS
PICKWICK ROOM.
MEUX &
LEATHER BOTTLE

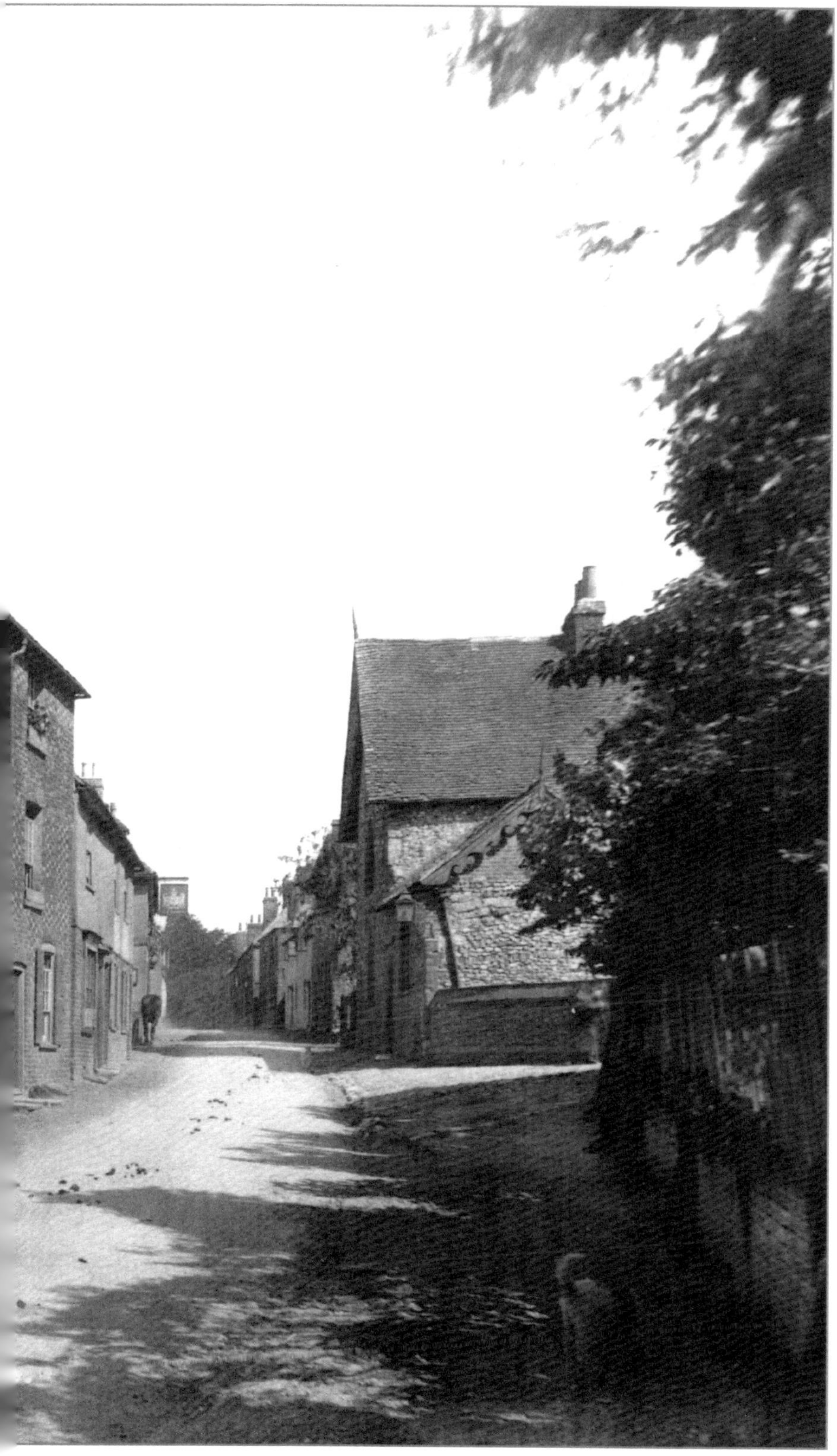

Cobham
The Leather Bottle
1899 44240
Cobham stands on Watling Street and was once a busy market centre. It was here that Charles Dickens wrote and set some of 'The Pickwick Papers', and where the 'clean and commodious ale-house' to which Mr Tuppence retried from the world could be found. Cobham Hall, near to the village, was lived in by the Earls of Darnley for some 200 years until the 1950s. It is now an independent school for girls. St Mary Magdalene's church in the village contains the county's first collection of monumental brasses, commemorating the Cobham family.

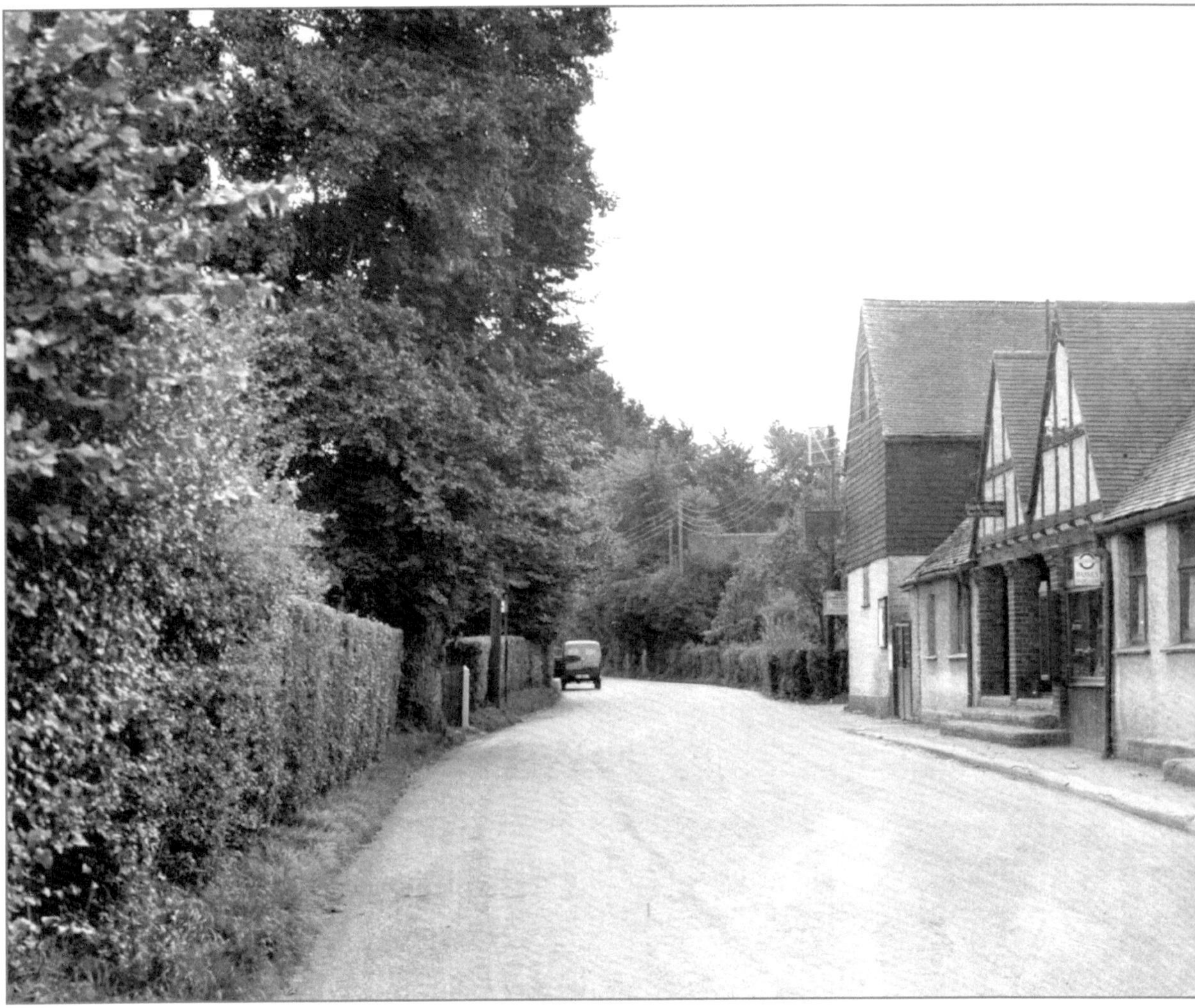

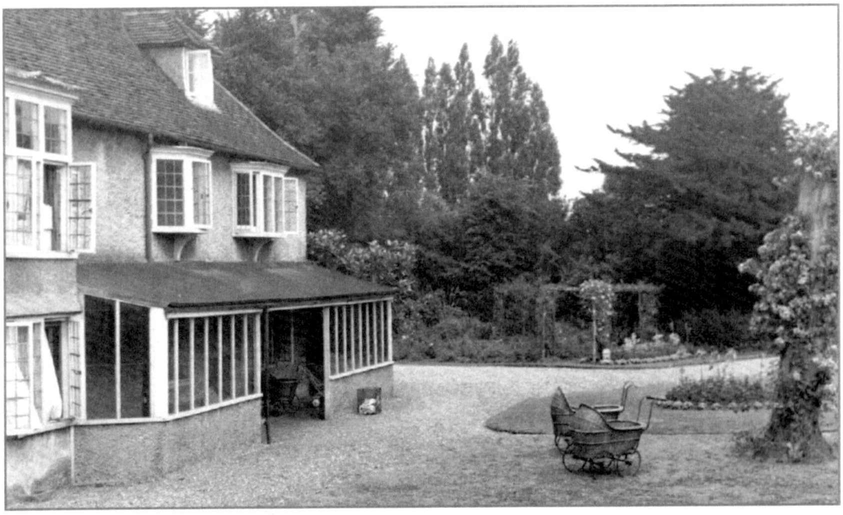

◄ **Hartley, The Fairby Grange Convalescent Home c1950** H462010
Fairby Grange stands in almost an acre of well tended gardens. In this view it must be a warm breezy day, for flowers are in bloom and curtains are fluttering at the open windows. Notice the old-fashioned basketwork prams.

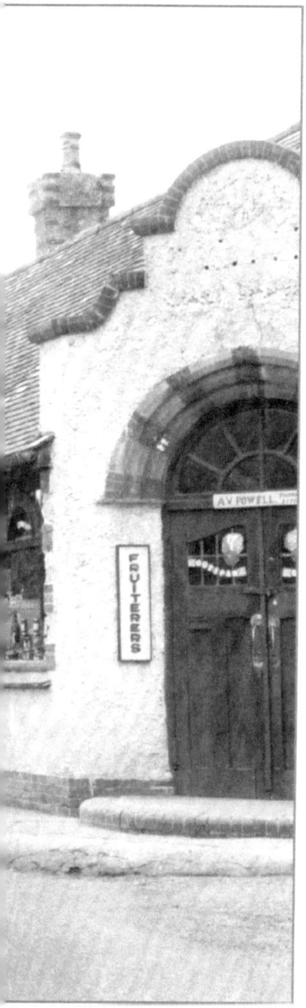

Hartley, The Village c1950 H462015
Hartley sits on high ground, six miles from Dartford, and enjoys expansive prospects all around. The much-expanded village rests on an ancient site - the remains of a Roman house were found here, and the church has Saxon foundations. A V Powell's fruiterer's shop is built in a curious style, with an arched corner entrance somewhat in the manner of a church hall or theatre. Next door are the twin half-timbered gables in the antique style of the Fairby Stores and Post Office and, beyond, a lofty weatherboarded barn. In 1895 the population was small - only 272.

Hartley, The Black Lion c1950 H462017
Daniel Defoe lived in a cottage that was once part of this fine old inn. It is said that he wrote 'Robinson Crusoe' in a back-room above the wash-house. Henry Treadwell was one of several generations of yeoman farmers in the village, and was the landlord of the inn during the second half of the 19th century.

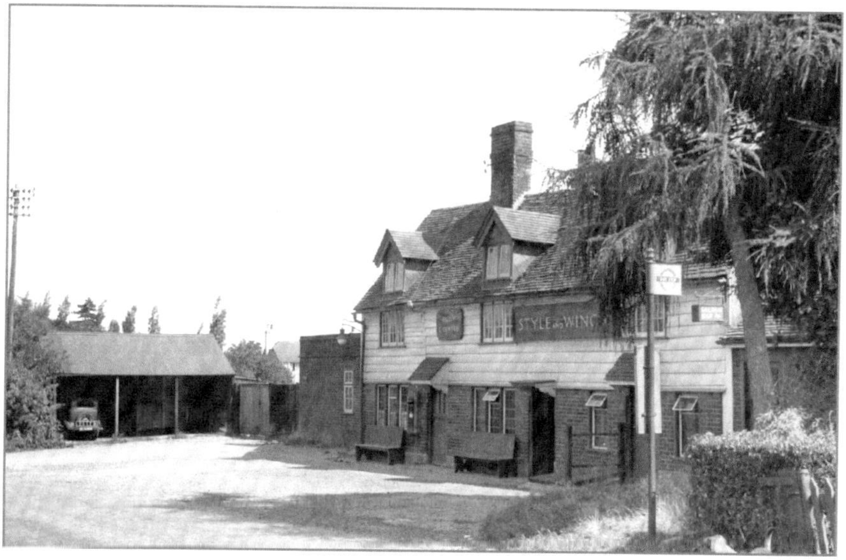

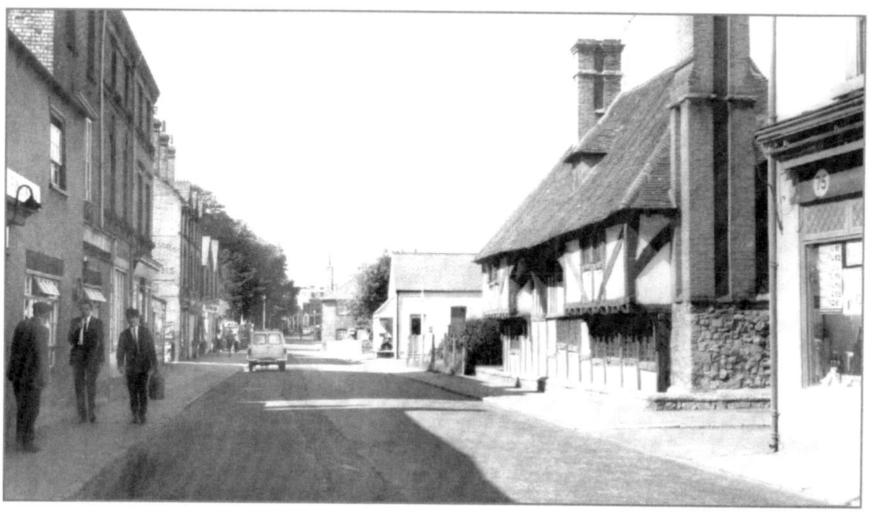

Snodland, Mulberry Cottage c1965 S535032
The village stands on the River Medway in a somewhat blighted industrial landscape. In 1895 there were already extensive lime and cement works in the neighbourhood, as well as a large paper mill. However, this view of the village street shows that there are still some historic buildings left in Snodland, despite its massive expansion. There is now a bypass which takes traffic away from the centre.

▼ **Wateringbury, Oast Houses c1960** W399024

By Victorian times there were orchards, hop gardens and two sizeable breweries in the village. Here we see an excellent example of the Kentish oast house, which was used for storing the hops picked from local fields. Wateringbury suffered a remarkable freak storm in August 1763. Hailstones said to be ten inches across fell, and lay in heaps for up to a month, attracting visitors to the village. Travellers still come by boat and tie up at the riverside here.

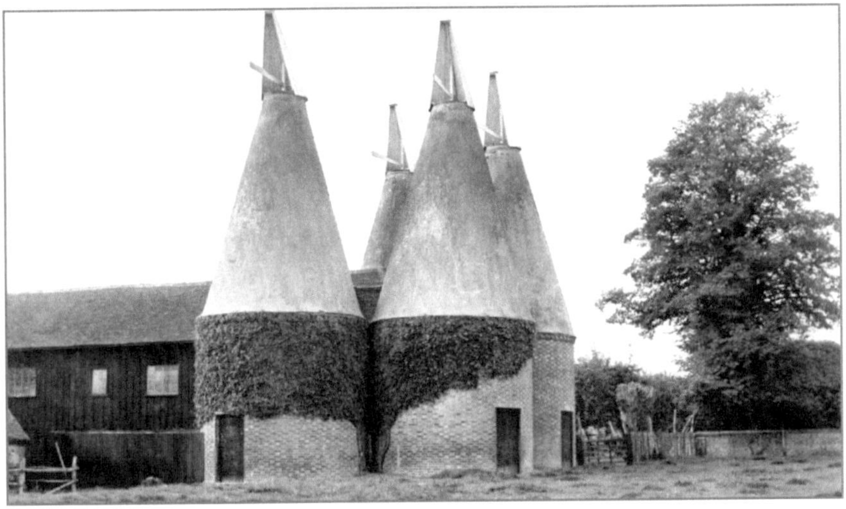

▼ **Yalding, The Medway c1960** Y35005

Yalding stands near the confluence of the Medway, Beult and Theyse rivers, and has long been popular with the sailing fraternity. Barges plying the Medway once tied up here. The building next to the tree is the Anchor Inn: for years, the Anchor has been the destination for an annual raft race from East Peckham. Yalding was once a substantial market centre, but was desolated by the plague four times in the 16th century.

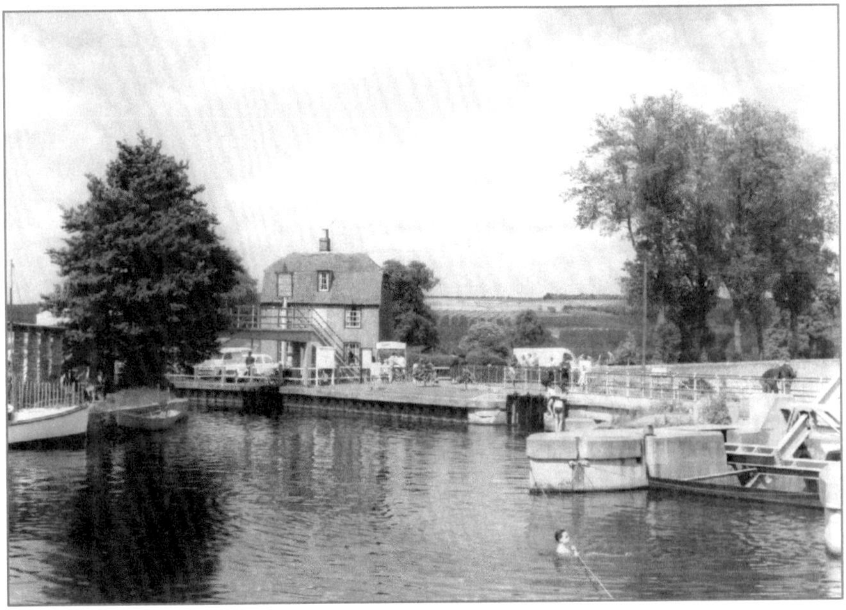

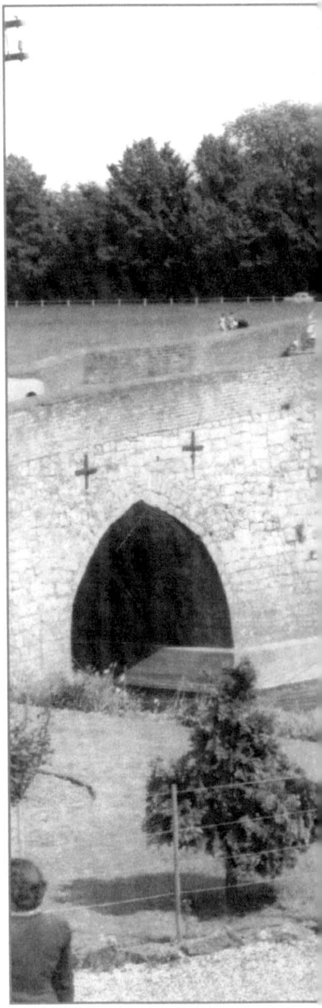

▲ **Yalding, The Bridge c1960** Y35006

Yalding boasts the longest bridge in Kent, crossing two rivers over 150 yards. This photograph was taken on a summer's day, when the river was low. A different scene was to be witnessed in October and November 2000, and again in February 2001, when the river was in full flood on a number of occasions. Yalding has suffered frequently as a result of its proximity to the three rivers.

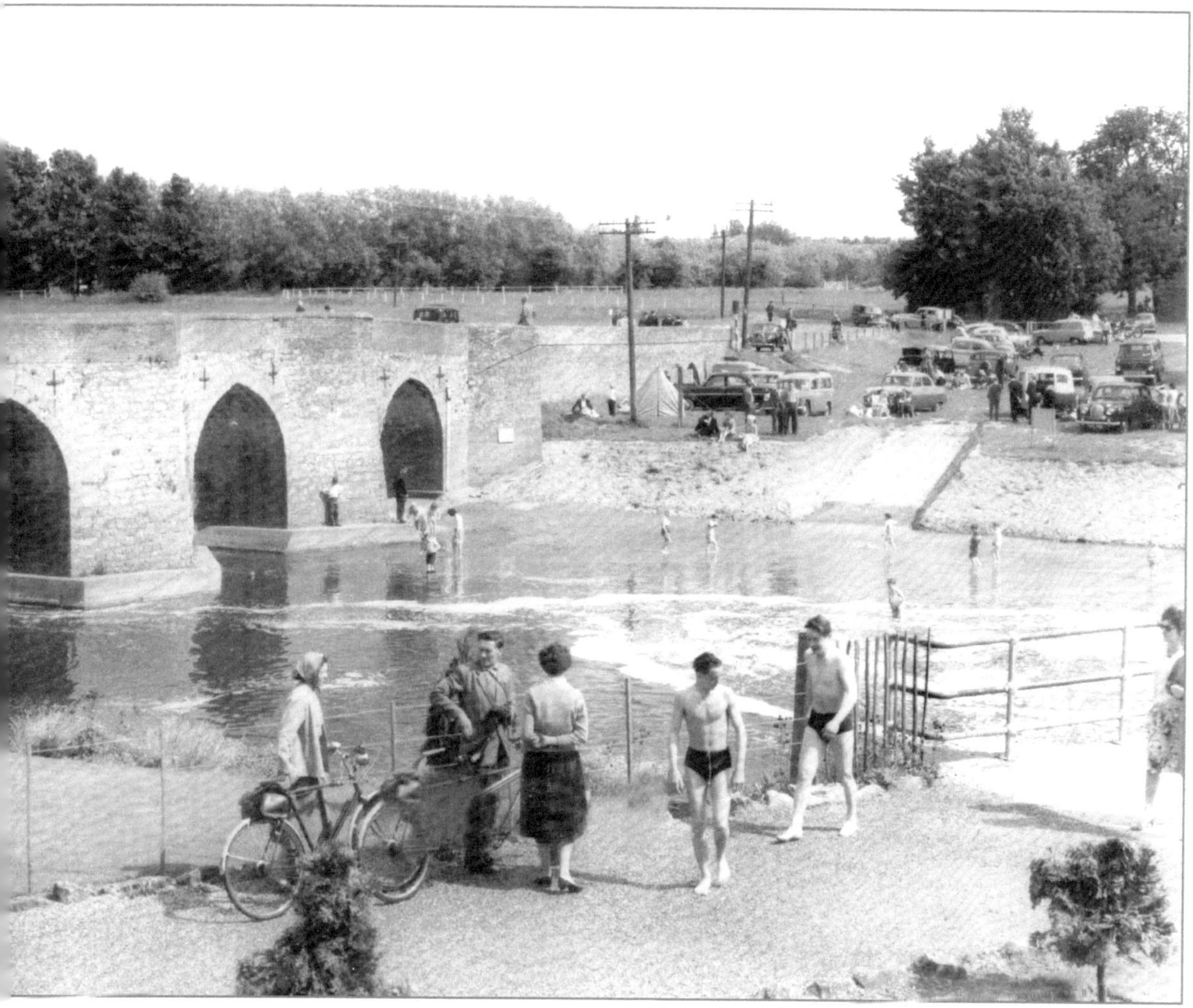

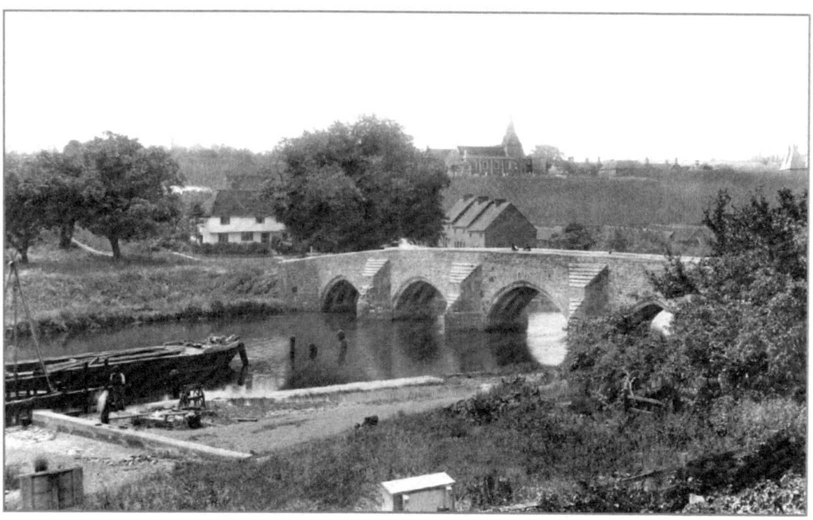

East Farleigh, The River Medway 1898 41556
The village sits high above the flood plain of the Medway. This peaceful scene shows the 14th-century five-arched ragstone bridge, which is considered by some to be the finest in the south-east. Violent and unhappy events took place here in earlier times, however. Cromwell's men marched across the bridge on their way to capture Maidstone from the Royalists. At St Mary's Church, on the hill, there is a cross commemorating 43 hop pickers who died of cholera in 1849.

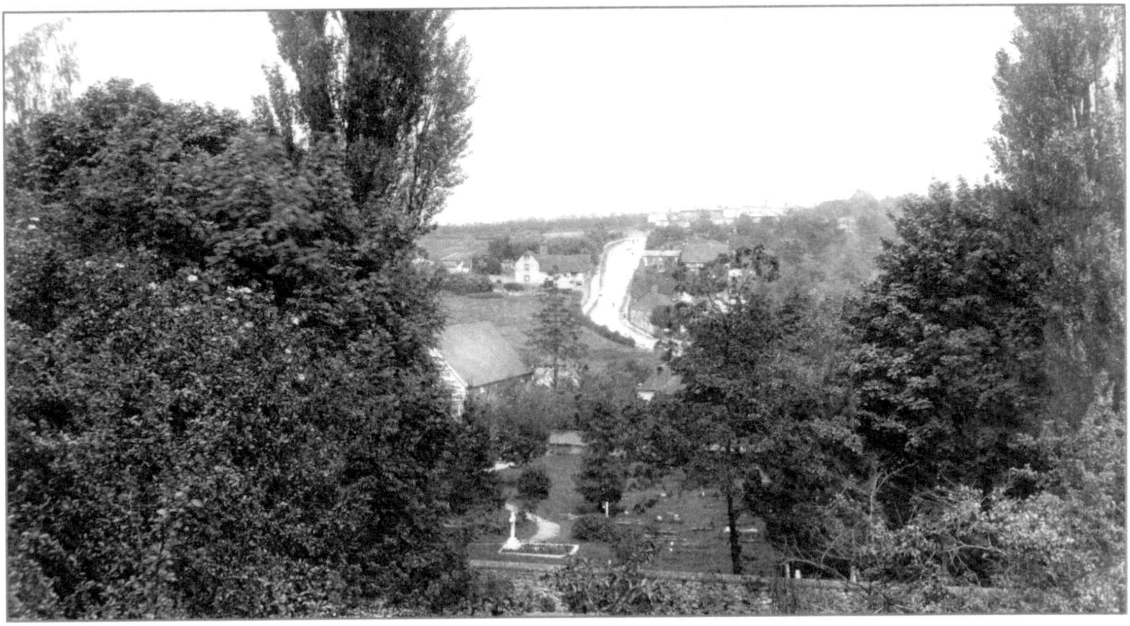

Loose, The Valley 1898 41561
Loose is situated just south-east of the Medway; it is an unusual village that spills down the hillside towards the valley bottom, and is surrounded by hop and fruit gardens. There is an attractive causeway across the Loose stream which is sometimes covered by flowing water in the winter. It drove several paper and corn mills in Victorian times.

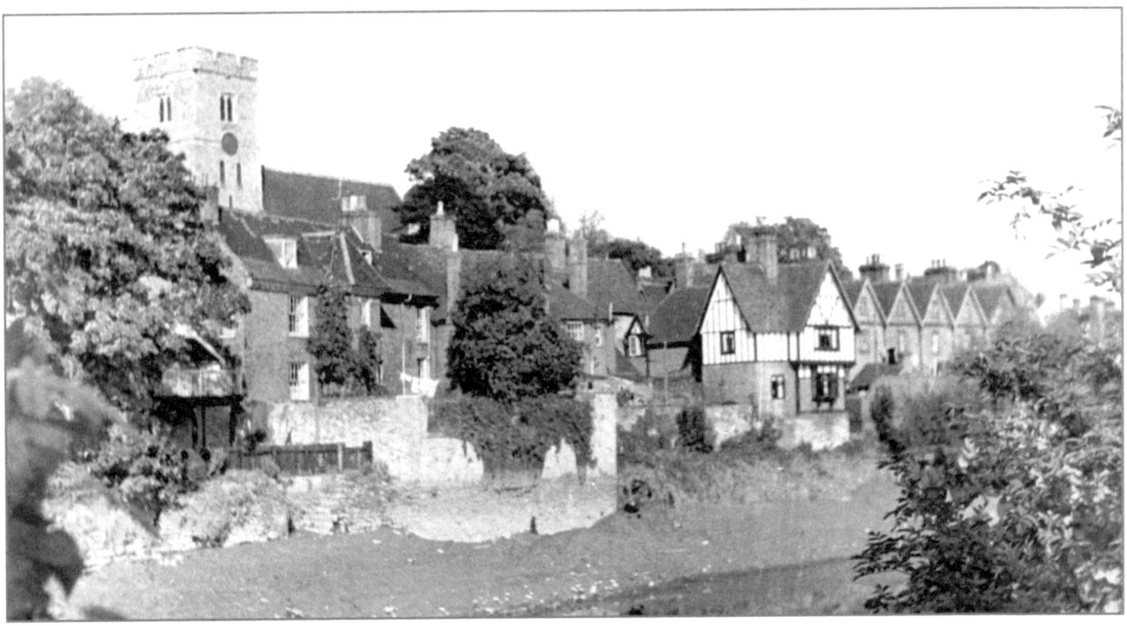

Aylesford, The Village from the River c1960 A85005
One of Kent's most ancient villages, Aylesford occupies a strategic crossing of the Medway, and dates from the time of the Saxons. The parish church crowns a hillock and is principally Norman. The tower was raised in height in 1892 in the memory of H A Brassey. Just down the road to the west is a Carmelite friary, which is much visited by those in search of tranquillity and meditation.

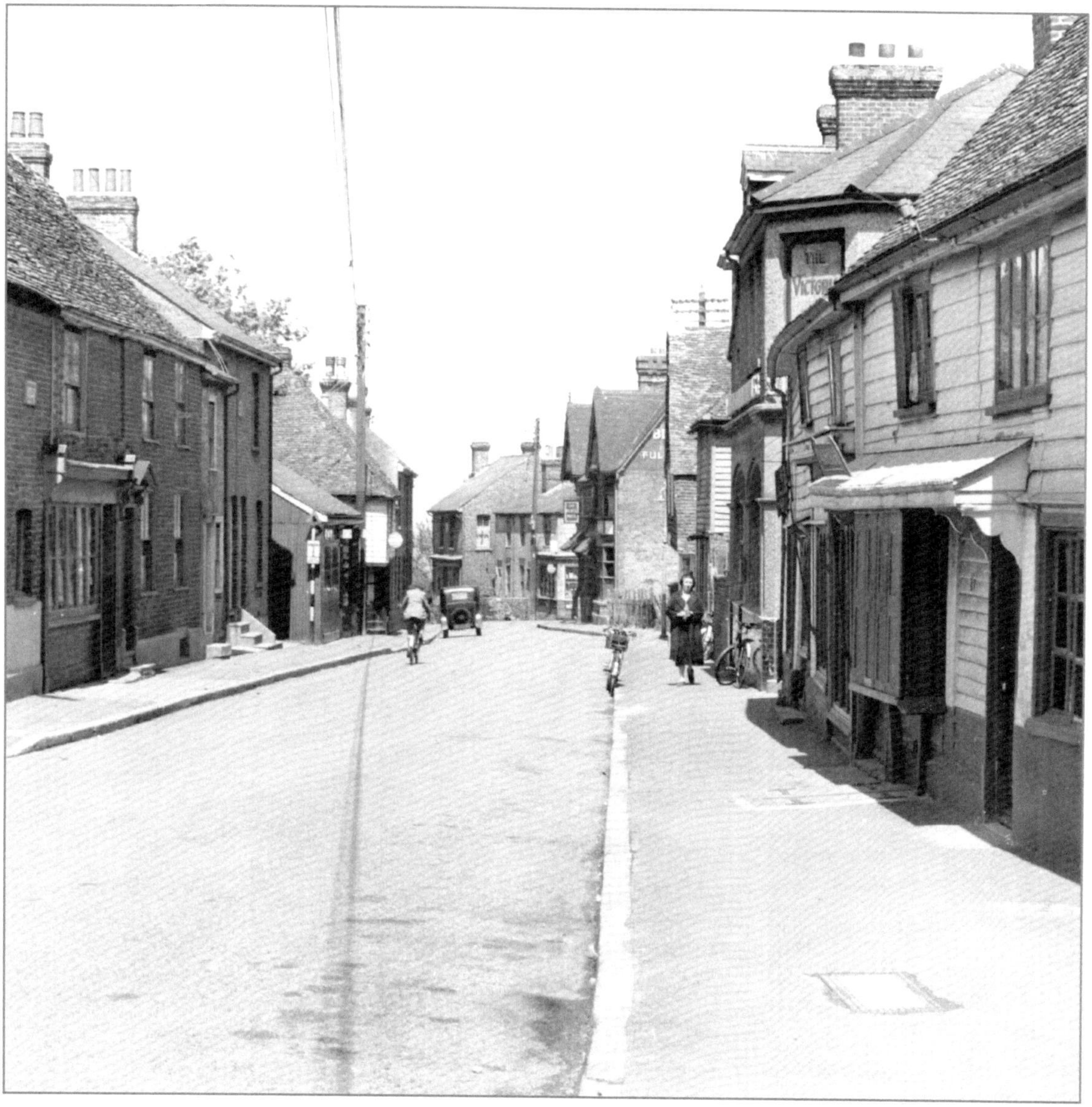

Cliffe, High Street c1950 C464014

Cliffe perches at the end of the long chalk ridges, overhanging the marshes of the Thames. It was formerly an important place until a fire in 1562 gutted the town. Various industries flourished here in Victorian times: chalk was quarried, whiting and cement made, and a canal allowed passage through to the Thames. It is now an unprepossessing village, with some pleasing weatherboarded houses in the High Street. On the right are two public houses - the Victoria and the Black Bull. In the foreground, Parker's store is advertising Brasso, Silver Shred marmalade and Cherry Blossom shoe polish.

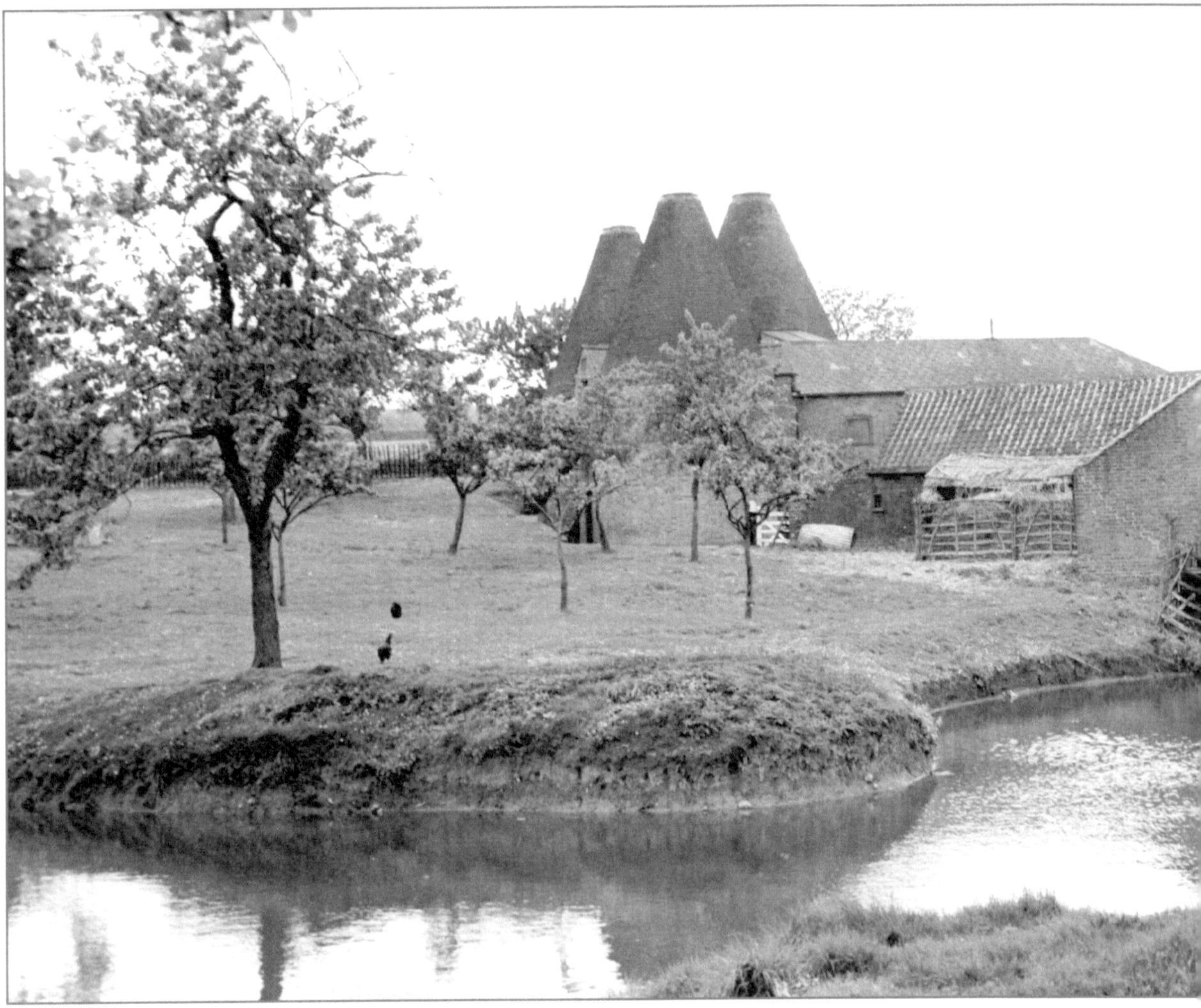

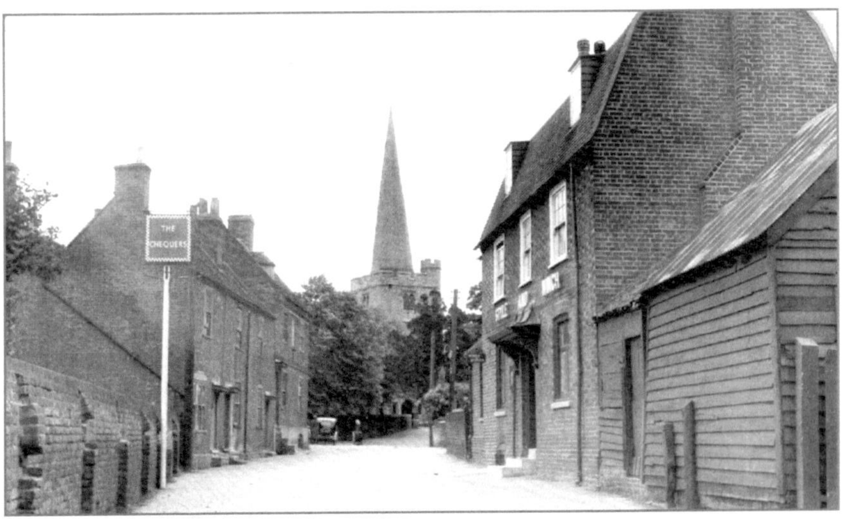

Hoo, The Church and the Chequers Hotel c1950 H356006
Since 1968, this village has been officially known as Hoo St Werburgh; it is named after a Saxon princess who became a nun, and who was buried on the site of the present church. The impressive shingled spire of the parish church rises above the thick yews, and acts as a useful landmark for shipping on the Medway.

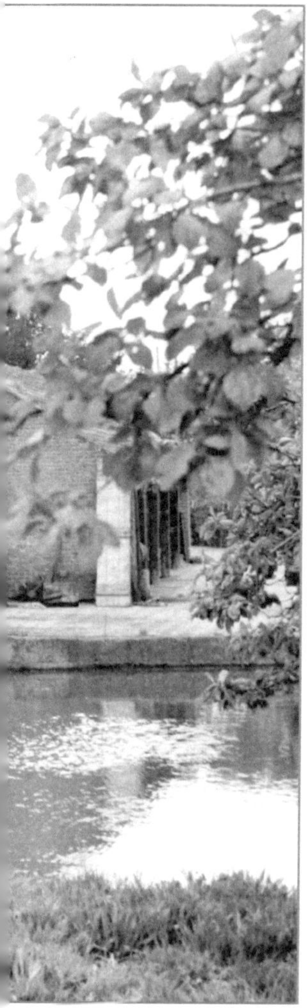

◄ **Cliffe, Oast Houses c1955** C464012
This beautiful scene of blossoms and oast houses was obviously taken in the spring. These oasts are of a slightly different design to those seen at Wateringbury earlier in this chapter.

▼ **Allhallows, The Rose and Crown c1950** A229002
Allhallows is in the hundred of Hoo, close by the Thames. It looks as if the Rose and Crown might have at least one customer taking refuge from the cold winds of this exposed part of the Hoo Peninsula. Isolation led in the past to the area being a hotbed of smuggling. Today, once away from these few houses, you cannot avoid the dominating presence of the Isle of Grain power station chimney.

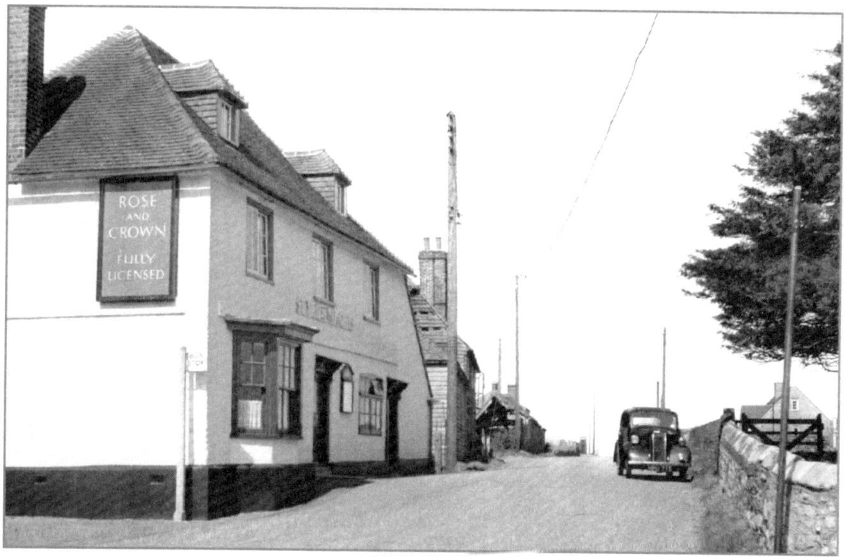

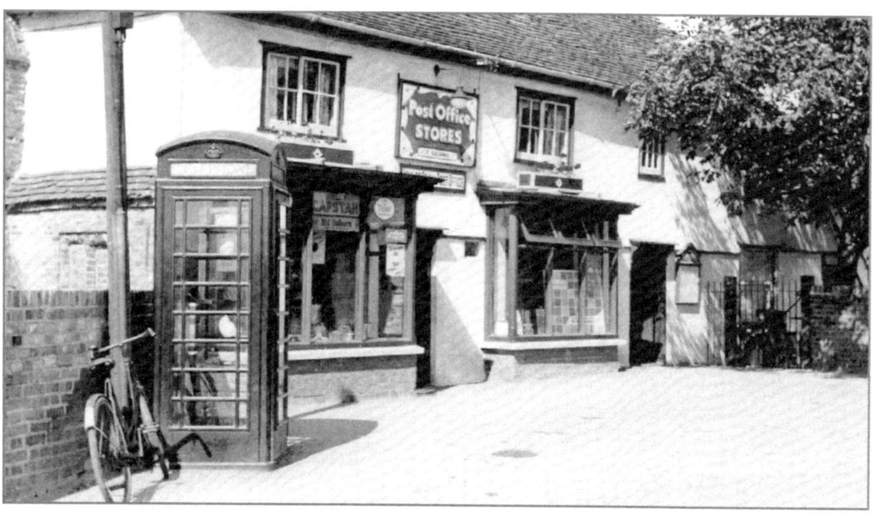

◄ **Isle of Grain The Post Office c1955** I52006
Set between the Thames and the Medway, Grain was once an island. Now it is connected to the mainland by road. The village sits on high ground, and unlike much of the parish which sits on more marshy land, is protected from flooding by embankments. It is now much industrialised. The little post office no doubt did a brisk trade, doubling up as a general store.

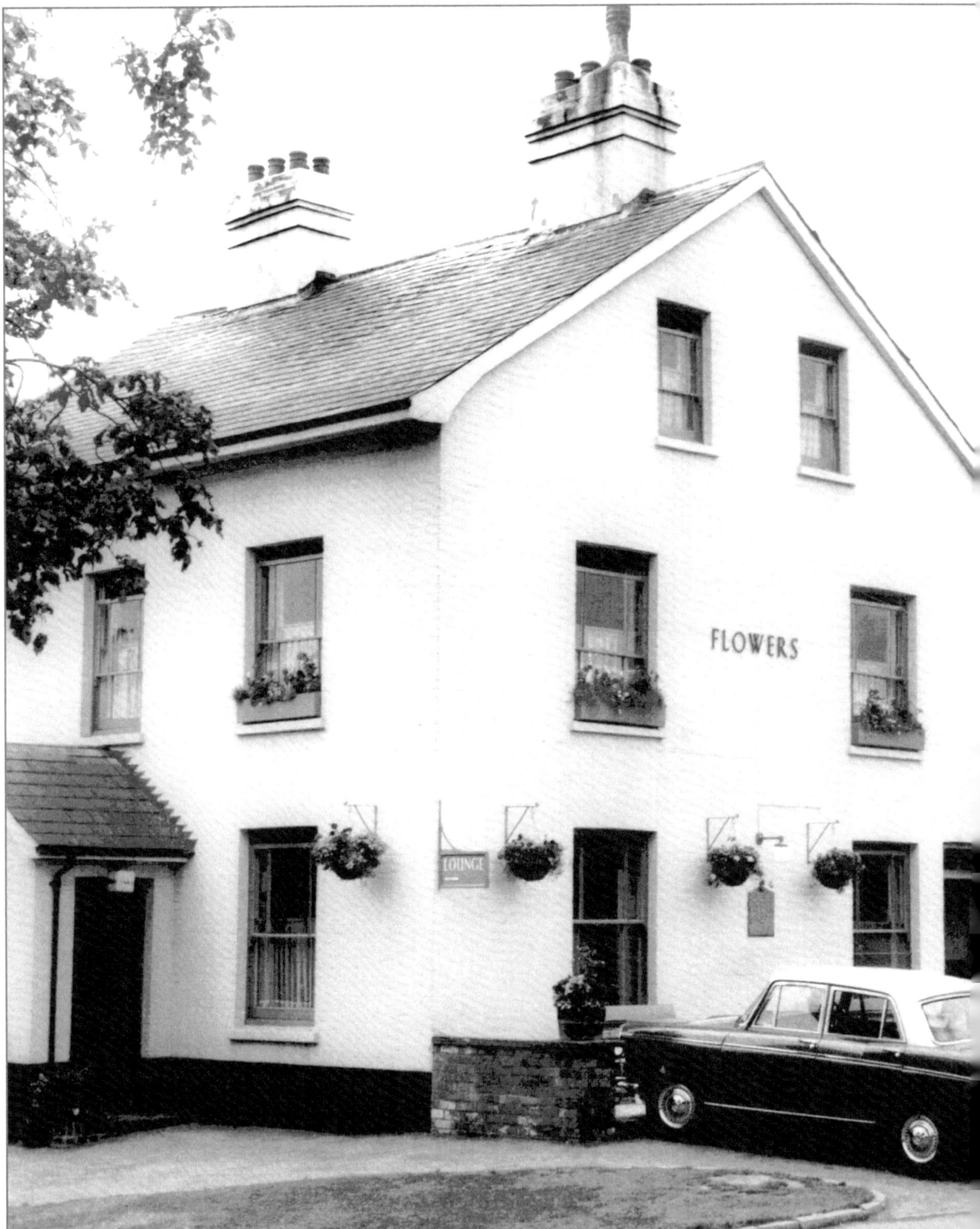
FLOWERS
LOUNGE

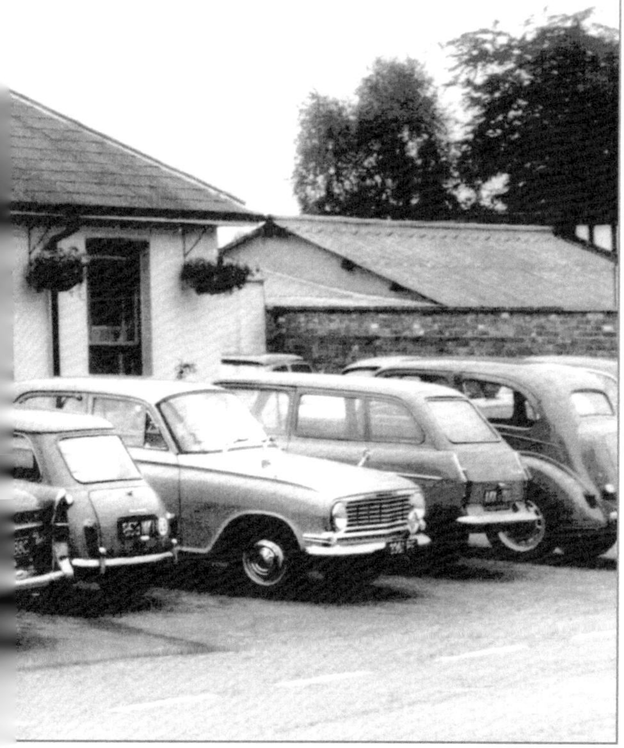

The Weald of Kent

Bidborough, The Hare and Hounds c1965
B87008
This village is set high up close to the Sussex border. The village pub, the Hare and Hounds, has barely changed since this photograph was taken 35 years ago. Look at the car to the far right of the line: it is remarkable how old-fashioned some cars still being driven in the 1960s now look. Bidborough's claim to fame is a rare form of chestnut tree that only grows around the village. Predictably, it is known as the Bidborough chestnut.

Langton Green The Village Green c1950 L324008

This leafy suburb of Tunbridge Wells boasts a broad and spacious green, fringed by cottages and trees. It was a popular place to live in Victorian times, containing several 'gentlemen's seats and neat villas'. The village sits three miles west of the Tunbridge Wells on the East Grinstead road, which is much busier today than when this picture was taken some 50 years ago.

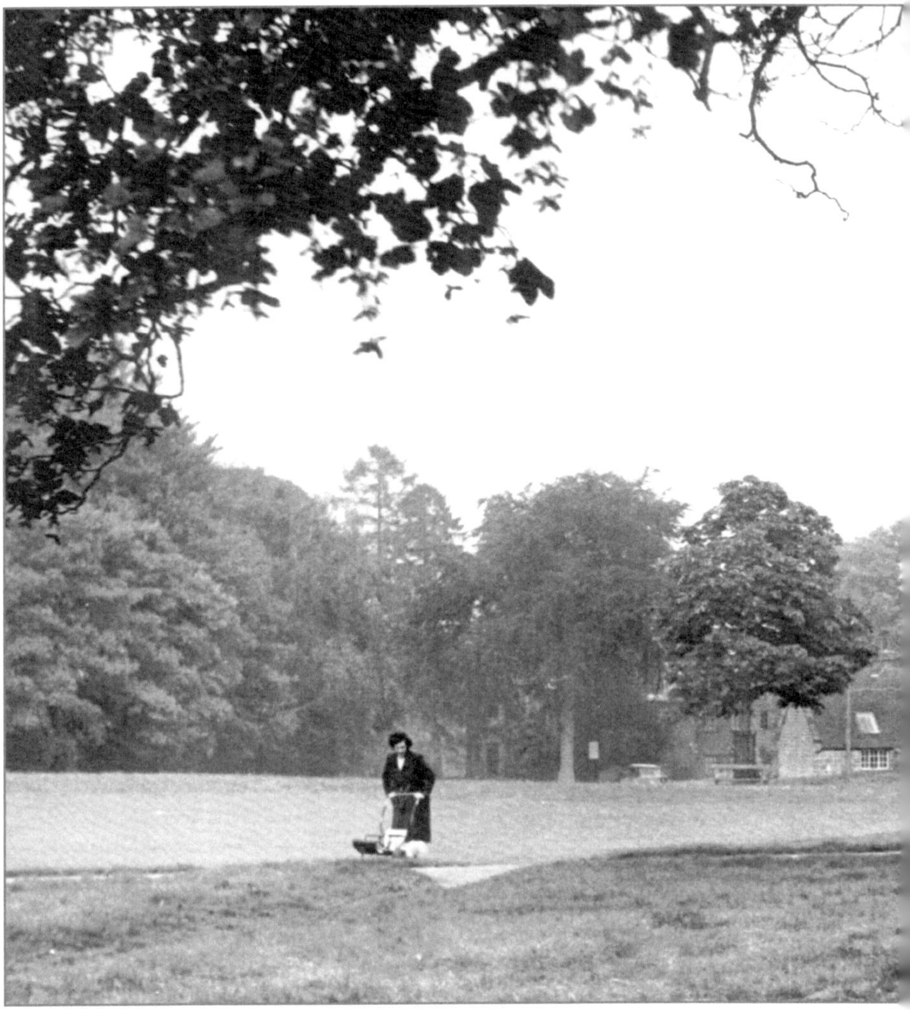

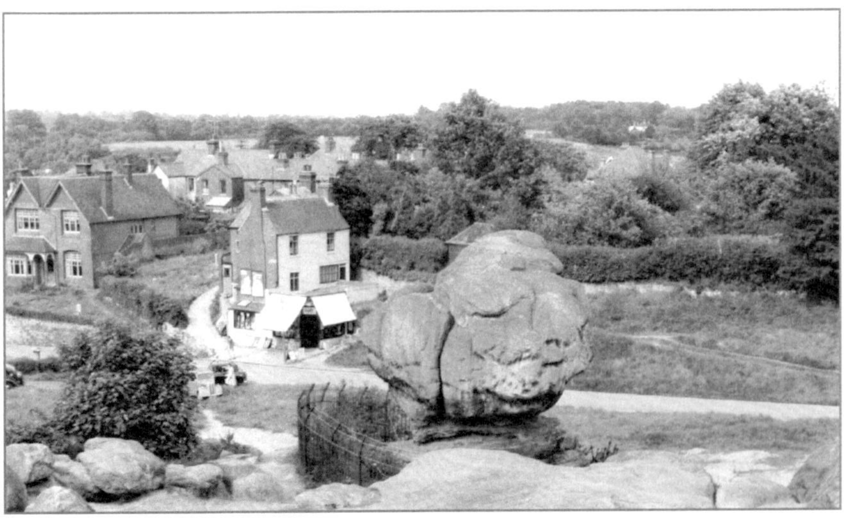

Rusthall, Toad Rock c1950 R320030

Rusthall is now little more than a Tunbridge Wells suburb. Rusthall Common is an extensive open waste studded with massive singularly shaped rocks. Toad Rock, perched precariously above the cottages below, is a remarkable logan-like cluster.

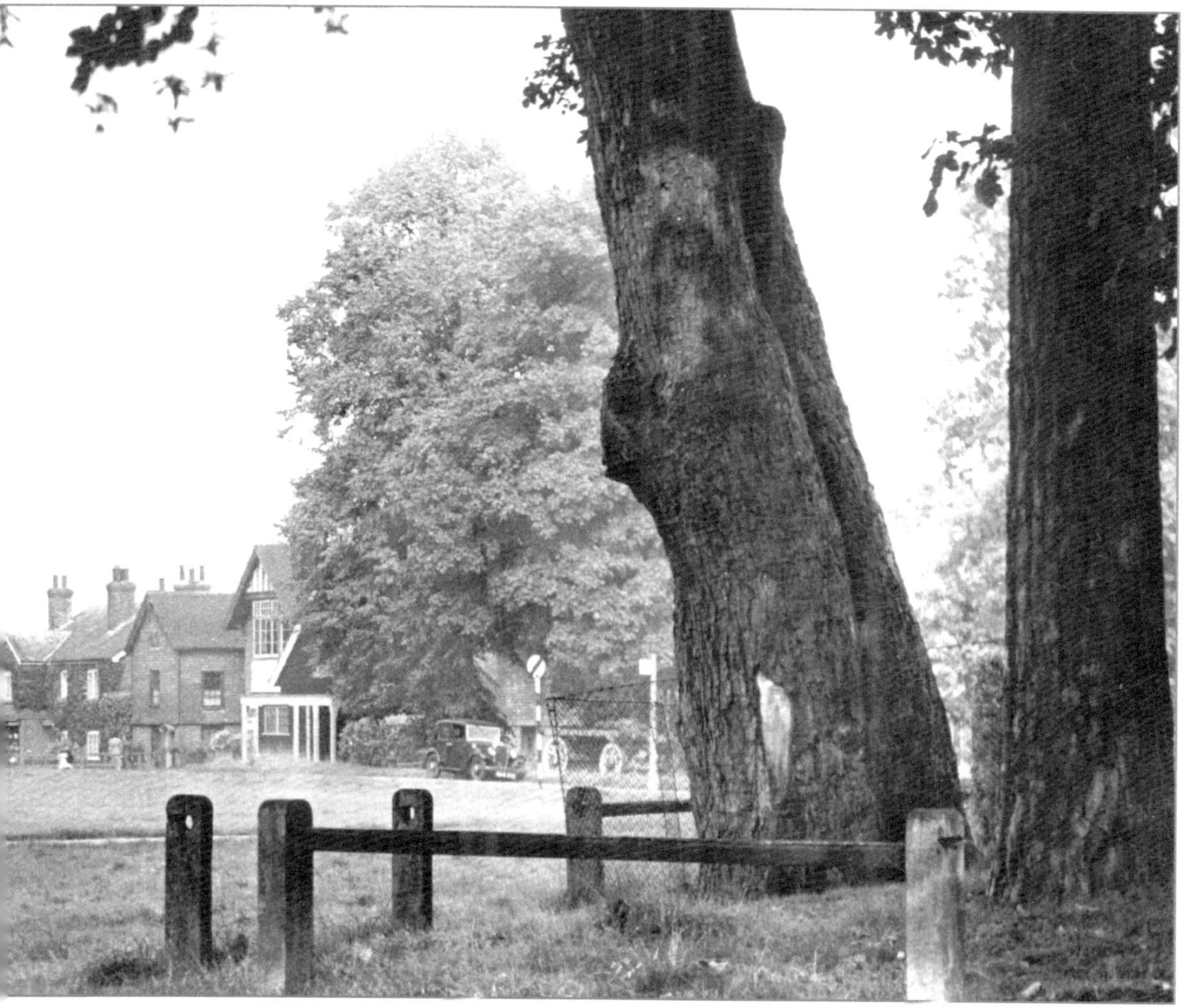

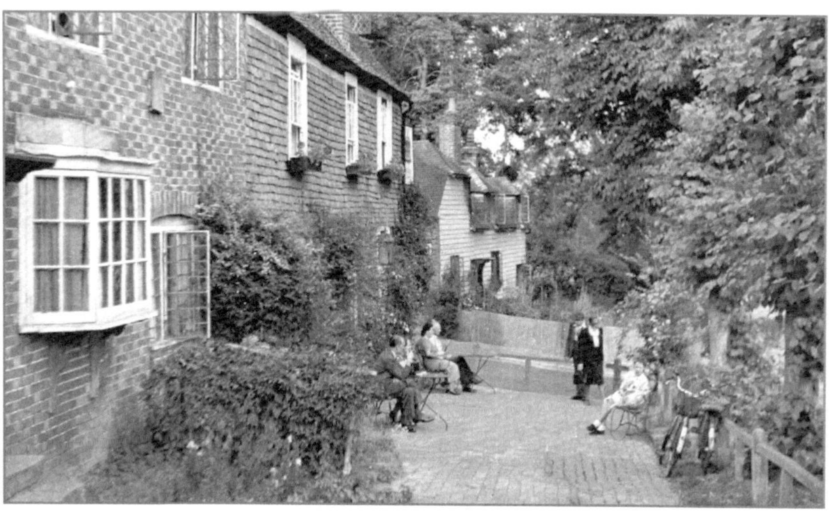

◄ **Groombridge, Cottages c1955** G216003

This beautiful village of brick and tile-hung cottages clusters about its small green. On the extreme left we see cottage walls constructed in the popular Flemish bond. A simple decorative effect is gained from the incorporation of differently coloured headers. Sir Arthur Conan Doyle set some of his Sherlock Holmes story 'The Valley of Fear' at nearby Groombridge Place, where there is now a museum dedicated to this great writer's most famous creation.

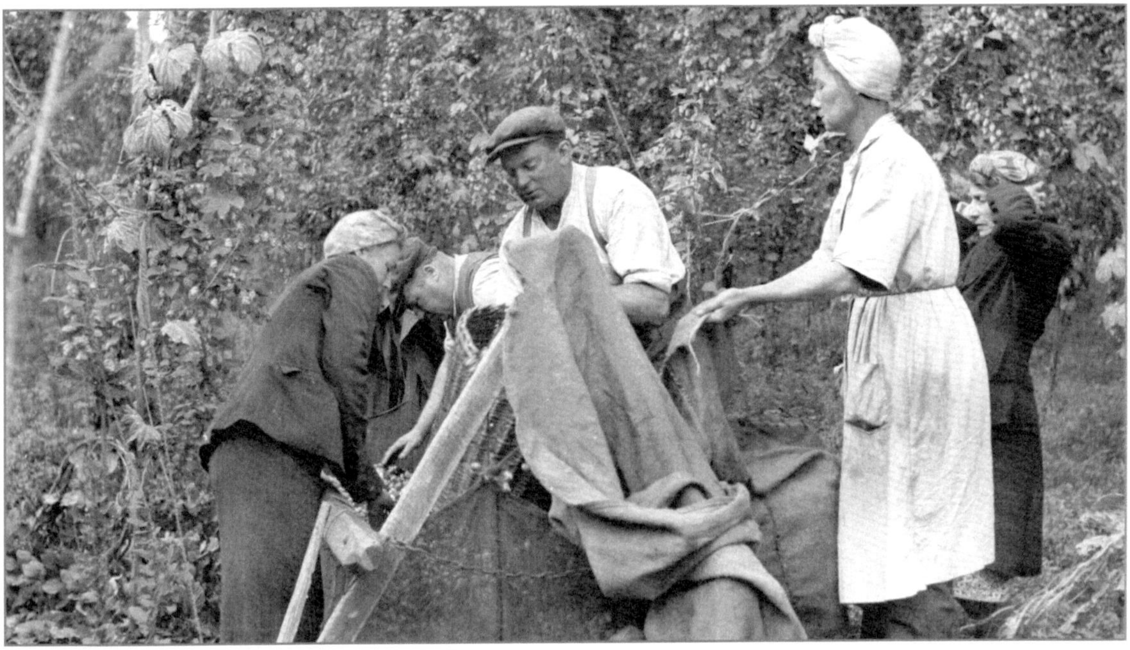

Paddock Wood, Measuring the Hops c1950 P220008
This village was the hop picking 'capital' of Kent. At one time, every September hordes of workers with their families would arrive and camp out for the season. As well as earning some money, it was a way for some families to have a cheap holiday. Hop picking is today largely mechanised.

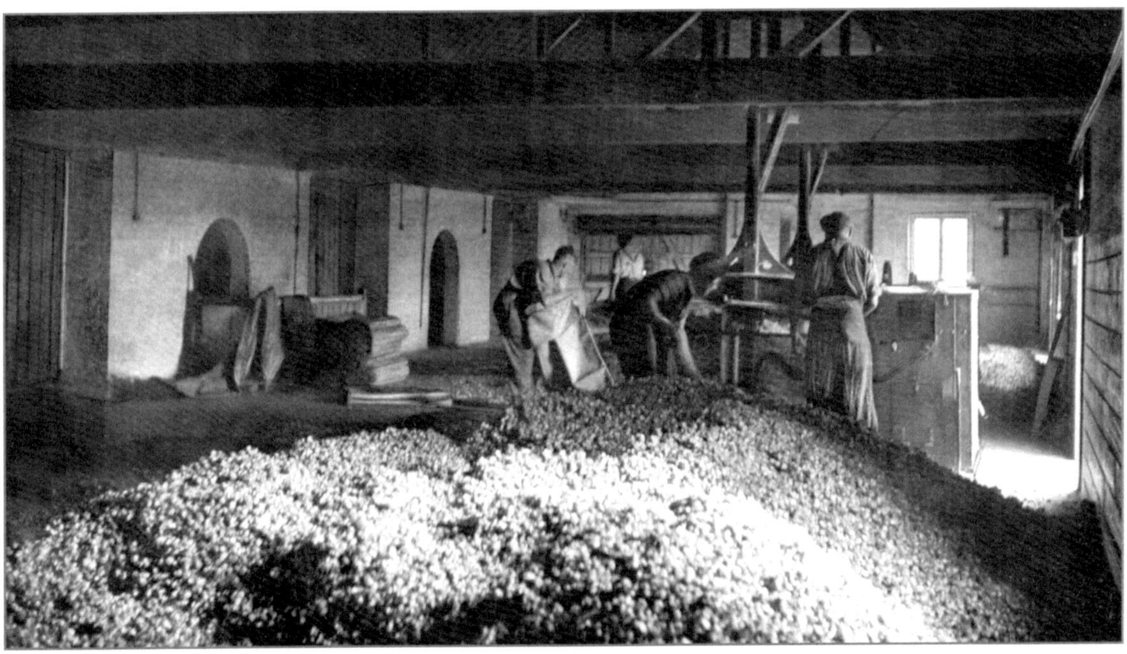

Paddock Wood, Pressing the Hops c1950 P220016
Here we see piles of hops prior to pressing. Kentish hops were much in demand, particularly of course by Kentish breweries such as Mackesons and Shepherd Neame. So many hop pickers came to the Paddock Wood area that a hospital called the Little Hoppers Hospital was built in the late 19th century.

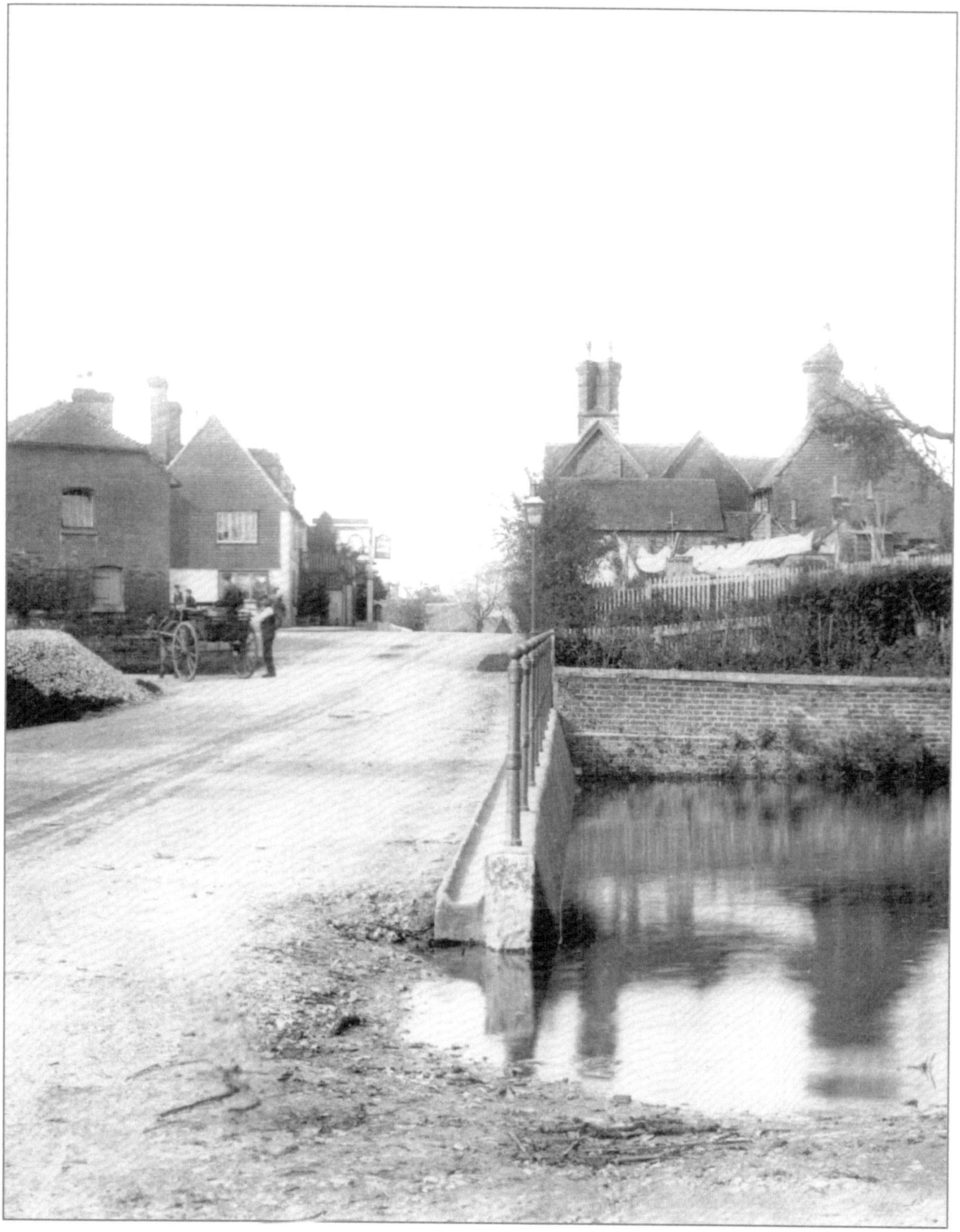

Horsmonden, The Village 1903 50550
Once a major ironworking centre, this village also boasts the first Fuggle hops to be grown. It was also the birthplace of a useful invention: John Read of Horsmonden invented the stomach pump here, not the most glamorous association for a village! Bricks were made here in Victorian times, and there were several flour mills.

Horsmonden
The Green 1903
50551

Horsmonden's cottages and houses surround a spacious green. The village boasts a wealth of old buildings and timbered cottages. The curious building on the left, with the quaint bell tower and decorative geometric detailing is the Working Man's Club. In the middle of the picture a customer is entering Harvey's village shop.

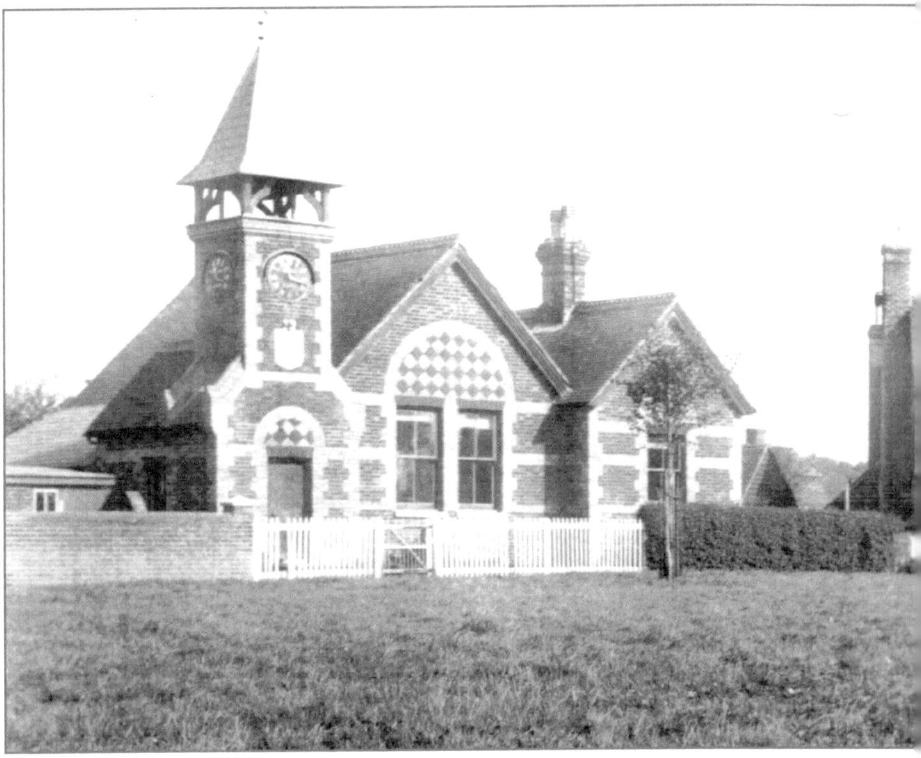

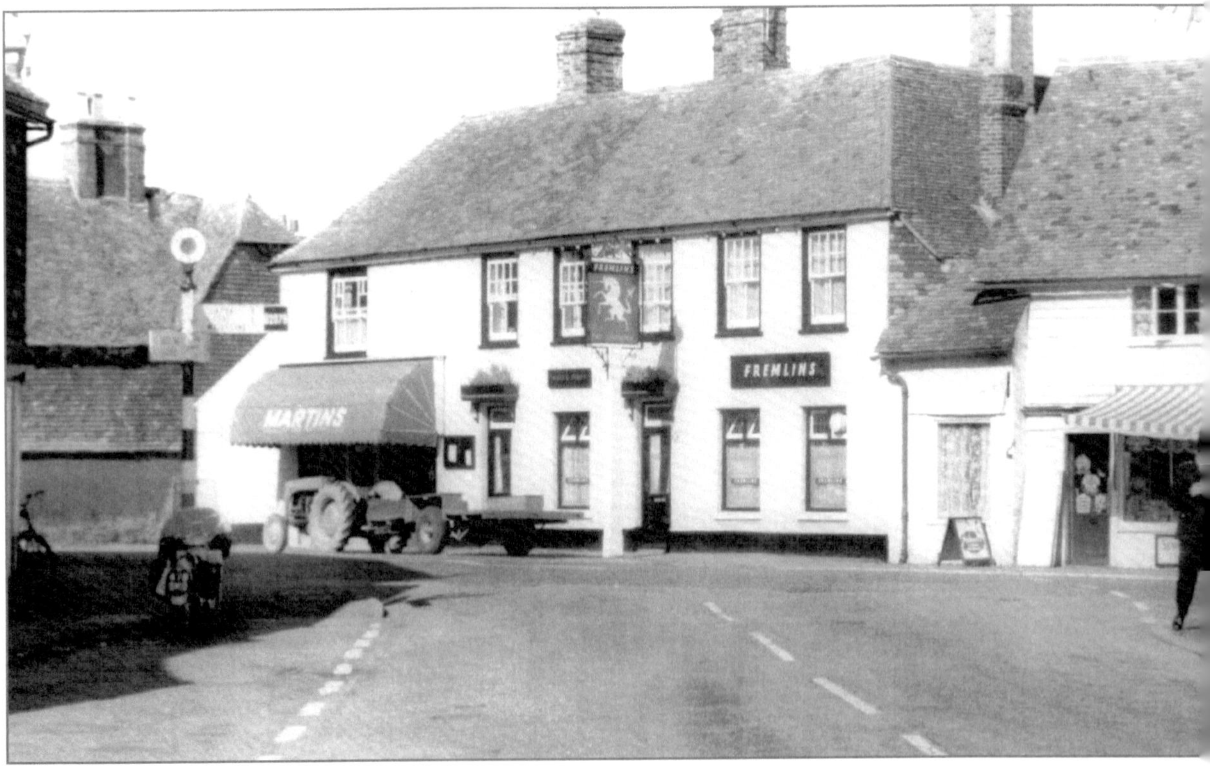

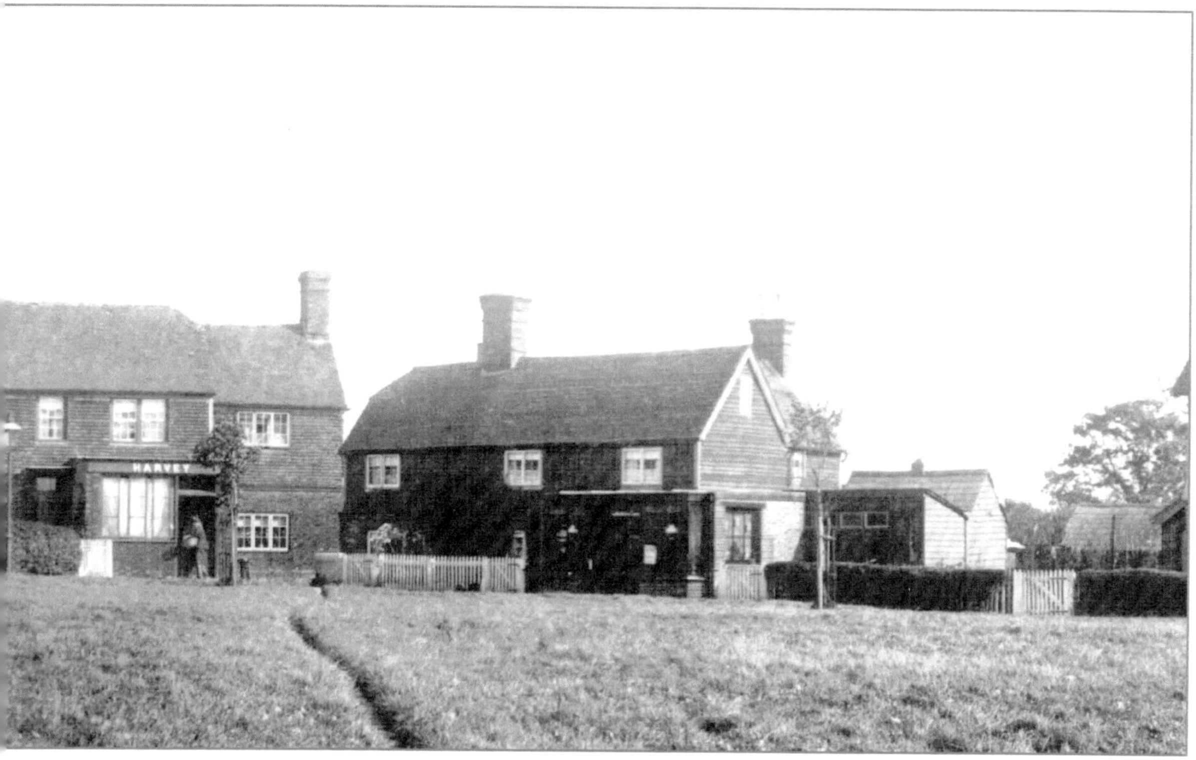

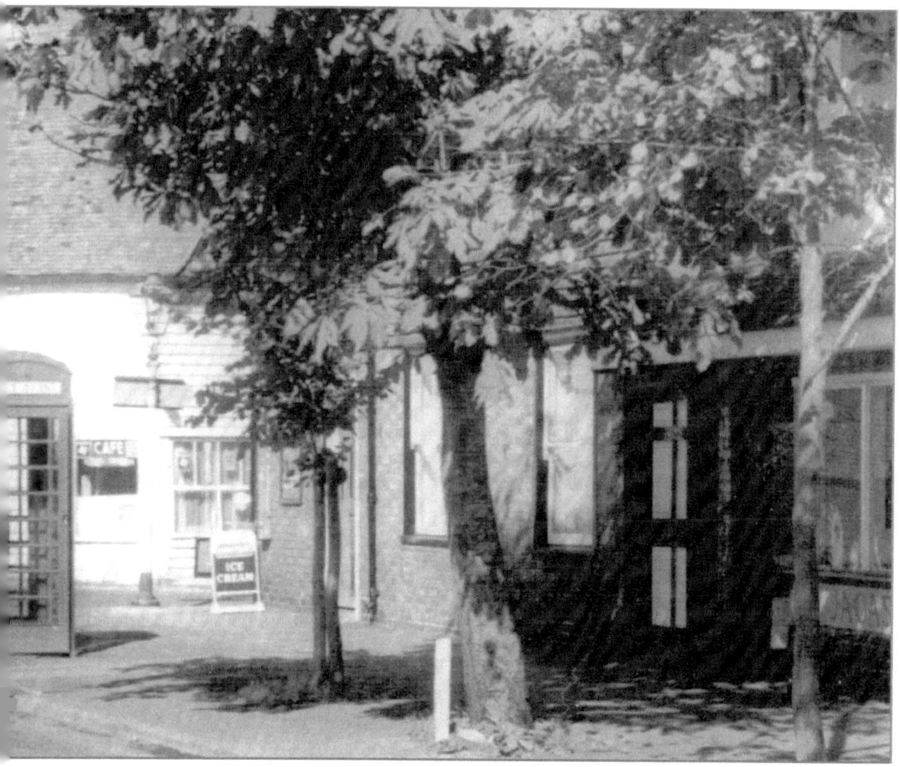

Marden, High Street c1955 M252014
Mardcn lics ninc miles south of Maidstone. In this quintessential village scene, we see the village bobby standing next to the red telephone box, with a café selling ice creams behind. The white Unicorn public house shows in the distance with a tractor and trailer parked outside. There used to be 14 pubs in the village, but since the decline of hop picking, many have gone out of business. In the churchyard can be found a well-preserved set of stocks, which were once used for the punishment of local offenders.

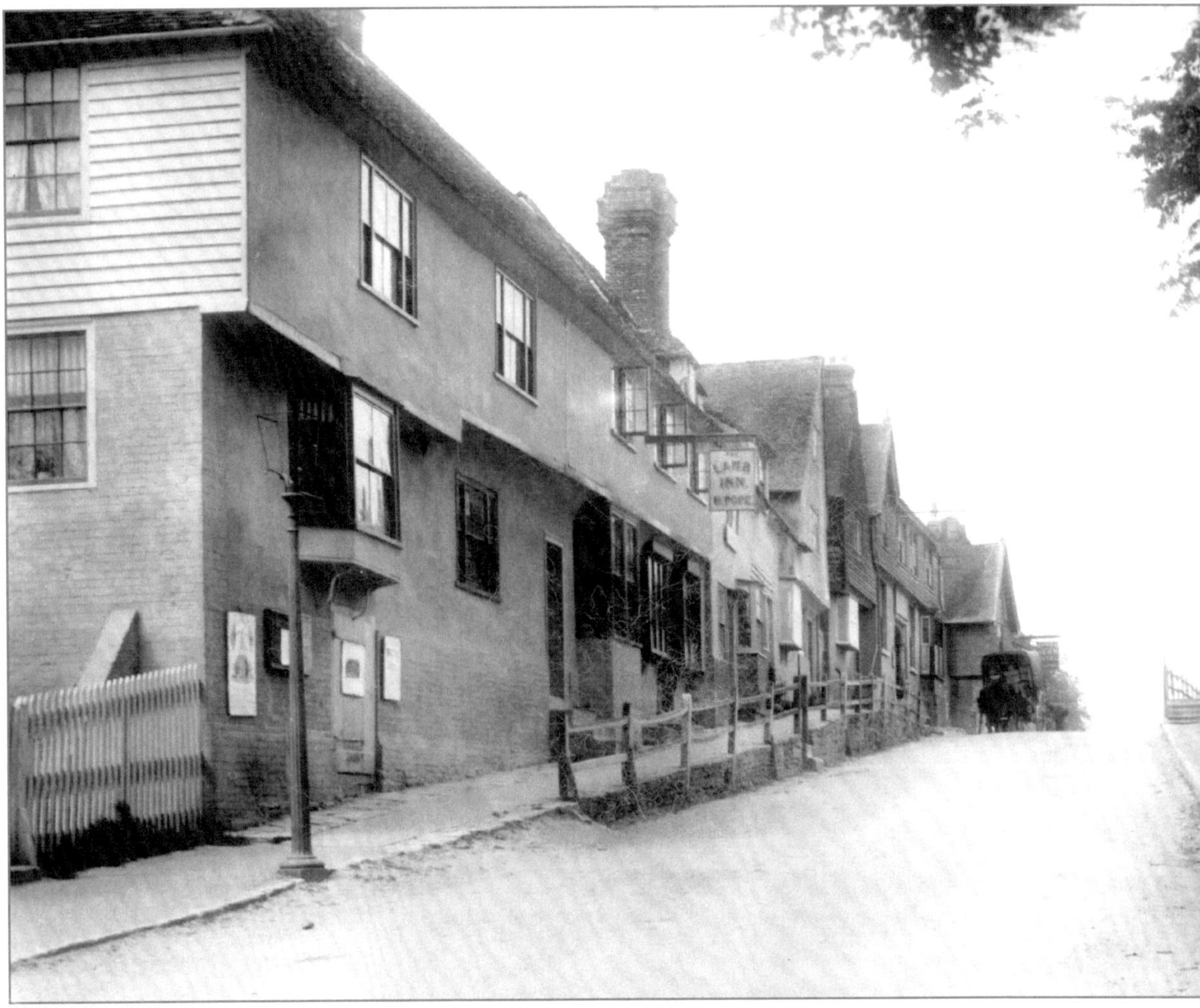

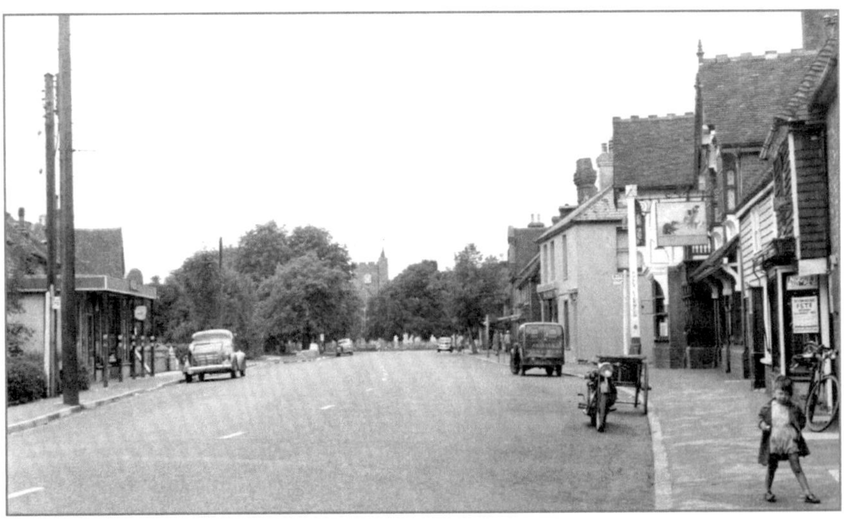

◄ **Headcorn, High Street c1955** H58007
Headcorn stands on the River Beult and is a large village with a single broad, straggling street. On the right outside the George and Dragon is a motorcycle with an unusual basketwork sidecar. The church, at the end of the village, is noteworthy on account of the ancient oak in its churchyard, which has a girth of 40 feet and is said to be nearly 1000 years old.

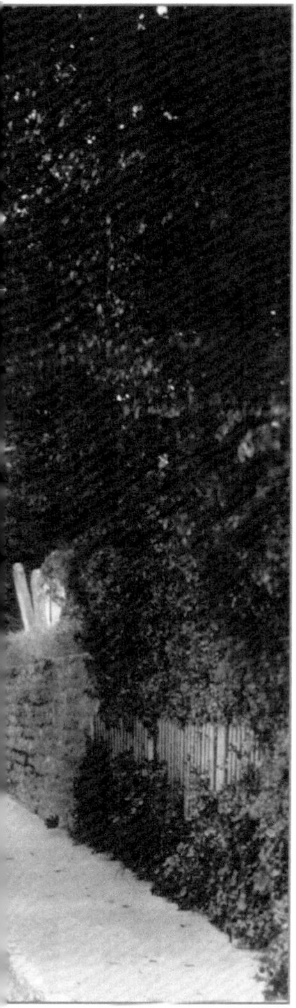

Staplehurst, The Village 1903
51073
This Wealden village lies on a Roman road. It benefited from the spread of the cloth industry in medieval times, and its prosperity led to the building of many solid timber houses for clothiers and yeomen. Staplehurst grew as a result of being on the South Eastern Railway's route from London to Dover. One notable commuter was the banker Henry Hoare, who was responsible for restoring the 12th-century church in 1853. On the left of the photograph is the Lamb Inn.

Smarden, The Street c1950 S533008
Smarden is an attractive Wealden village in H E Bates country, with a number of fine old timbered houses. At one time it had a substantial trade in linen and woollen goods. The 15th-century Chequers Inn has a ghost which has been seen on and off for many years. As recently as September 1997, a guest saw a small dark man who faded away when spoken to. It is thought the ghost is associated with a young French prisoner of war, who was lodged at the Chequers and was murdered for reasons unknown.

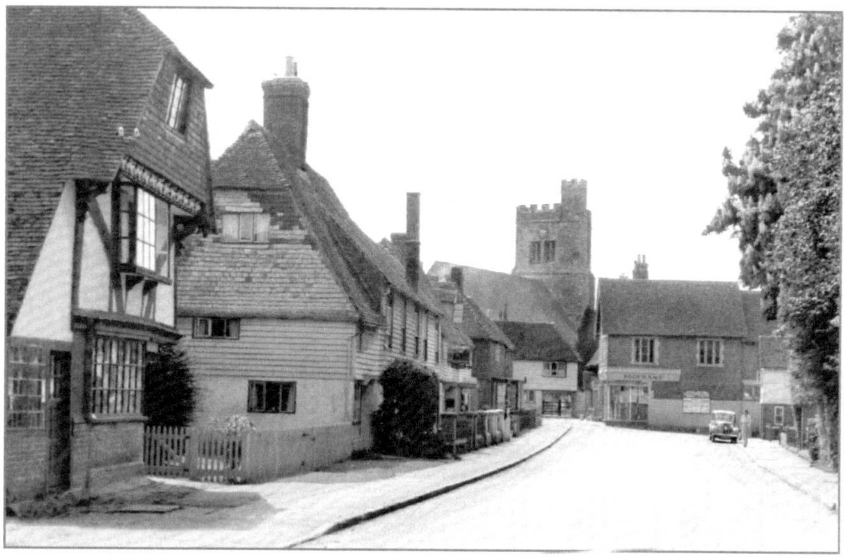

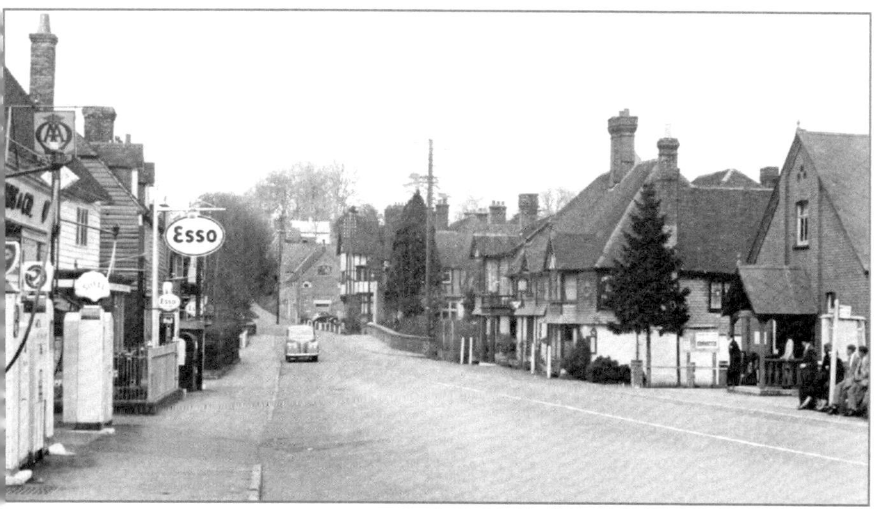

Lamberhurst
The Village c1955
L323025
Lamberhurst sits in rolling downland in the beautiful Teise valley close to the border with Sussex, surrounded by orchards and hop gardens. The main road is a lot quieter here than it is today. The garage on the left is interesting for its old-style petrol and AA signs.

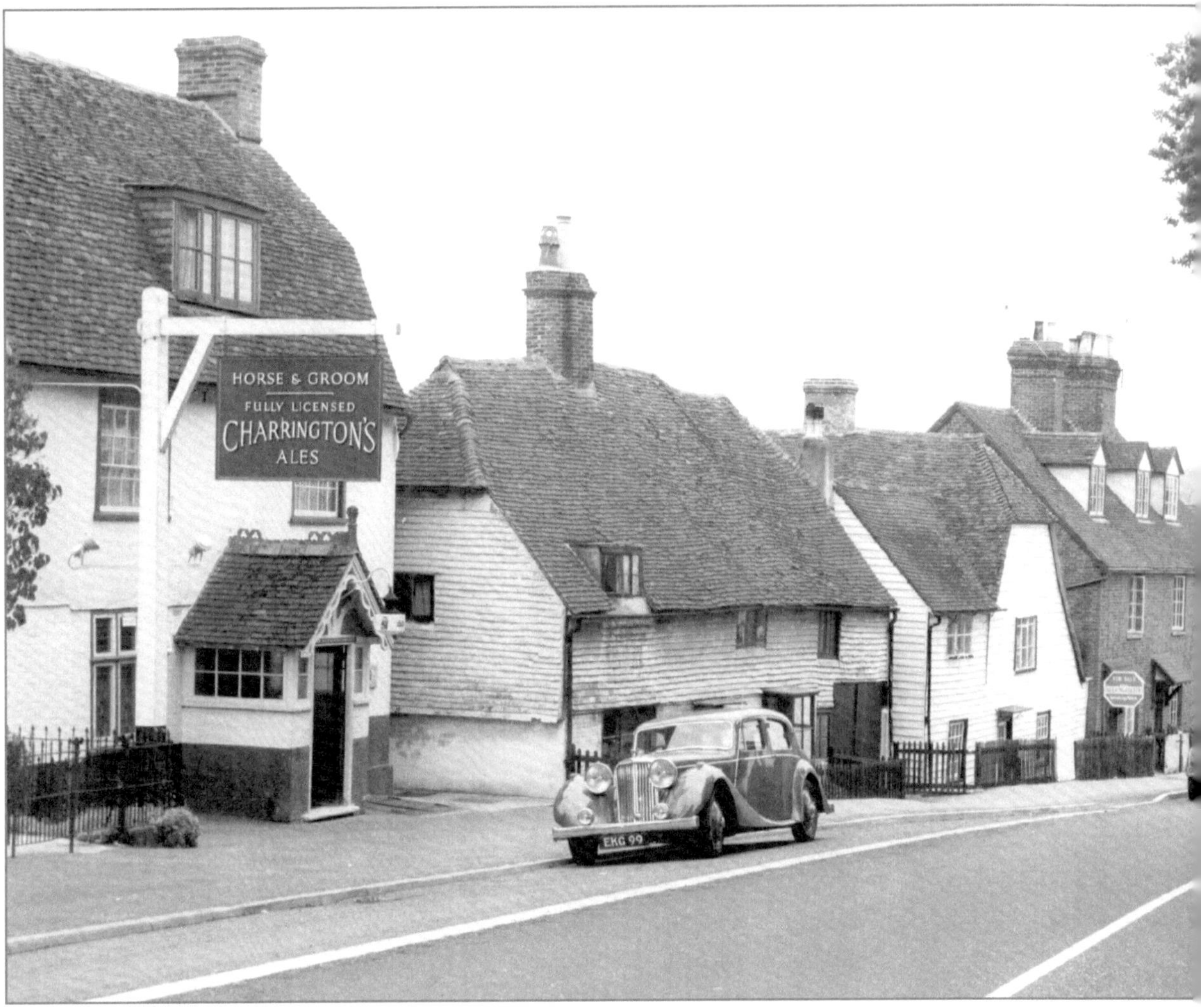

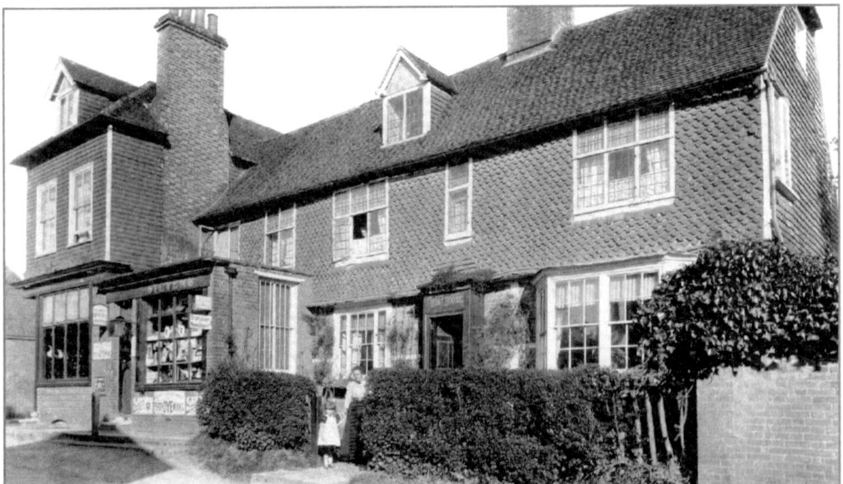

Goudhurst
West House 1901
46386

Here we see an attractive tiled house with Stevens' the newsagents attached to it. This shop also acted as an agent for the local dye works. Goudhurst originally prospered as a result of ironworking, and then later cloth making and dyeing. Flemish weavers were encouraged to settle in the locality, as they were in several other Wealden villages.

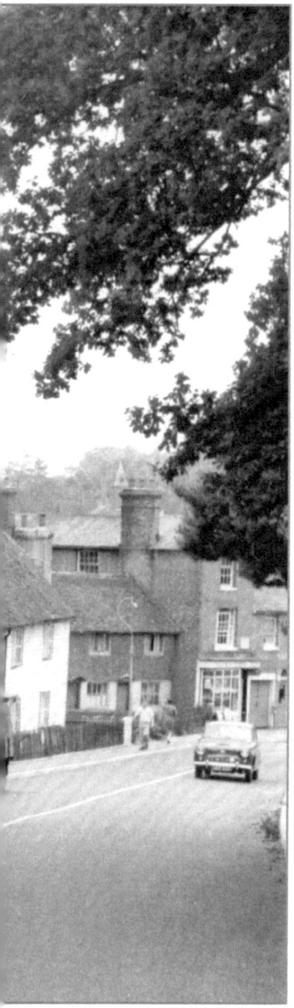

Lamberhurst, Old Hill and High Street c1955 L323051

This scene shows the delightful variety of sizes and styles of weatherboarded houses in the village. The Horse and Groom pub is now a private house. Once a centre of the Wealden ironworking industry, Lamberhurst is today known for its fine vineyard of 32 acres, for the 770-acre Bewl Water Reservoir, and for the attractive fairytale Scotney Castle, the seat of Archbishop Chicheley. It was rebuilt by Inigo Jones.

Goudhurst, Hope Mill 1901

46398

This peaceful scene shows schoolboys boating near the mill. By the 20th century, Goudhurst has quietened down considerably compared to earlier times, when the iron smelting and cloth making industries were at their peak. Fishing has been popular on the Teise since Victorian times, with grayling and barbel sought from Finchlock's Bridge along to Hope Mill. A station was built here in the 1890s for the Cranbrook & Paddock Wood Railway.

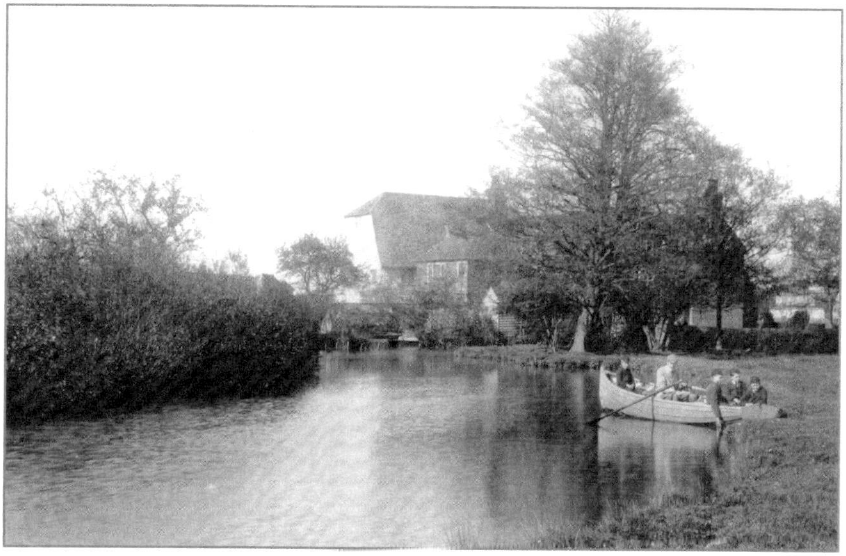

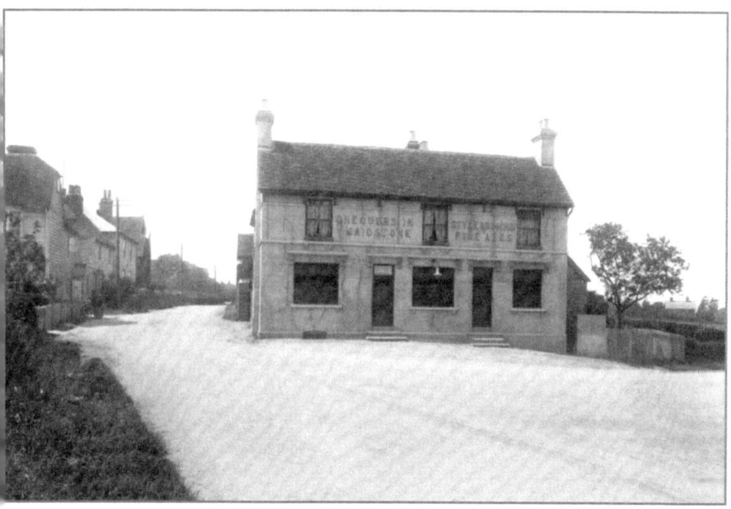

Goudhurst, The Chequers 1902

48303

At the time of this photograph, Thomas Bathgate was landlord of the Chequers, serving Style and Winch ales. During the 18th century, many of the pubs in the Weald were frequented by vicious smuggling gangs that dominated the area. Most notorious was 'the Hawkhurst Gang', which included the three Kingsmill brothers, residents of Goudhurst. Eventually the village had enough of the gang, and under the leadership of Corporal Sturt challenged the 100-strong gang to a pitched battle on 20 April 1747. Known as the Battle of Goudhurst, this resulted in the deaths of three of the smugglers, including one of their leaders.

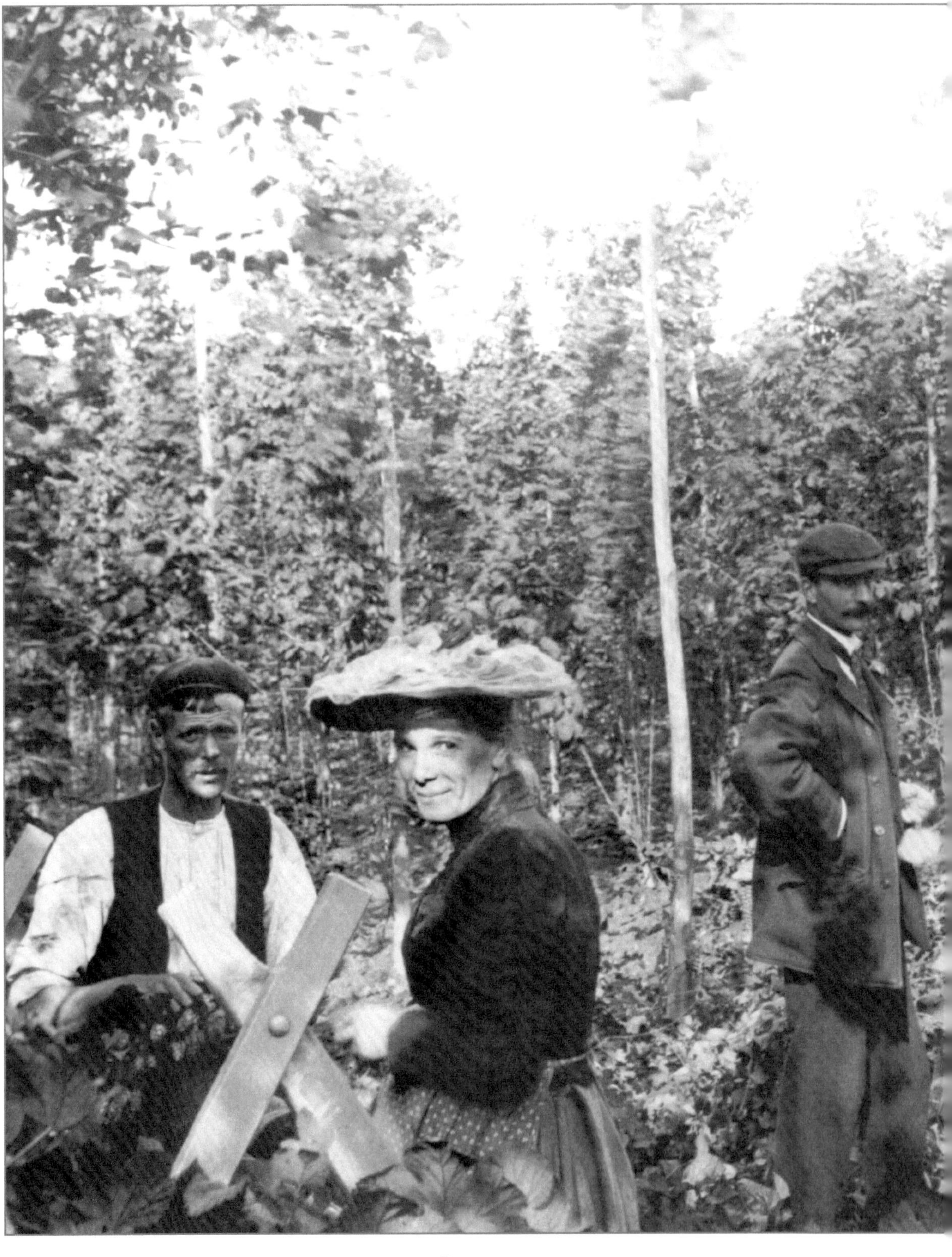

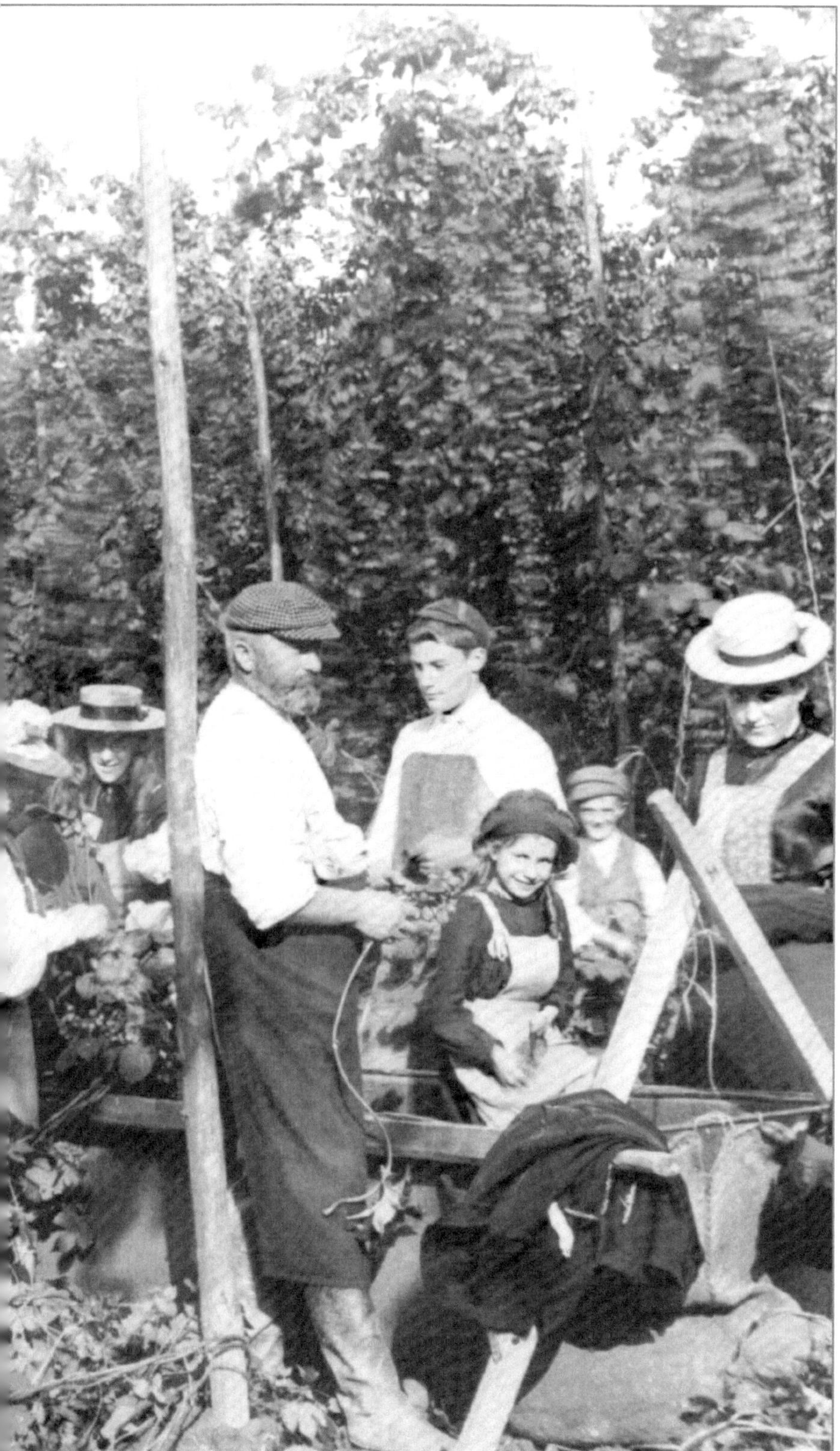

Goudhurst, Hop Pickers 1904 52569
During the first half of the 20th century, whole families from the poorer parts of London travelled down to the hop picking areas of Kent for a week or two's 'holiday' whilst earning money hop picking in the fields. Many camped on site, and have fond memories of halcyon days spent in the bright summer air. These workers seem so neatly dressed that they have surely put on their best clothes for the photographer!

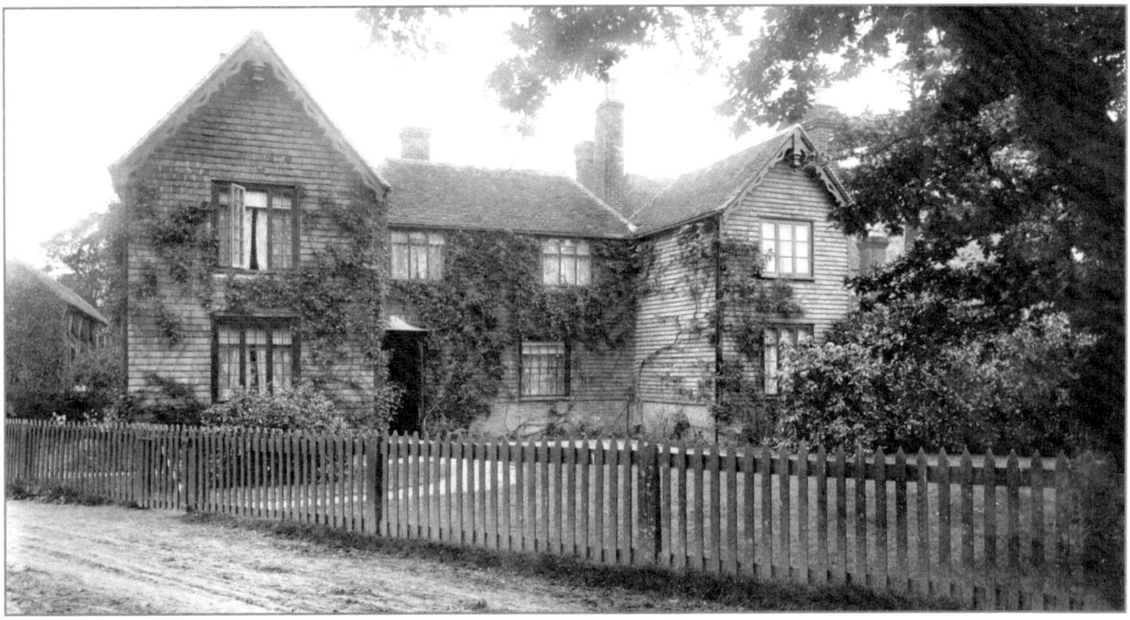

Bedgebury Park, The Farm 1902 48320
The fine old farmhouse sits on a brick base and is hung with tiles and swathed in creeper. The Manor of Bedgebury, near Goudhurst, had a foundry in the 16th century; it cast the guns for the fleet that fought the Spanish Armada in 1588. Today the forest around here contains an interesting pinetum, a nursery for pine trees of various types.

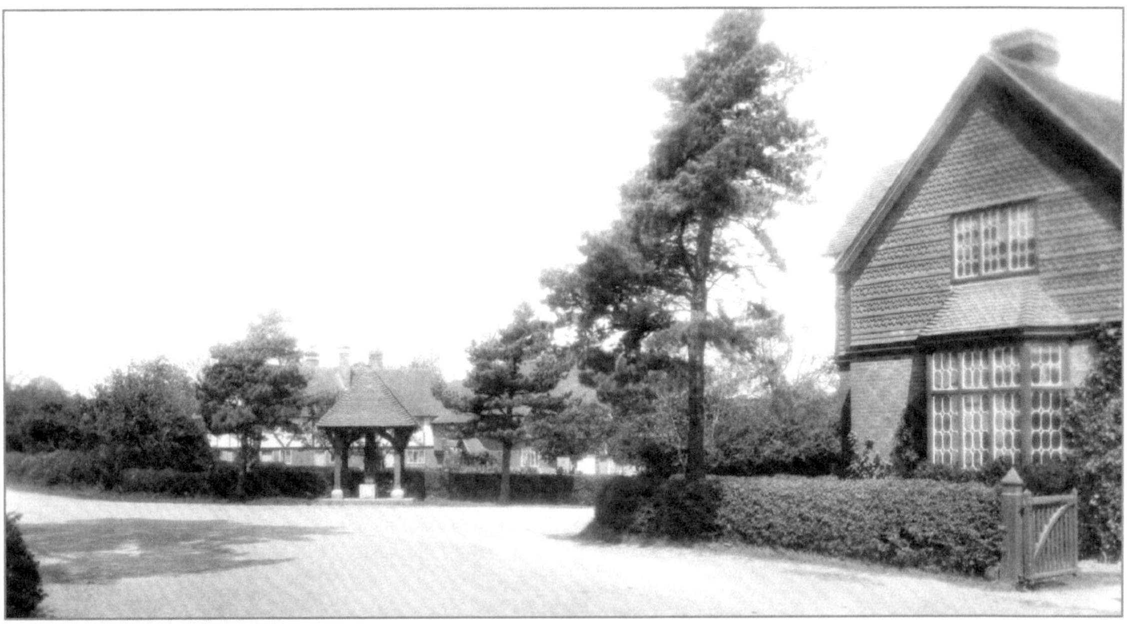

Benenden, The Village 1901 46450
This pleasant, tucked-away village, three miles from Cranbrook, is open and scattered in structure, like others in this part of Kent. It was once noted for cloth manufacture. It is now best known for its Chest Hospital, which was founded in 1905 to look after Post Office workers suffering from tuberculosis. A beacon stood nearby during the civil wars, forming part of a line of communication between Kent and London.

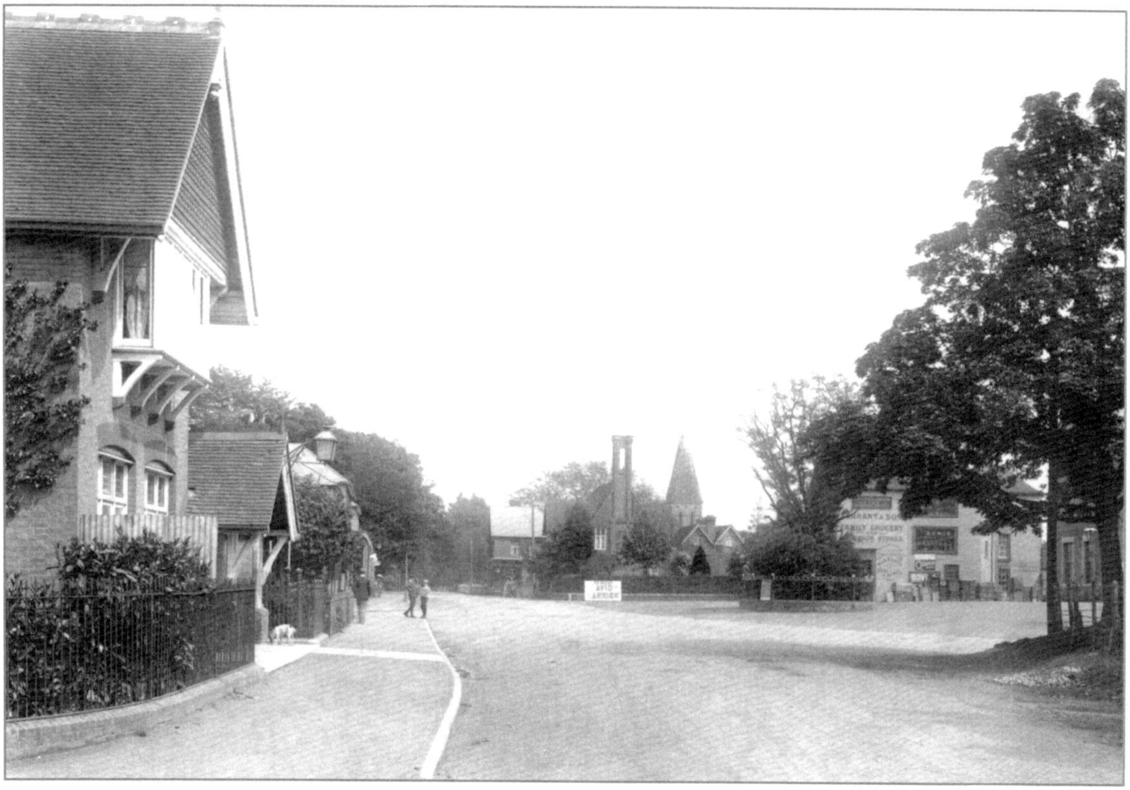

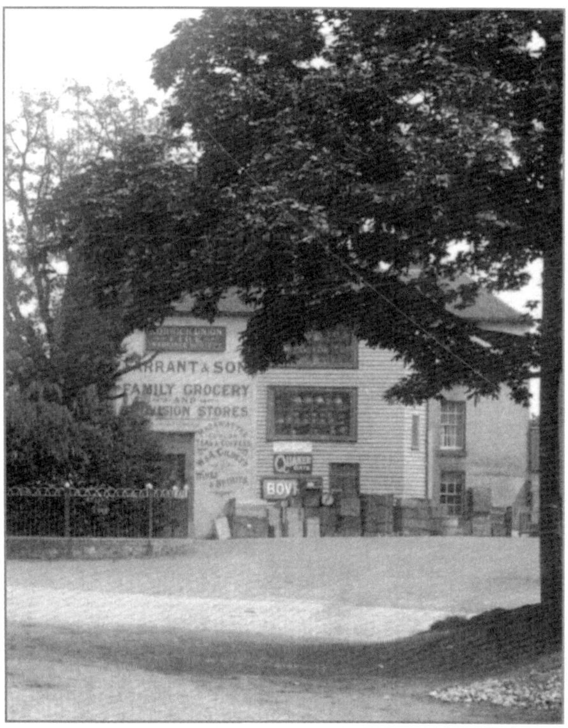

Hawkhurst, The Village 1902 48243
The village stands on the border with the neighbouring county of Sussex. It occupies rising ground and offers fine views across the Weald. It was once a substantial market centre, and in the 1890s had a small village hospital, a lecture hall and a reading-room. Babies' Castle, a nursery home for infants, was opened here in 1886 by Dr Barnardo. In the background is All Saints Church, erected in 1861 in the French Gothic style, with nave, aisles and lofty spire. Farrant & Sons, family grocers and local provision store, are advertising Mazawattee and Ceylon teas, as well as announcing that they are agents for Gilbey's wines and spirits. In the 18th century, Hawkhurst was the base of the dreaded 'Hawkhurst gang'. In the centre of the view is a bill board advertisement announcing the appearance of David Garrick, presumably in the hall behind. Does anyone remember who he was?

Hawkhurst, Highgate 1902 48244
This broad, open street is the newer part of Hawkhurst, seen in the days before modern motor traffic took over. The only vehicle visible is the fine coach parked up on the left by the tree.

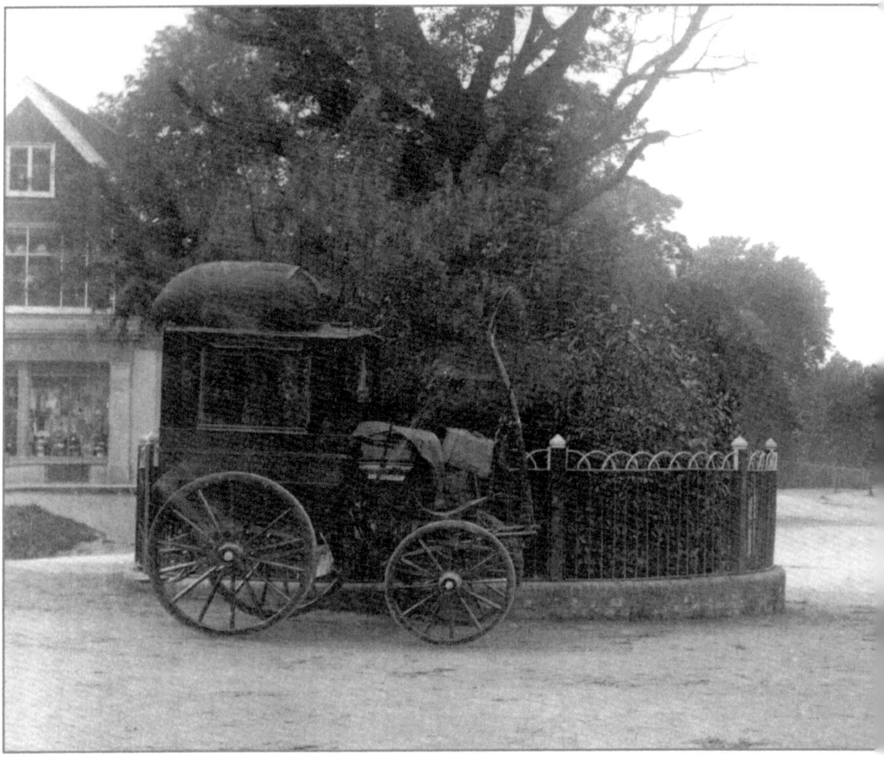

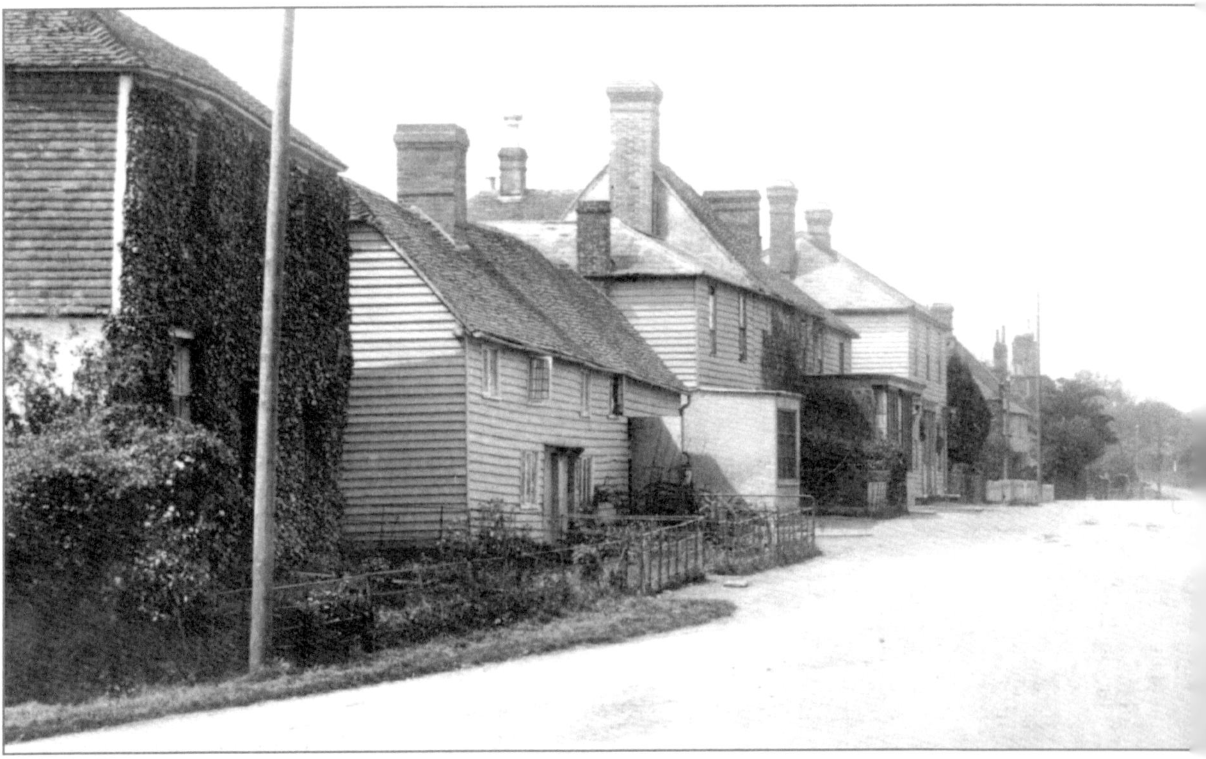

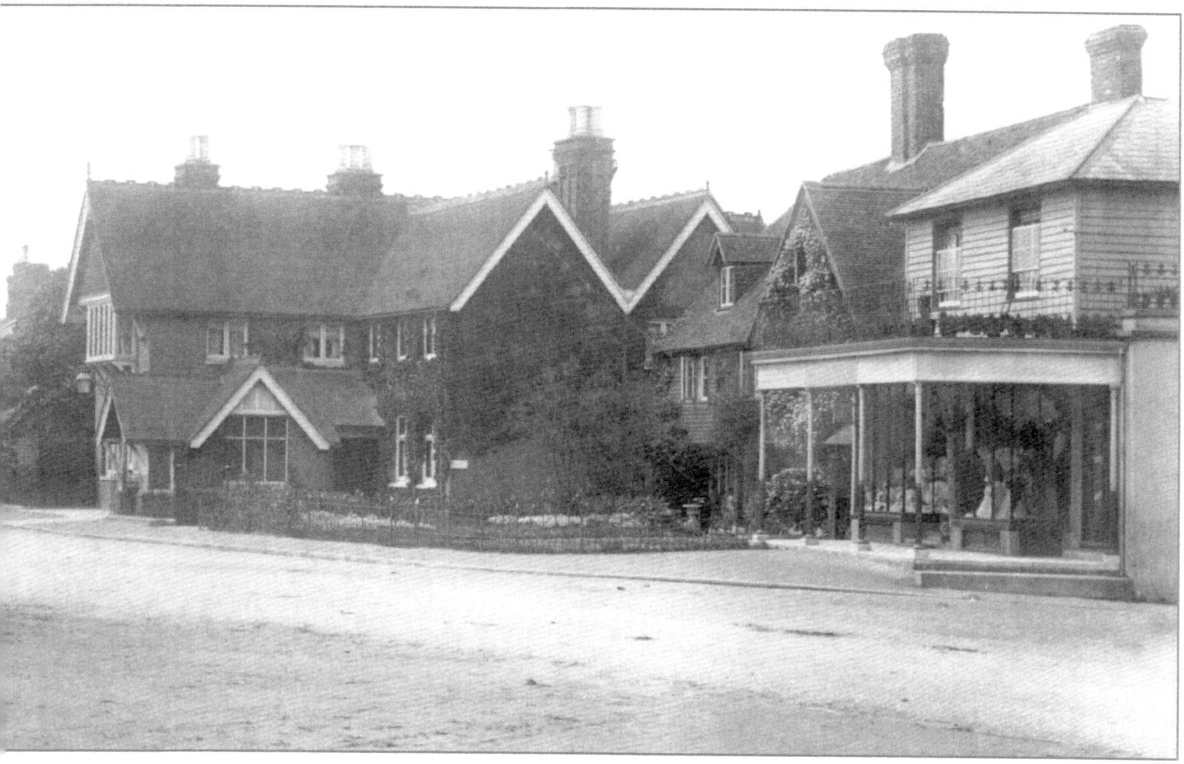

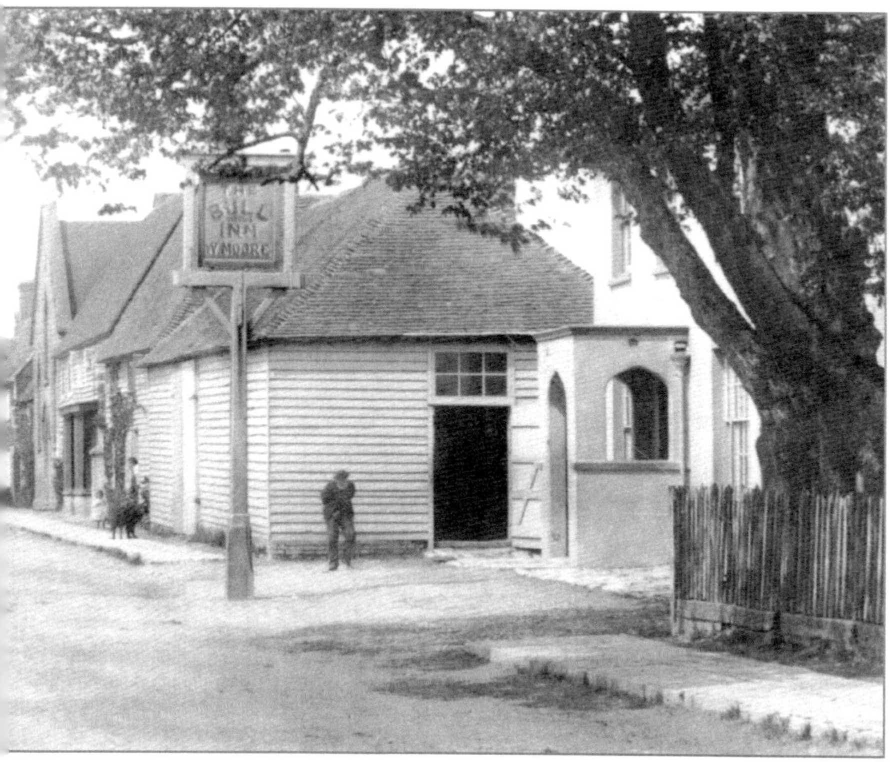

Sissinghurst
The Village 1903
51021

Here we see a fine display of weatherboarding along the empty and dusty main street. The faded pub sign is for the Bull Inn. Not far outside the village are the twin towers of Sissinghurst Castle with its beautiful gardens, once home to the author Vita Sackville West. Whilst at Sissinghurst she wrote her novel 'All Passion Spent', as well as poems and magazine articles.

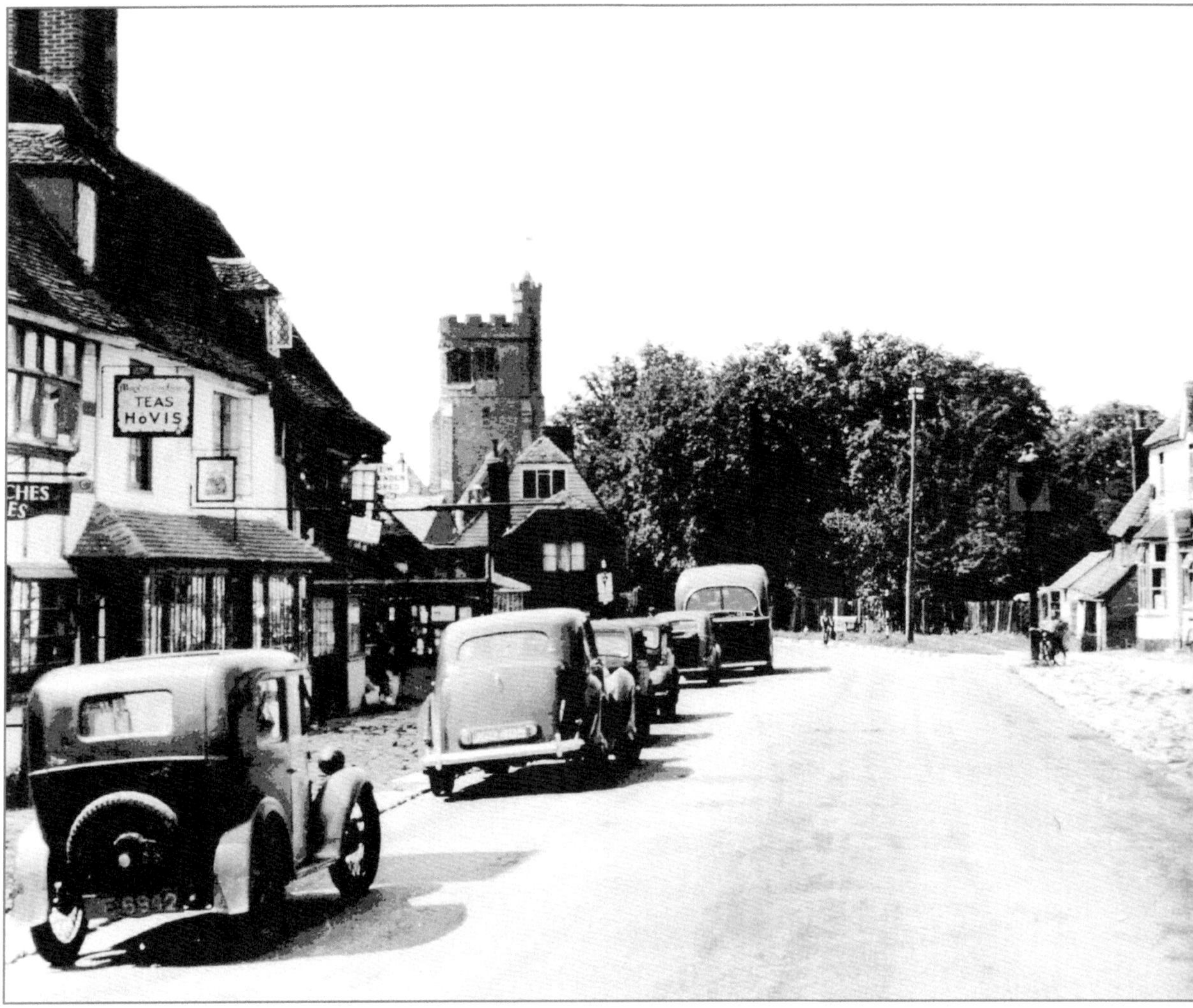

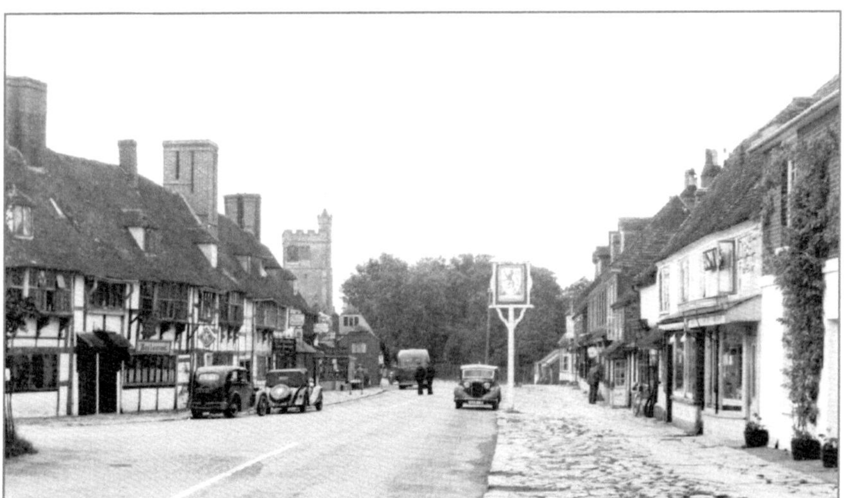

Biddenden, High Street c1950 B88009
Biddenden is a classic Wealden village with an unspoilt main street, lined with a range of fine medieval and 17th-century buildings. Half-timbered weavers' houses, with broad first-floor work-room windows, can be found on the south side. The Red Lion, on the right, is said to have been built by a soldier returning from Agincourt in 1415.

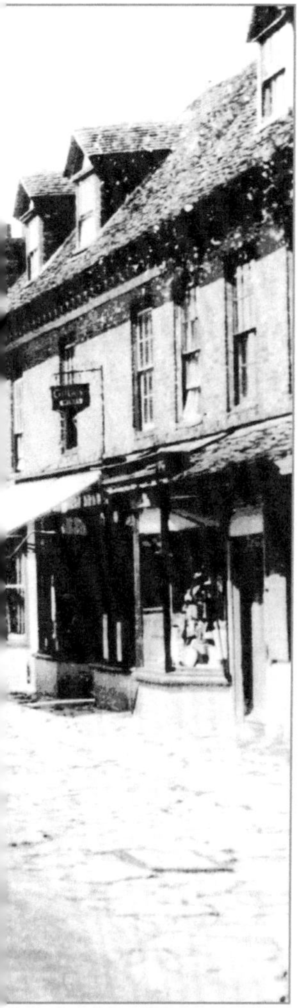

◄ **Biddenden, The Village c1950** B88005

An interesting collection of old cars can be seen along the left-hand side of the road next to the tea rooms on the main street of this pleasant village. Its claim to fame are the Siamese twins pictured on the village sign (not visible on the photograph); known as Eliza and Mary, they were born joined at the shoulder and hip and lived together like this for 30 years. When one died, the other refused to be separated, and died a few hours later. There is no trace of their burial in the village churchyard. The church itself was restored in 1857, and has features dating from the Early English to late Perpendicular periods.

▼ **Bethersden, The Village c1955** B571003

Now only a hamlet, this village was once well-known for the quarrying of Bethersden marble; apart from being used locally, it was used for interior work in both Canterbury and Rochester cathedrals, and in a number of local medieval churches. Before modern road surfaces spread to the countryside, Bethersden had the reputation of having the worst, most boggy roads in Kent.

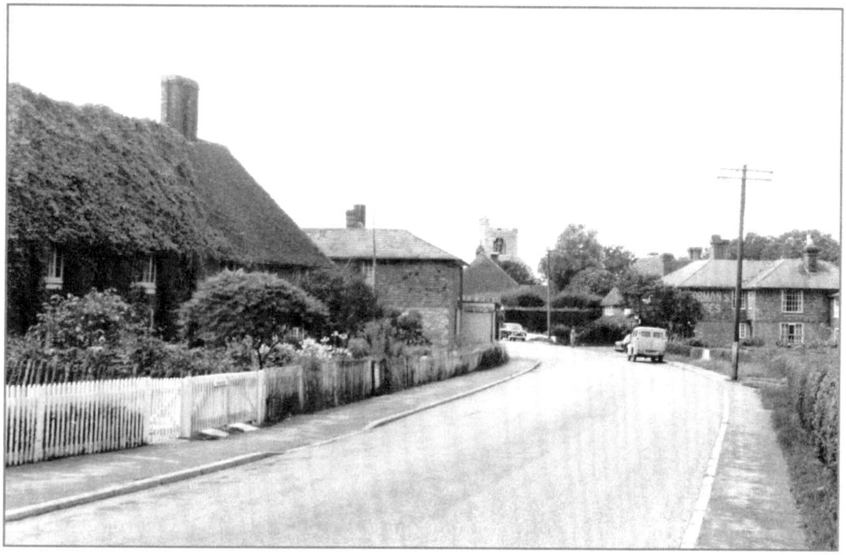

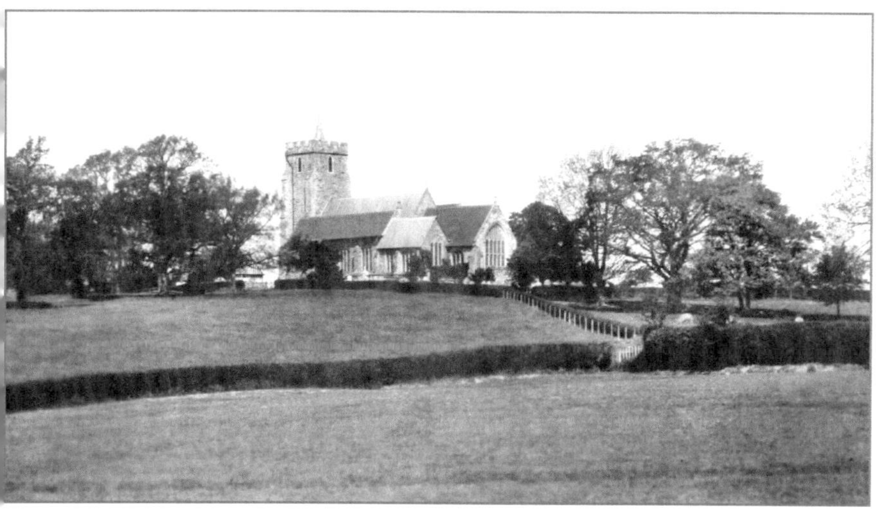

◄ **Rolvenden The Church 1901** 46454

The attractive church stands in a wide open space in this pleasant village on the edge of the Weald. In centuries past, Rolvenden was by the sea, but it is now well inland. At Great Maytham Hall to the south of the church, Frances Hodgson Burnett wrote 'Little Lord Fauntleroy'; the Hall was also the setting for her tale of 'The Secret Garden'.

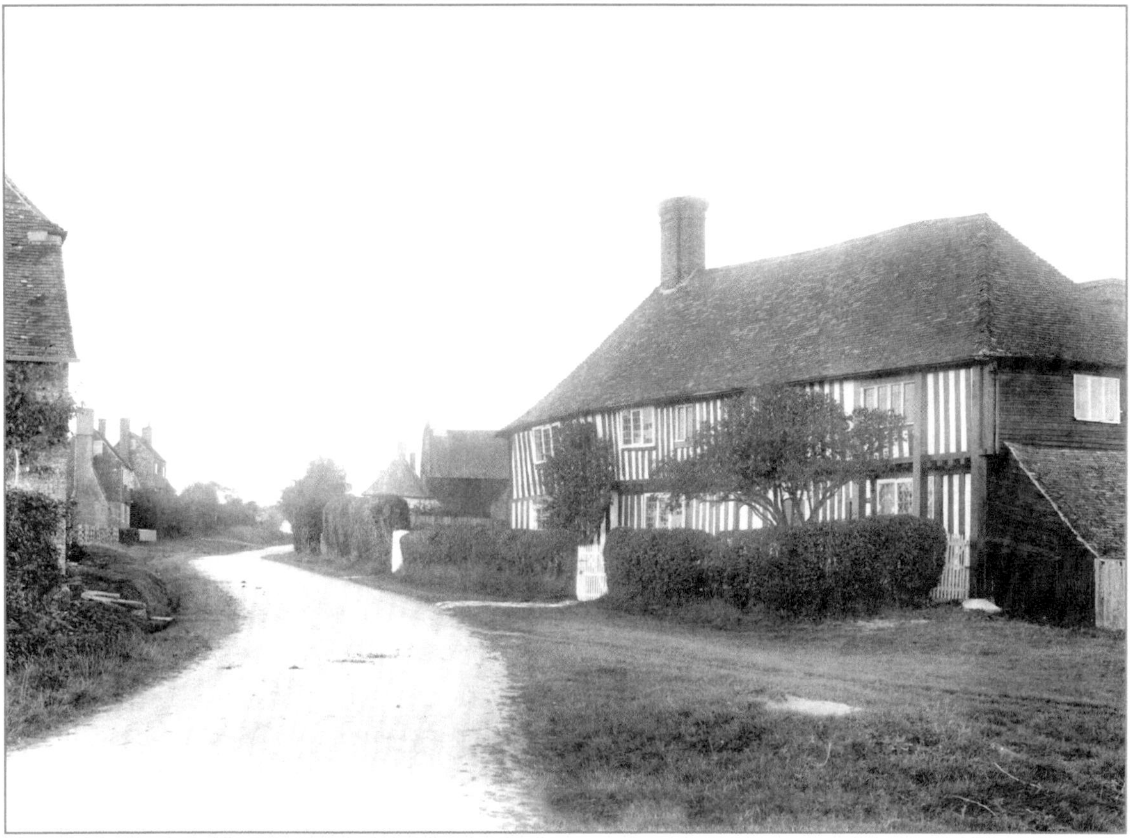

Smallhythe, The Village 1902 49083
Smallhythe was a harbour as late as the 16th century, when the sea came up this far from Rye. The long and spruce black and white cottage we see here was home to the harbourmaster. It was built as long ago as 1480; more recently, in 1919 it became the home of the actress Ellen Terry. Today it is a National Trust Memorial to Miss Terry. A collection of memorabilia was gathered in the kitchen, including Garrick's stool, a girdle once owned by Sarah Bernhardt and a variety of playbills from Ellen Terry's performances in theatres all over Britain. Beyond the house, on the right, we can just glimpse a chapel.

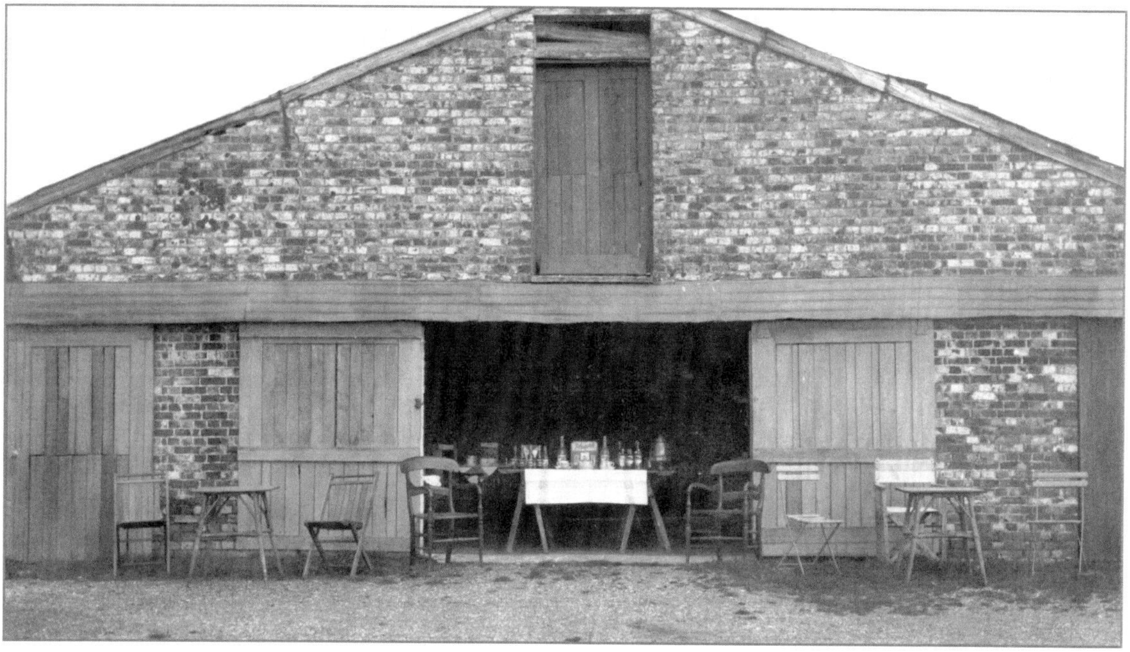

Leigh Green c1960 L336001
This interesting old building of uncertain vintage is located in a small village near Tenterden. The door where a first floor may have been suggests considerable alteration. Or could an upper floor have been used for storing hay or flour? The hall seems to have been in use for local festivities at the time the picture was taken.

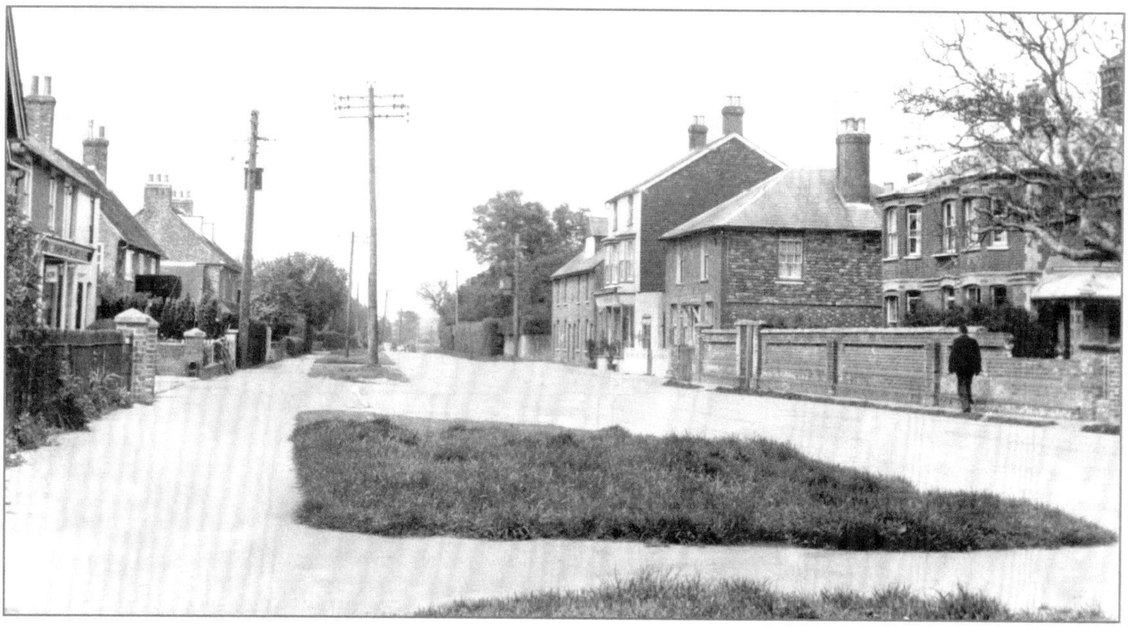

Appledore, The Street 1955 A231011
Appledore stands on a branch of the River Rother close by Romney Marsh. During the 9th century, it was an important Viking base. From here they penetrated far inland on destructive forays. More recently, Appledore became a wealthy village with its own harbour. However, in 1287 a storm changed the course of the river Rother and left the village landlocked. This picture shows the main through road, which is considerably busier today.

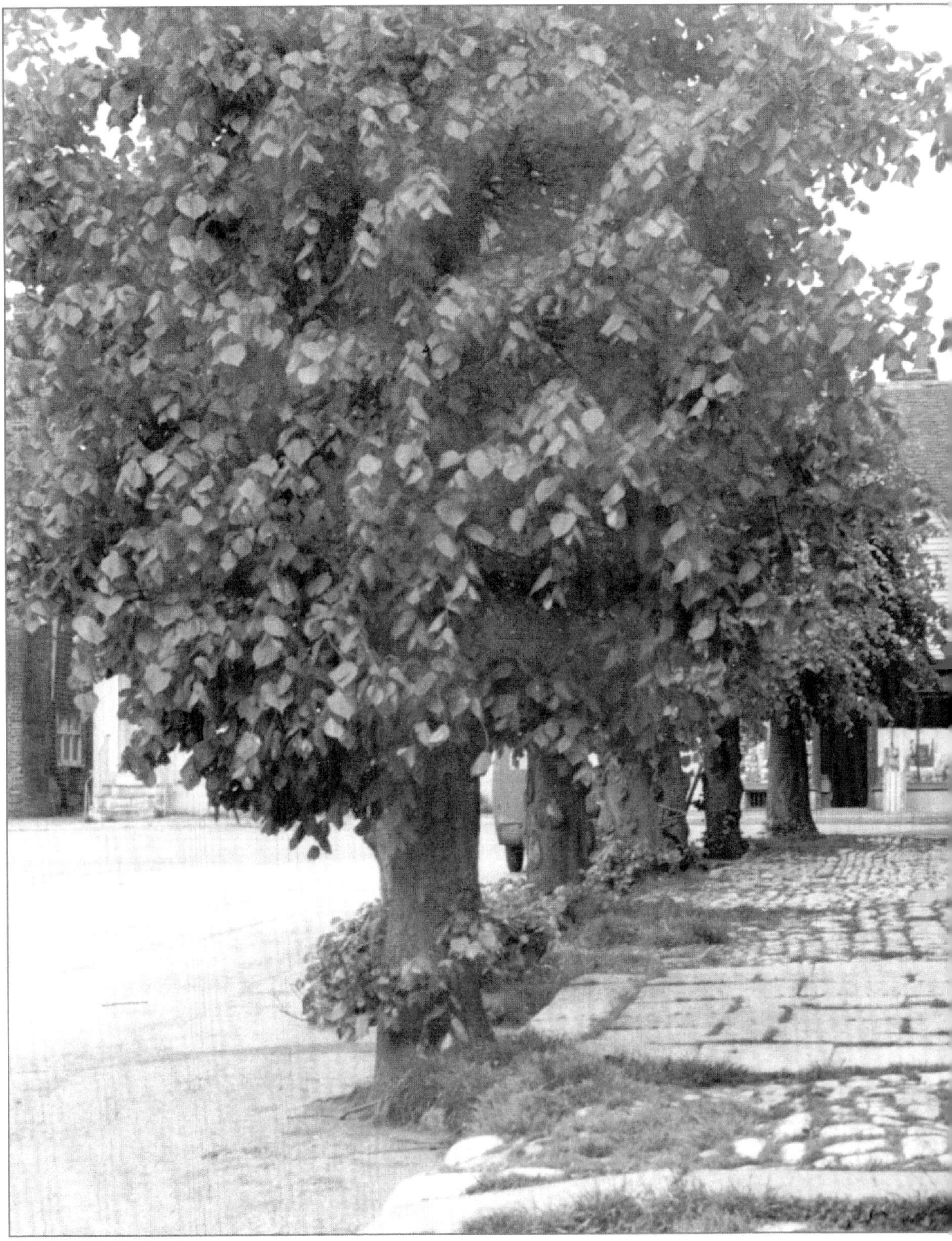

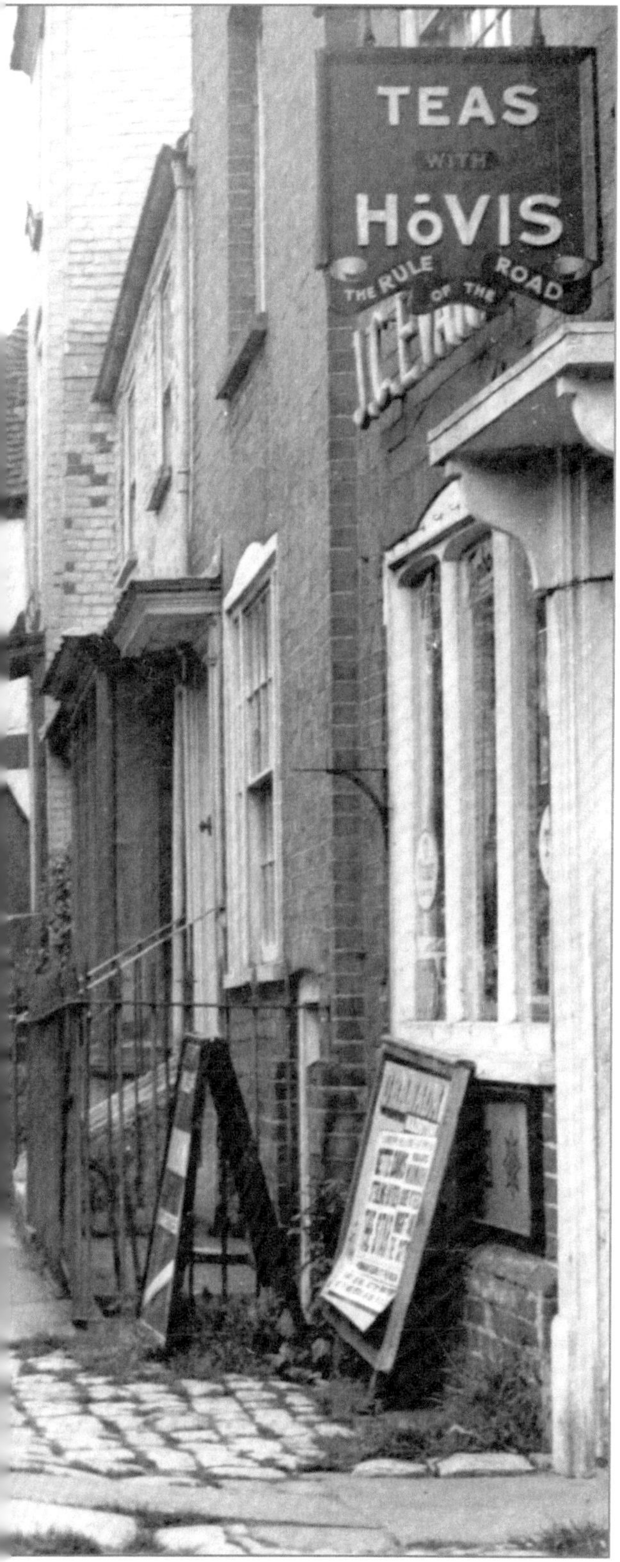

From the North Downs to Romney Marsh

Lenham, The Limes c1960 L322005
The village stands under the downs near the source of the Len and has a broad, attractive market square fringed with lime trees, which create a shadowed path over the uneven setts and cobbles. Fortunately, as the village is bypassed, it now escapes the worst ravages of modern traffic. In the background a Masons' dray is delivering beer to The Dog and Bear, an old traditional coaching inn built in 1602. Queen Anne stayed here in 1704, and her royal coat of arms is displayed above the front door. The church is partly Early English but mostly 14th century, with nave, aisles and two chancels.

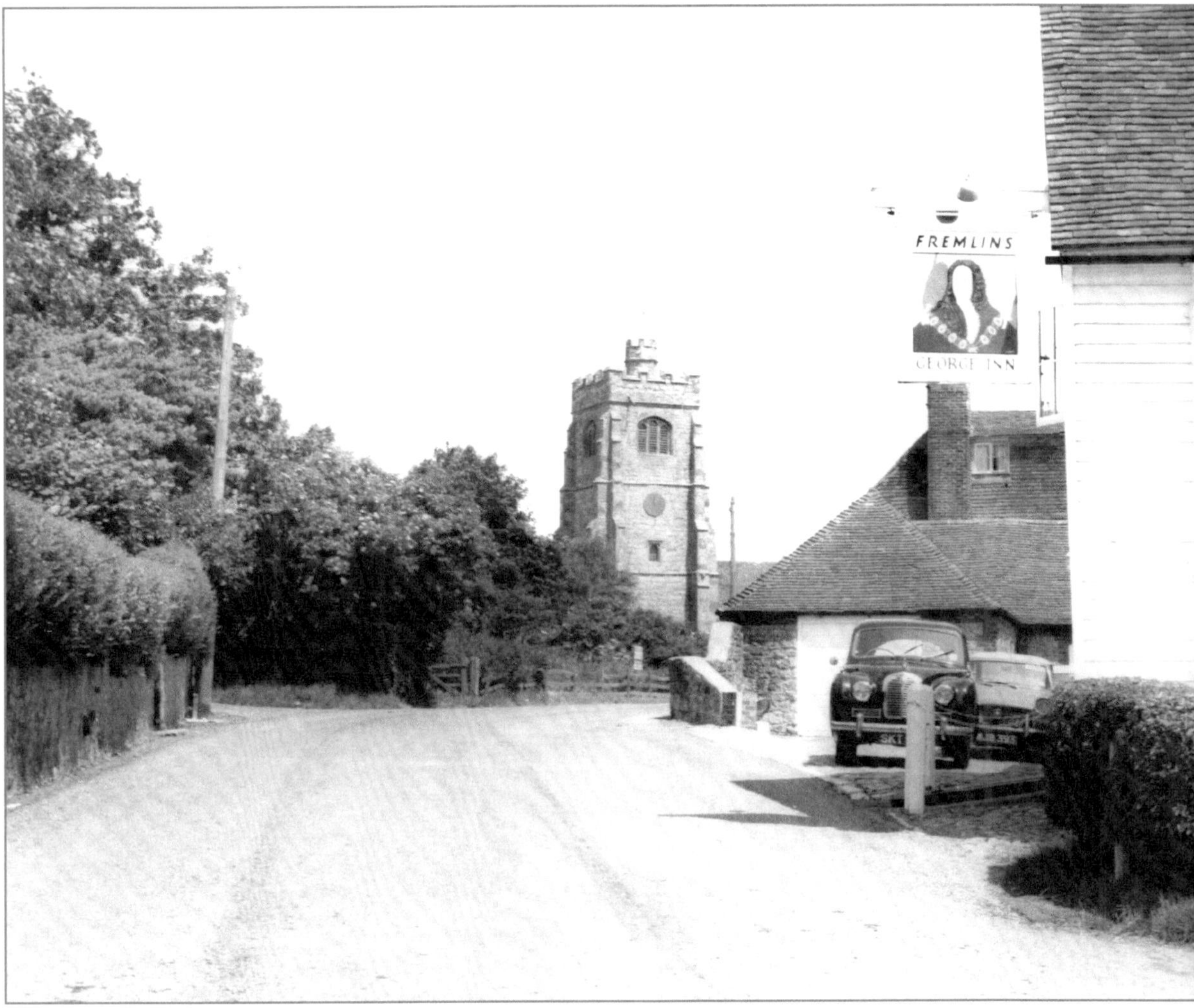

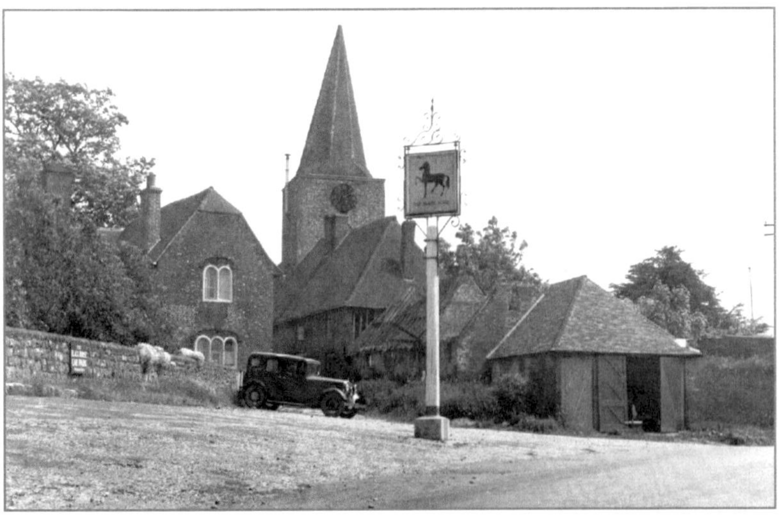

◄ **Pluckley, The Village Square c1950** P57001
This is one of Kent's most haunted villages. Ghost hunter Andrew Green recently looked into these tales for a new book, and found only one haunting still allegedly occurring. Apparently, a lady dressed in red is sometimes seen drifting around the graveyard of the church we see here. A barmaid from the Black Horse (we can see the sign) saw the figure pass clean through a gravestone! Recently Pluckley has become well-known and much-visited for another reason: the H E Bates story 'The Darling Buds of May' was filmed in the village.

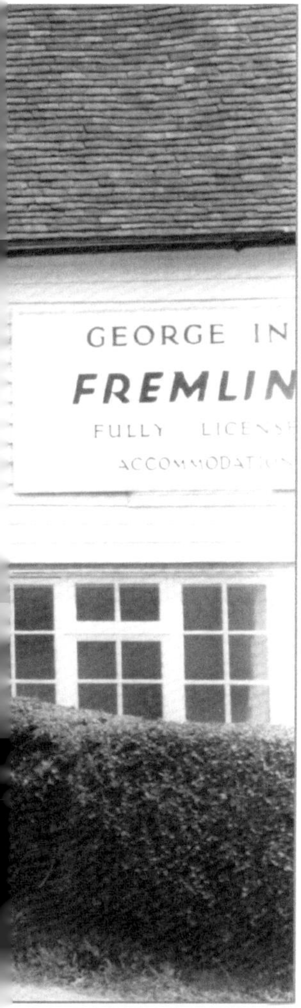

Egerton, The George Inn c1960
E155024
Egerton stands at the edge of the Weald on a high greensand ridge. The church is 15th-century and built of Kentish ragstone, and its gargoyled tower is a landmark for miles around. The George Inn was begun in 1576 during the reign of Elizabeth 1st. In its original form it was a farm dwelling with a barn and outbuildings, but has been added to and altered down the years.

Brook, A Corner of the Village c1955 B583019
Brook is still a beautiful village, despite being something of a dormitory for the expanding town of Ashford nearby. Here we see a group of picturesque old weatherboarded farm buildings. Elsewhere in the village a stream gurgles by the side of the road. The village church is a squat Norman building with a fine interior with ancient wall paintings.

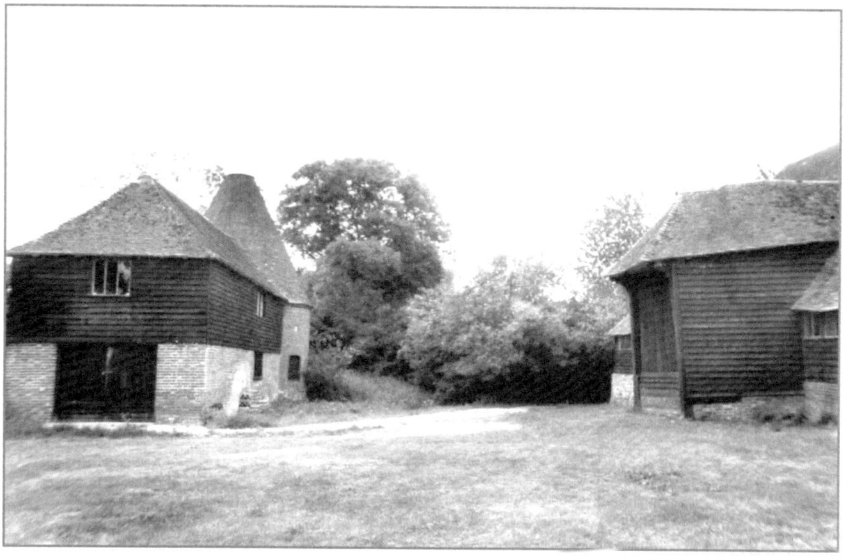

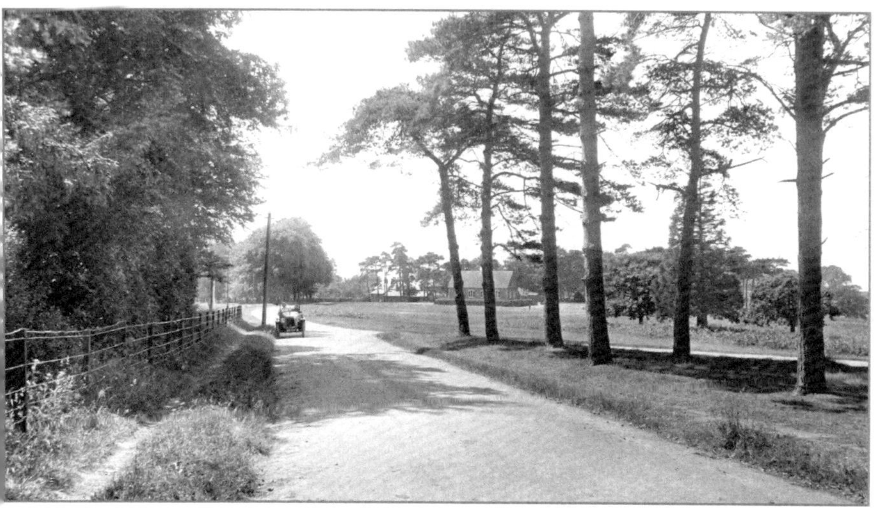

Hothfield, On the Common 1921 70317
Hothfield lies close to a branch of the River stour. Here we see a peaceful drive through a beautiful landscape of green commons and mature pines. The soils around are sandy and specked with bracken and gorse. Hothfield remains relatively unspoiled. The common is now a nature reserve with notable unusual plants and insects.

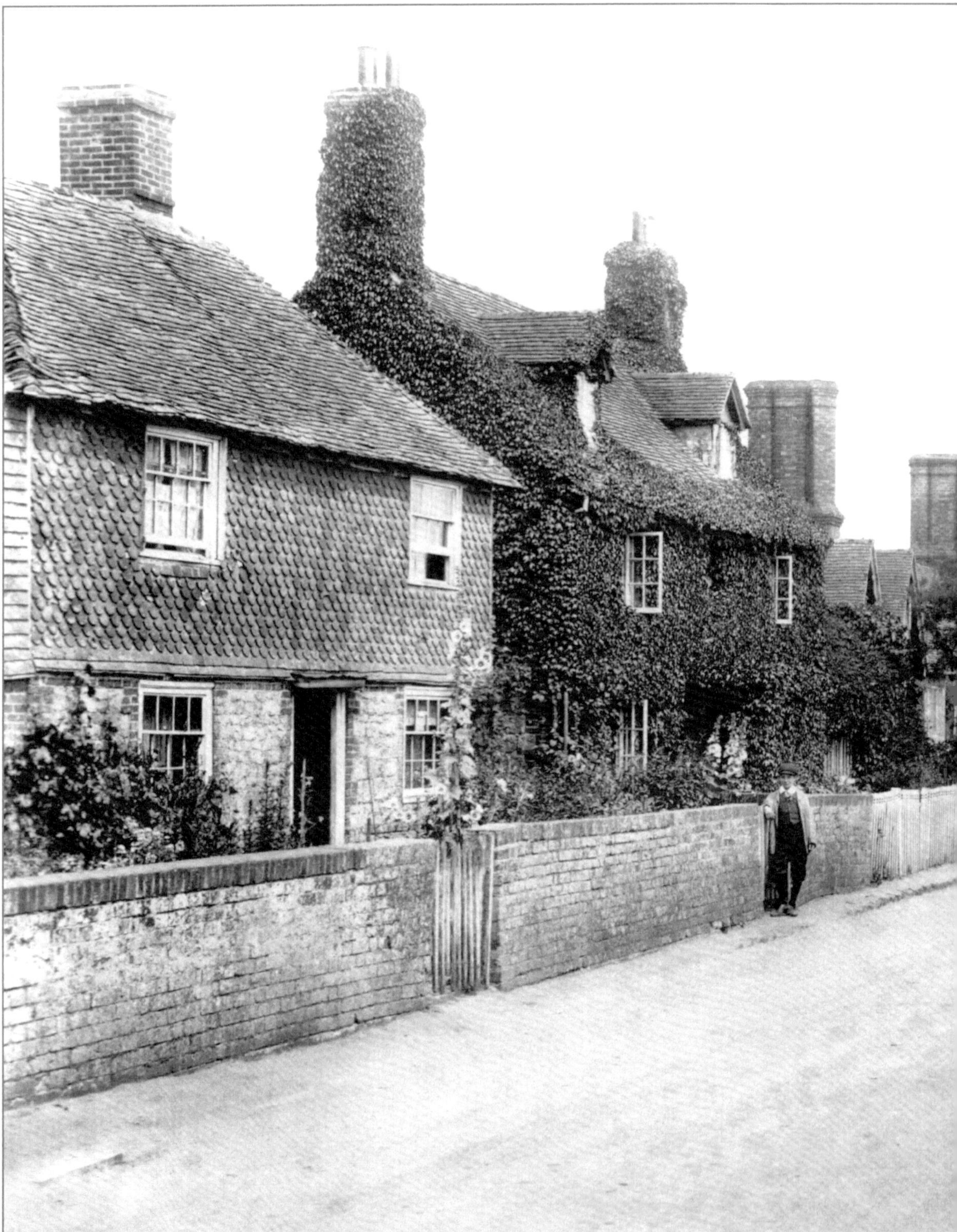

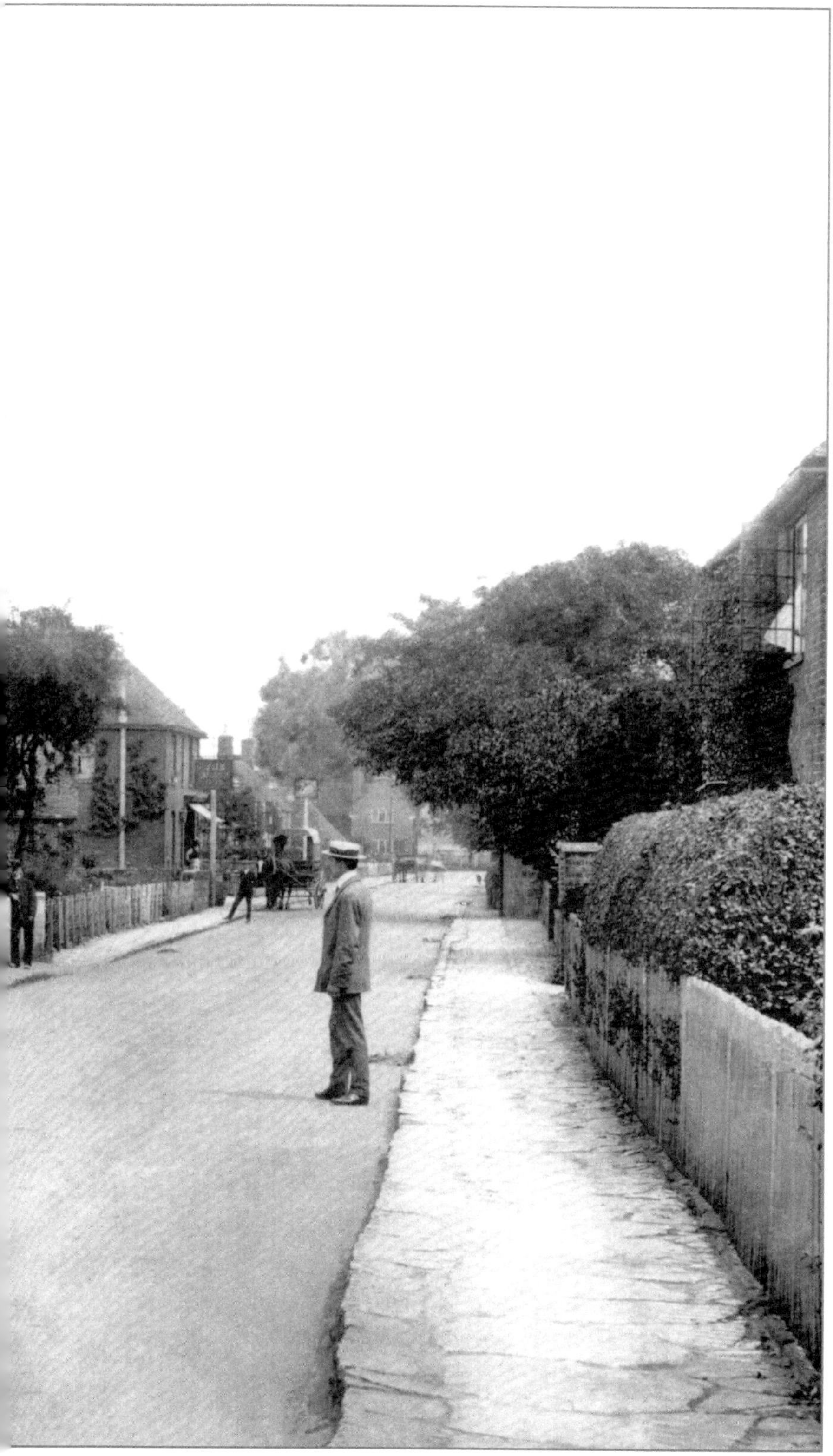

Great Chart
The Village 1908
60337

Although only just outside Ashford, Great Chart, along with its neighbour Little Chart, retains its traditional village character. However, it was once a more substantial settlement and a significant market centre for the locality. This street scene shows some fine red brick, tile-hung, ivy-clad houses with beautiful old chimneys, lining the left-hand side of the road. Various villagers have paused and are deliberately posing for the cameraman.

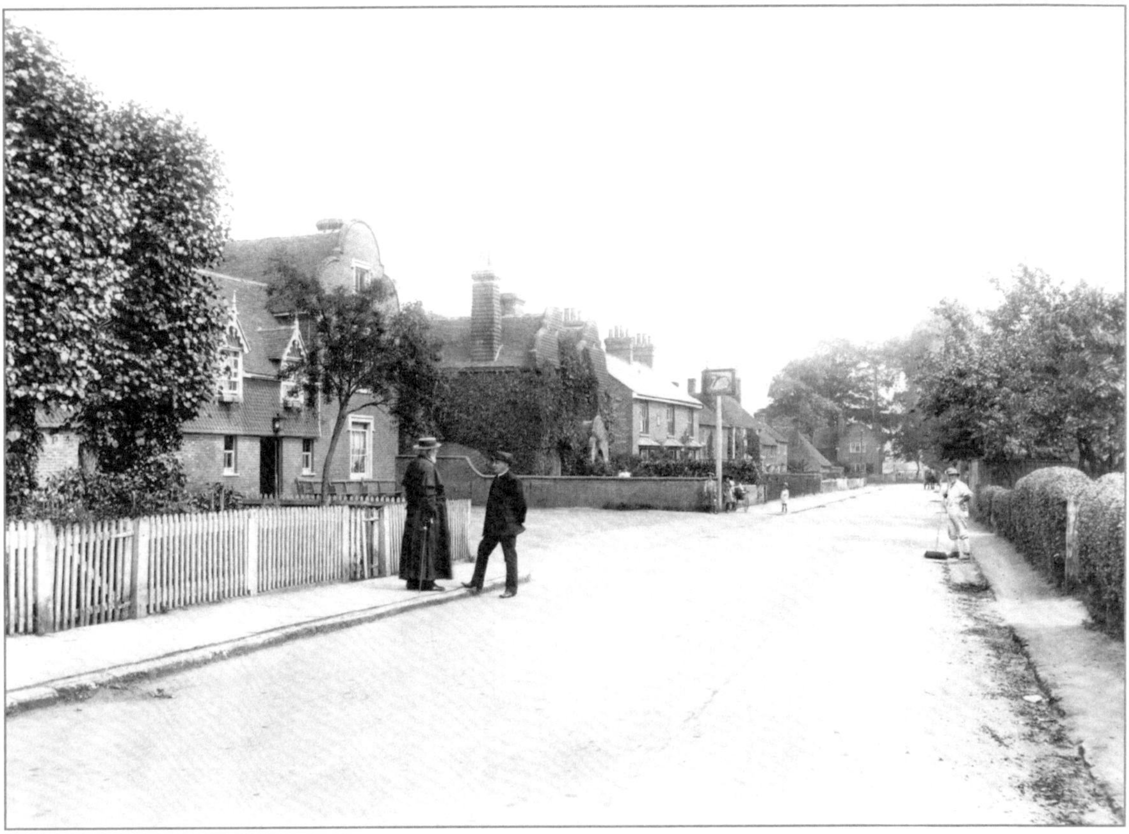

Great Chart, High Street 1908 60338
Here we see some fine brick houses, some with decorative bargeboards and Flemish-style gables. The landlord of the Swan Inn - the pub sign is in the centre of the photograph - was a Mr Beaney in 1908. The two men deep in conversation are clearly posed. Even the road sweeper has momentarily stopped work. Beyond the houses, across the fields, the roofs of Ashford can be seen.

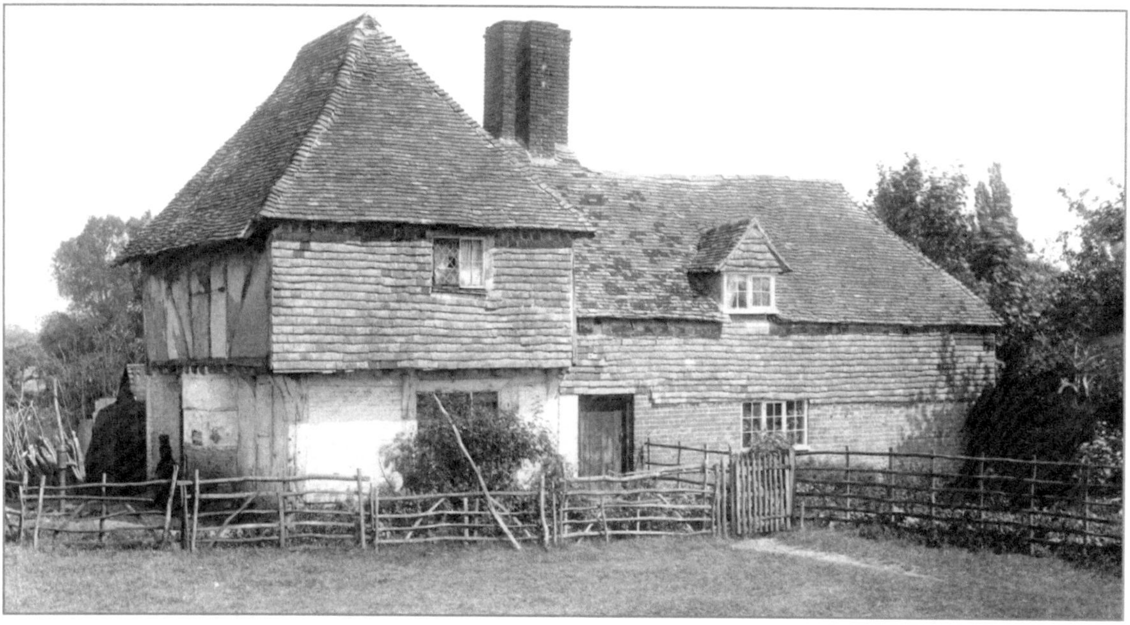

Kennington, An Old Cottage 1901 47542

This is a 16th-century building par excellence, much altered and added to down the centuries; it is timbered, tile hung and jettied, and bears a cluster of tall chimneys. Sad to say, Kennington is not very rural now; it has become ever more just a suburb of Ashford. In 1895 there were brick and tile works in the village. In the churchyard is an ancient yew tree, reliably dated at some 2000 years of age.

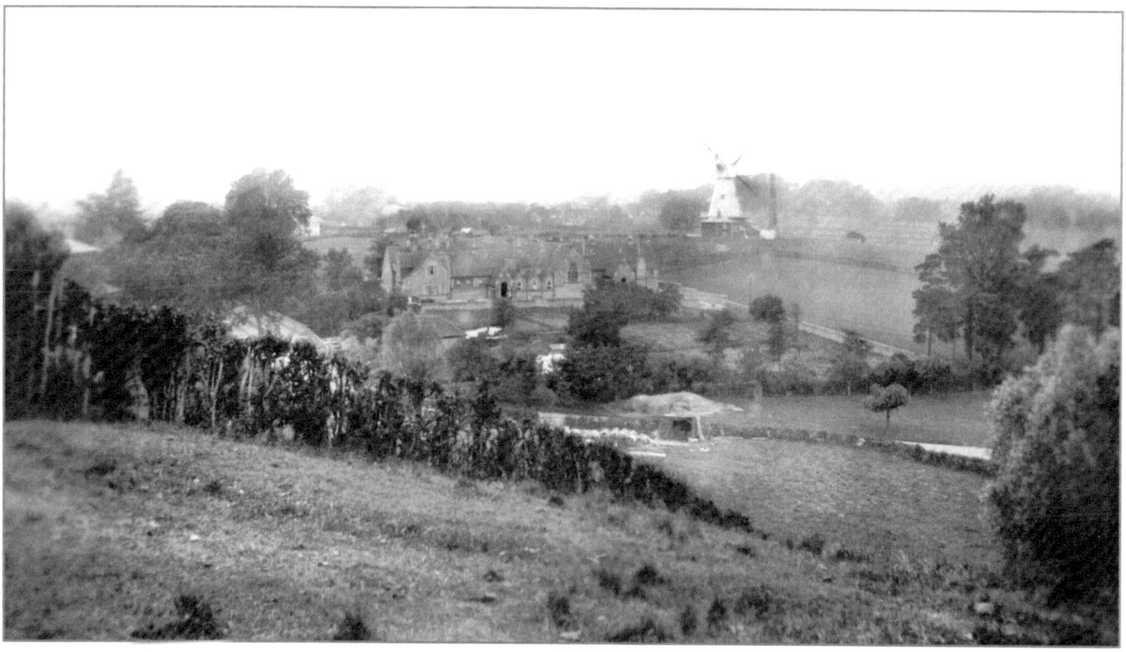

Willesborough, The Windmill and the Schools 1909 61558

This scene has now completely changed. The M20 now cuts directly across this picture, and new factory and housing developments fill the scene. However, the white smock windmill, built in 1869 by the Ashford millwright J Hill, still rises over the village roofs, and is of course now preserved.

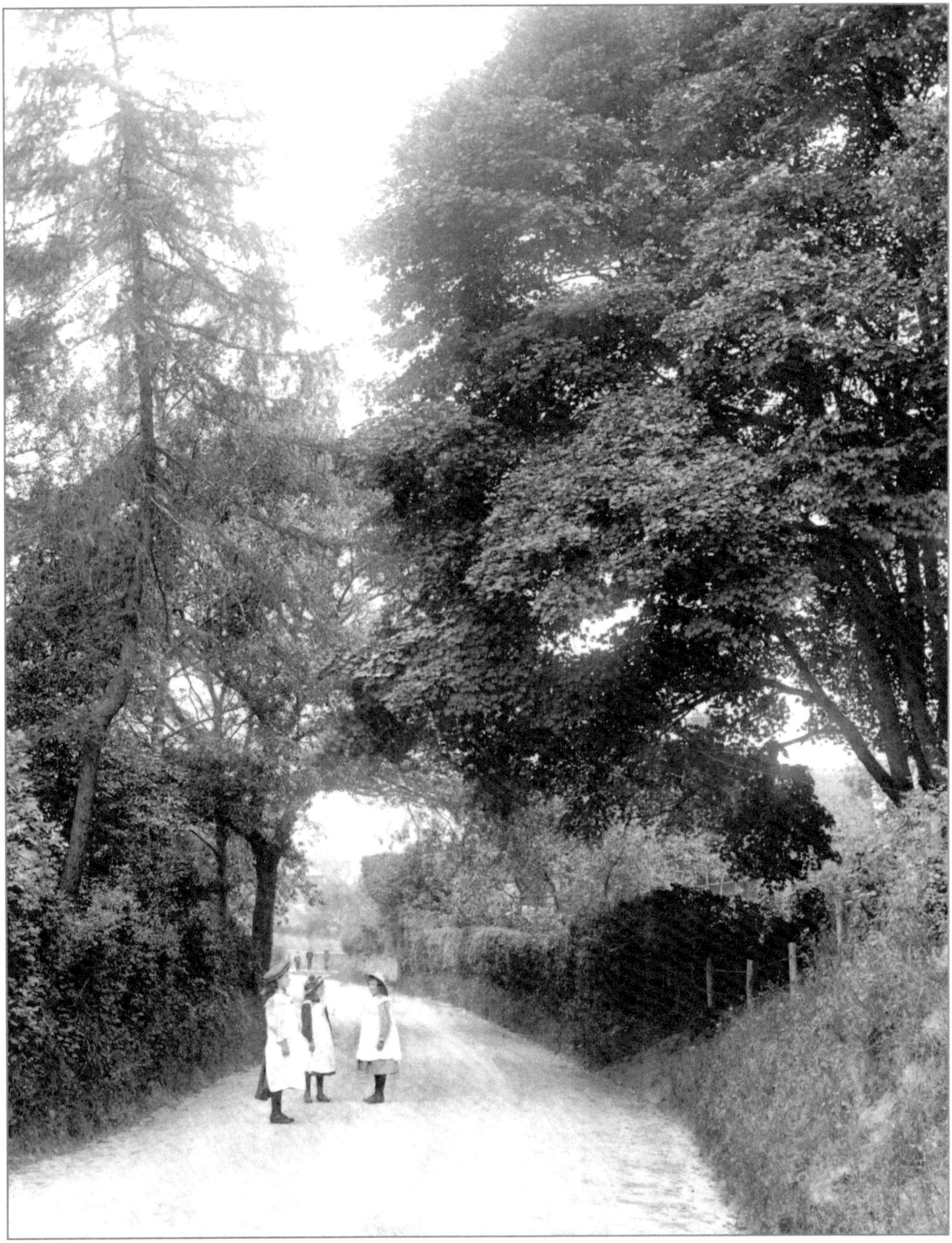

Willesborough, Sandy Lane 1909 61561
Perhaps these children were schoolgirls in their bright pinafore dresses and bonnets from the magnificent school building seen in photograph No 61558. They seem to be posing for the Frith photographer.

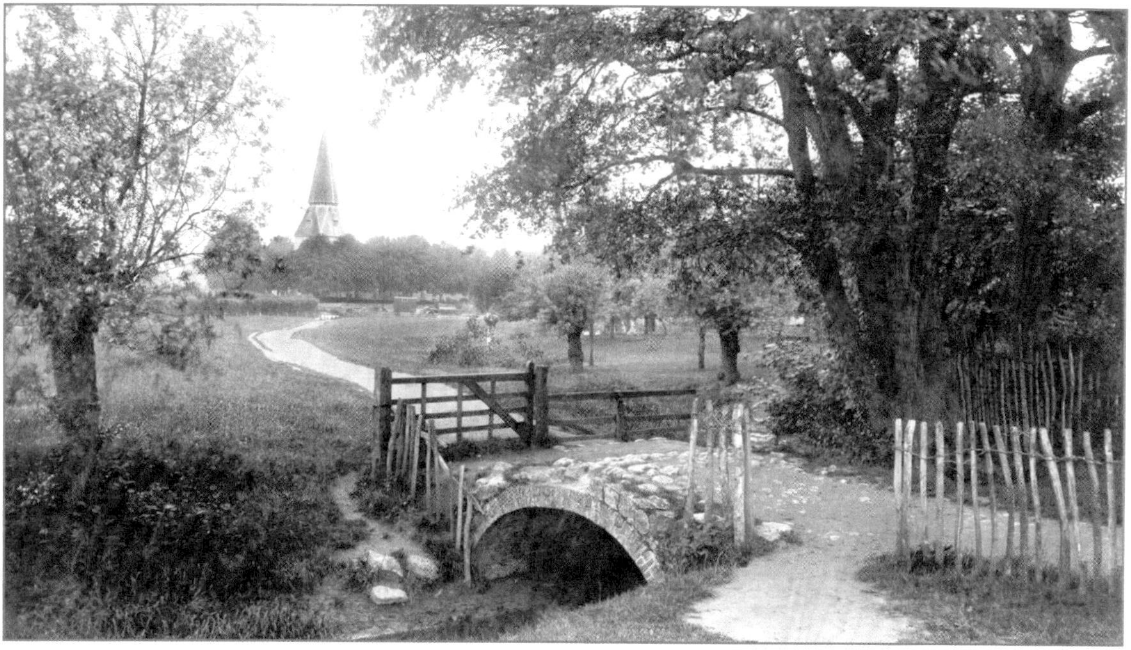

Willesborough, The Church 1909 61563
A narrow path leads through trees and across a small humpbacked bridge to the attractive shingle-spired church. The church is 15th-century, but its interior is much more recent. Most of the area we see is now smothered with modern housing, and the countryside cut off by the fast dual carriageway to Romney Marsh.

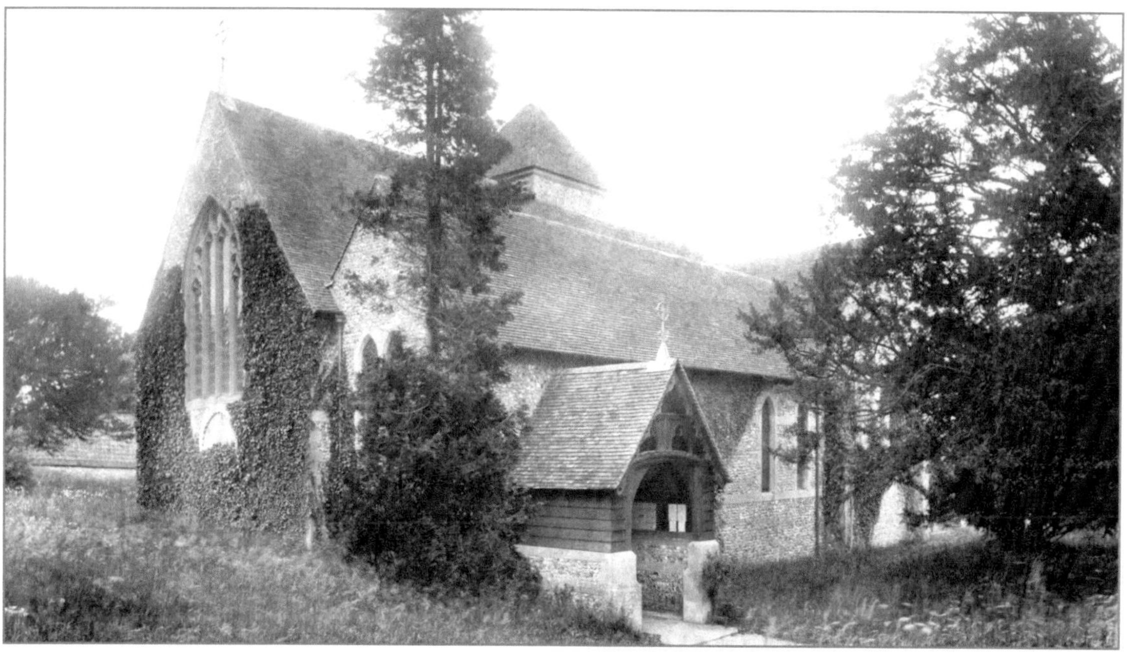

Godmersham, The Church 1909 61570
This neat church is basically Norman, and was so badly neglected during early Victorian times and was in such a poor state of repair that it was heavily restored in 1865. Inside there is a 12th-century stone bas-relief of Thomas Becket. There are stout flint walls, splayed Norman windows and arches, and a tympanum depicting a cross.

▼ **Godmersham, The Village 1909** 61566
This village stands alongside the River Stour, two miles south-west of Chilham. In the main street of the village, we see a nice picket fence and some typically ivy-clad buildings. Just outside the village is the beautiful 560-acre Godmersham Park, the home down the centuries of the Valoigns, Astyns and Broadnaxes. Jane Austen was a frequent visitor here.

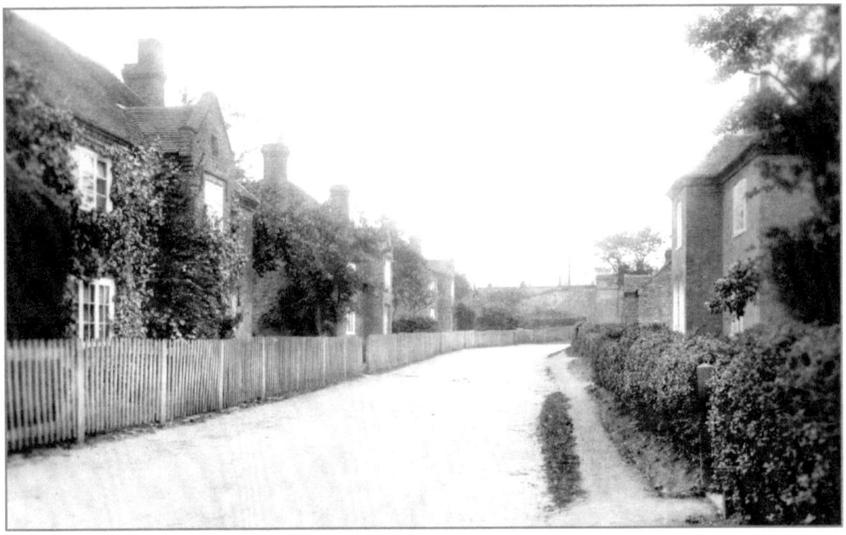

▼ **Chilham, Old Houses 1903** 50343
These steep-roofed houses on the way up into the village square are typical of the beautiful houses built in the local vernacular style to be found in this locality. However, because it is so picturesque the village suffers at weekends and bank holidays - it is often choked with cars.

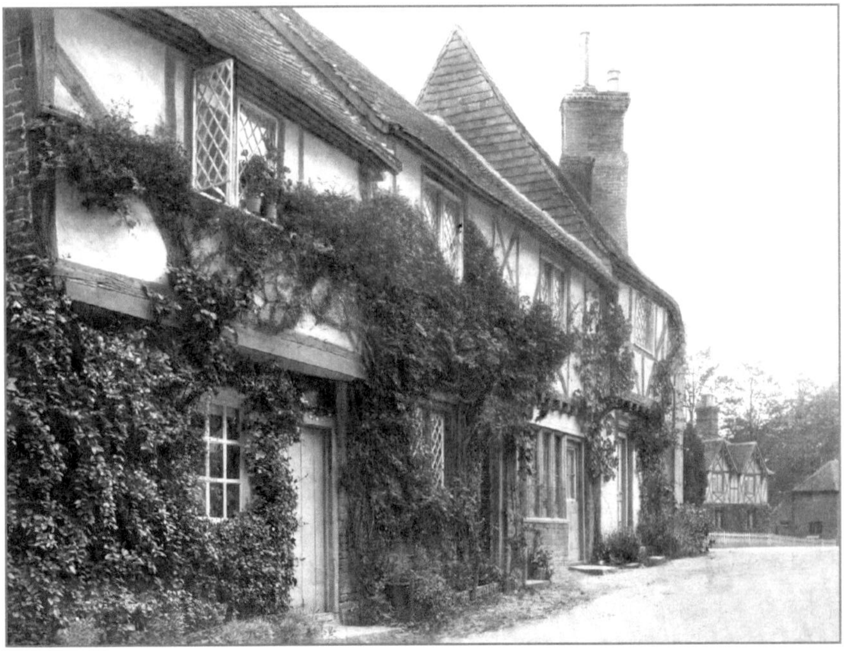

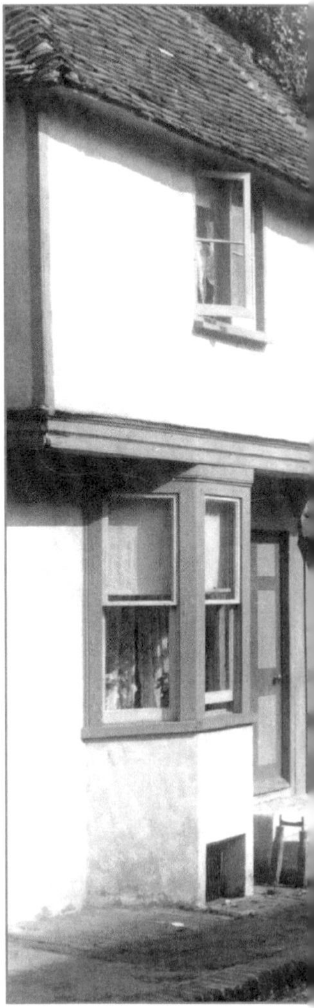

▲ **Chilham, The High Street 1903** 50345
Note the rough road surface, which had not yet been modernised with tarmacadam. In summer the dust would fly as horses and carts pressed their way through, and in winter the rains would turn it into a quagmire. On the right is Colman Stores – 'China and Glass, Furniture'. On the other side there is another shop; the notices outside advertise a farm auction and stock for sale.

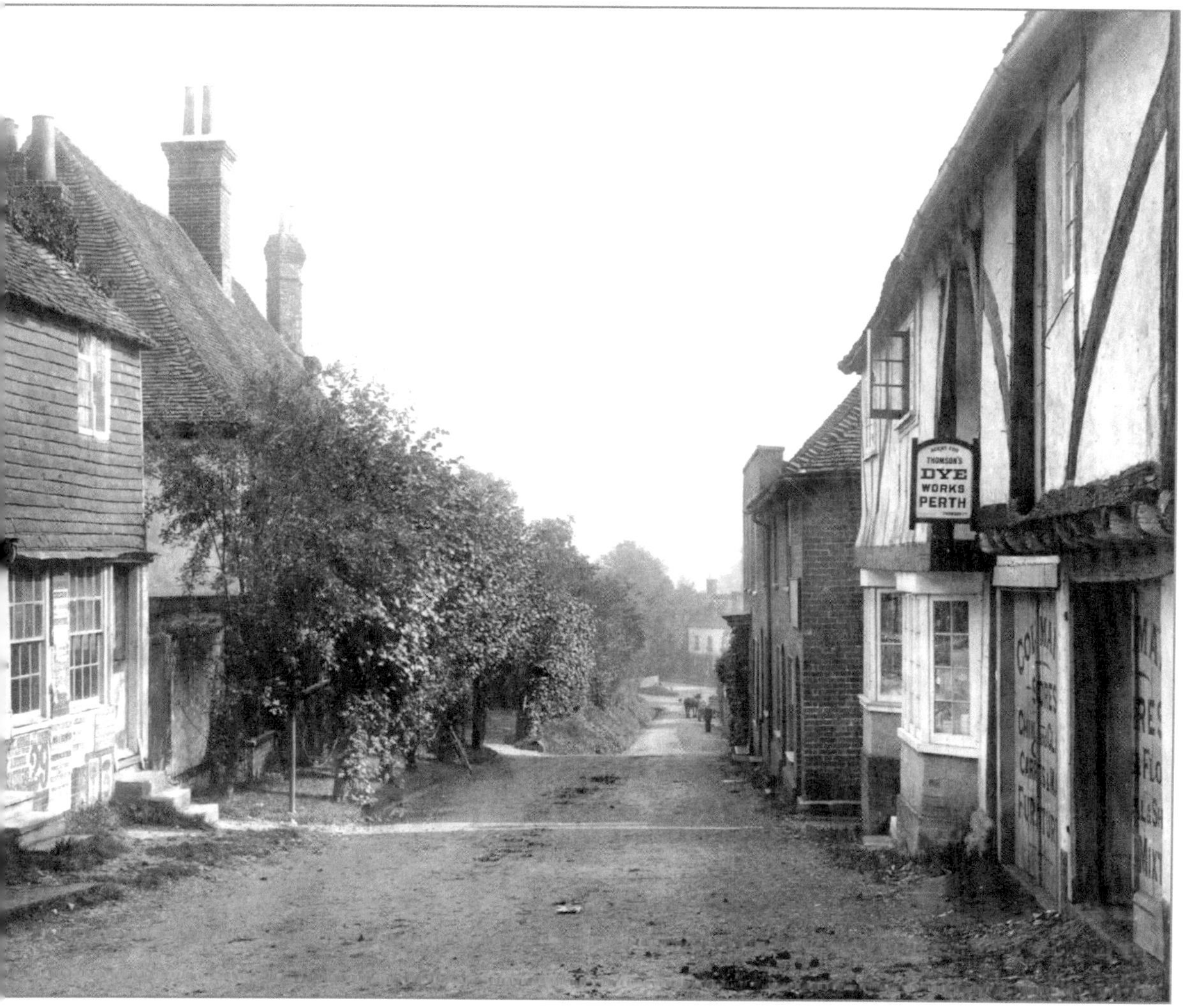

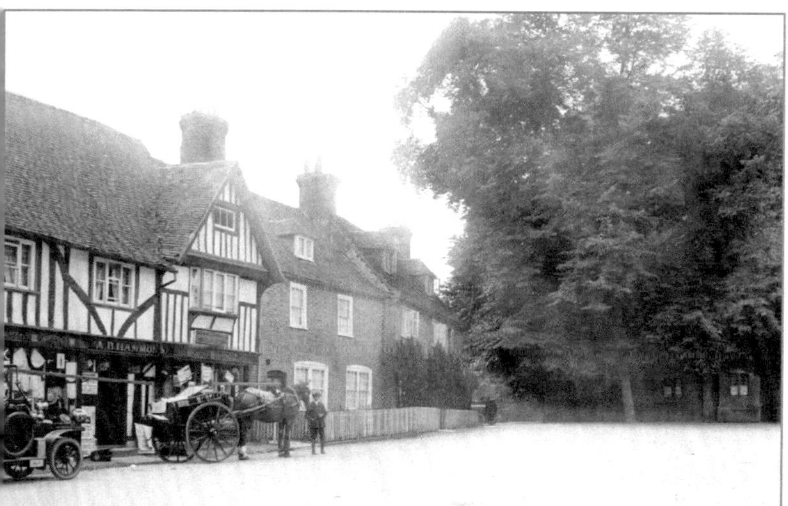

◄ **Chilham, The Post Office and Stores 1913** 65335

Both horse and cart and motor car are parked outside Wealden Hall House; at the time of the photograph it was trading as the Post Office, and advertising itself as selling 'Drapery, Outfitting, Grocery and Provisions.' The newspaper headline by the parked car reads 'Air Passenger Service in England.' This could, of course, refer to a service by airship, as heavier-than-air aeroplanes were still in their extreme infancy at this time. Hidden in the trees is the entrance to Chilham Castle, originally Norman. It is said to be haunted by a ghostly grey lady.

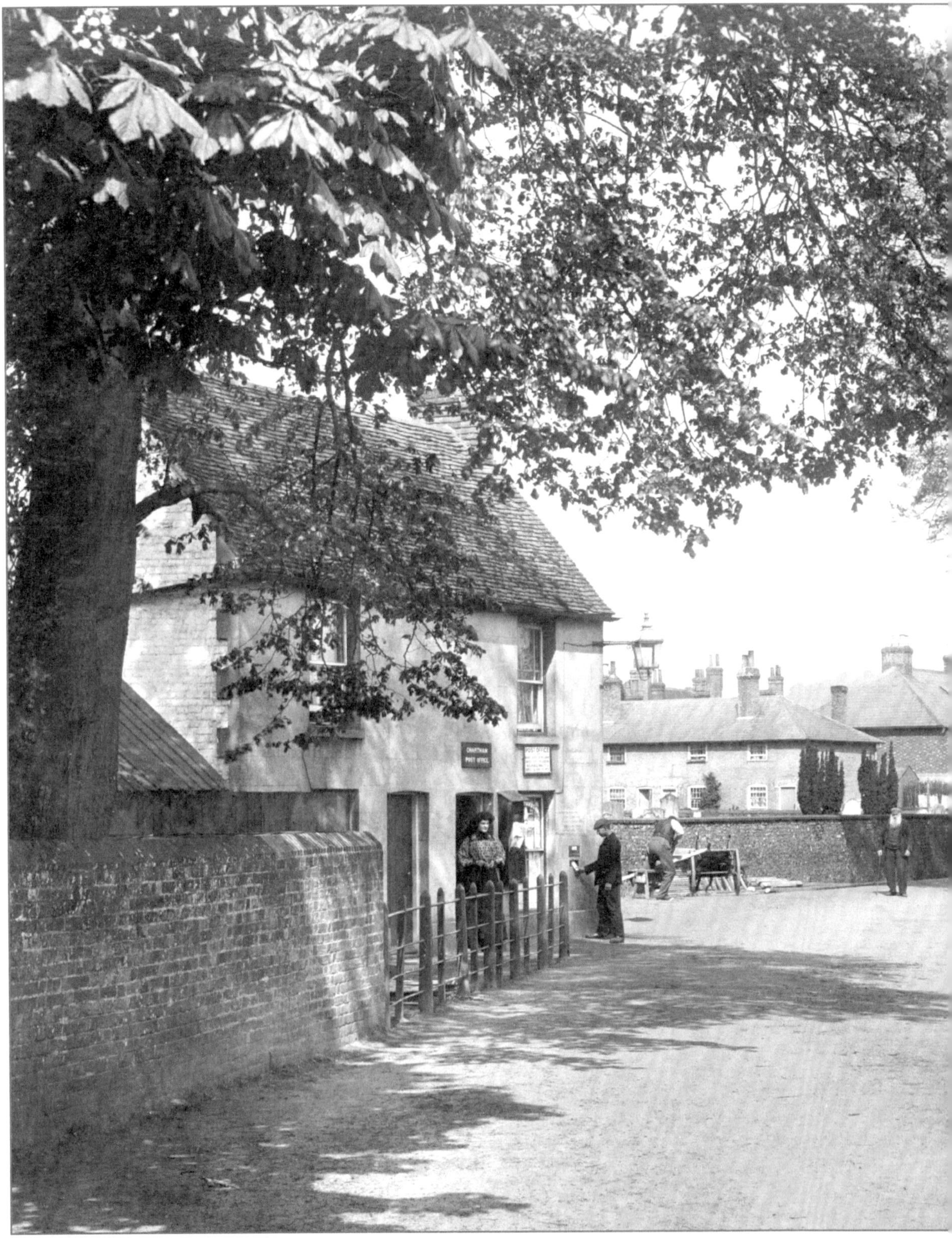
CHARTHAM
POST OFFICE
POST OFFICE

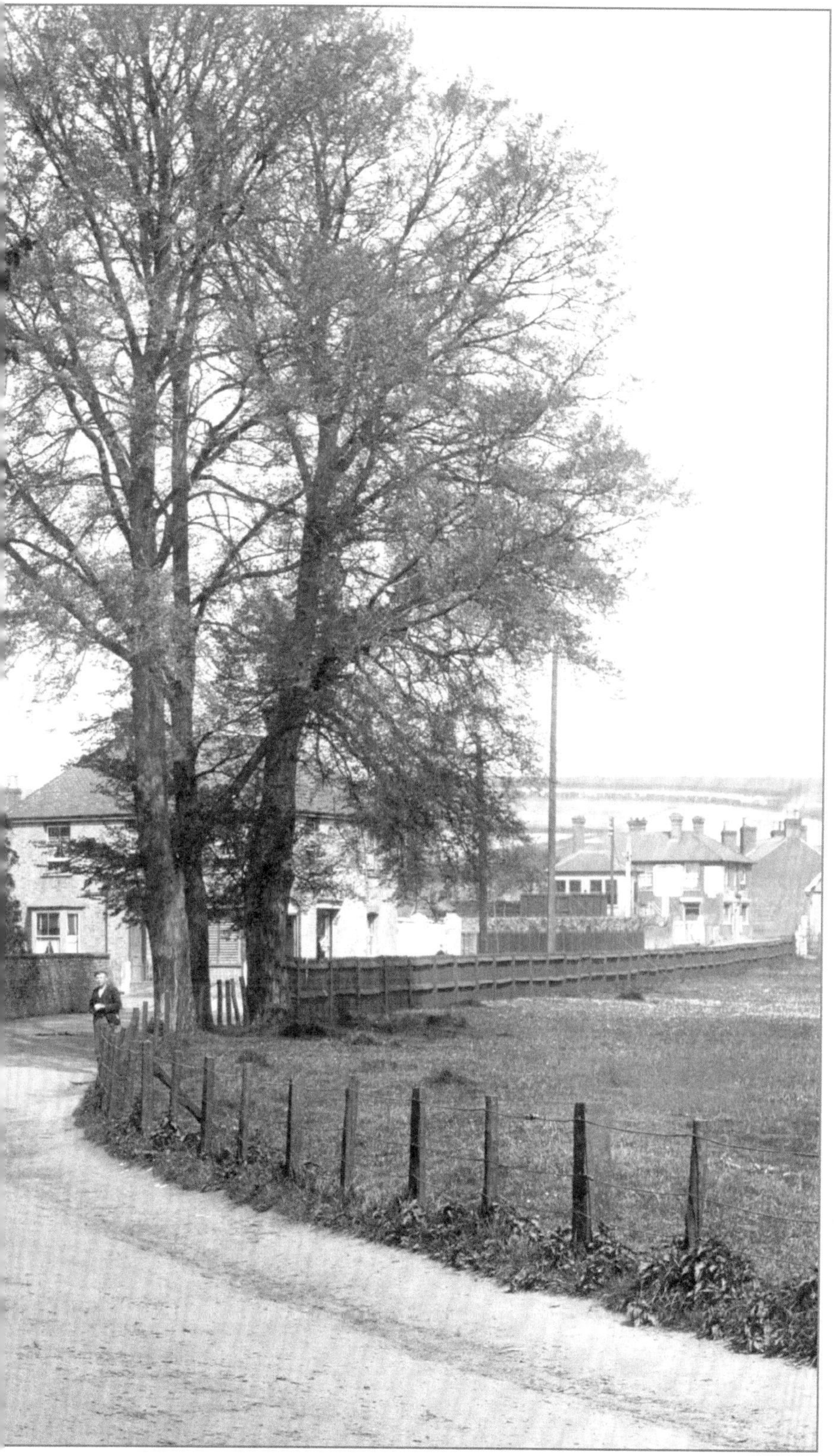

Chartham
The Parade 1905
53458
On the left a woman stands in the door of the Post Office, which in 1895 also acted as a money order and telegraph office. Just beyond a carpenter is at work. There is a sizeable stack of what look like floorboards piled against the wall. The downs can just be glimpsed over the rooftops - in 1875 the East Kent Lunatic Asylum was built here, and accommodated 900 patients.

▼ **Chartham, The Village 1903** 50352
Chartham occupies a low-lying site about a large green. Here we see the River Stour flowing through the village. The river has at various times proved indispensable to local industry. In 1949 Wiggins Teape reopened a local paper mill here, which specialised in producing tracing paper.

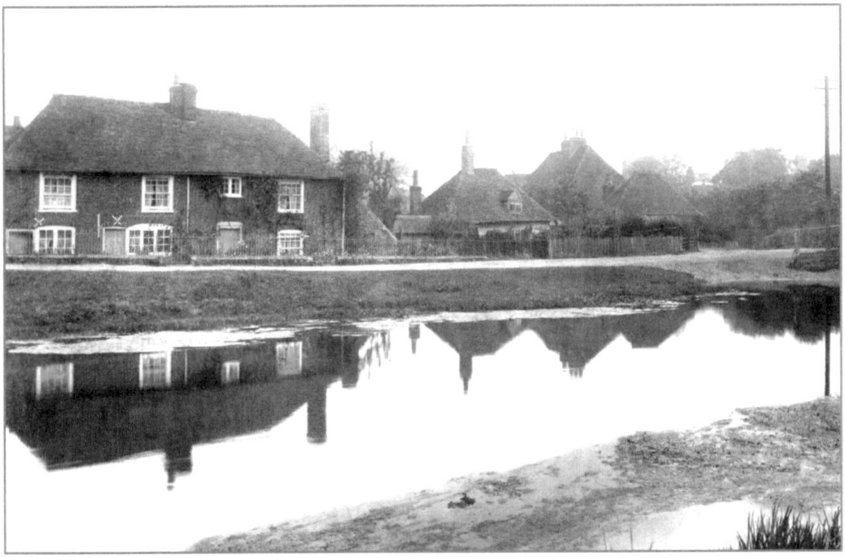

▼ **Petham, The Street c1960** P267005
Petham is a small village set in a valley just off the Roman Stane Street that runs from Canterbury to Lympne. There are remains of entrenchments here, constructed during the Roman invasion. On the right of the street can be seen W C Phipps and Sons, General Stores.

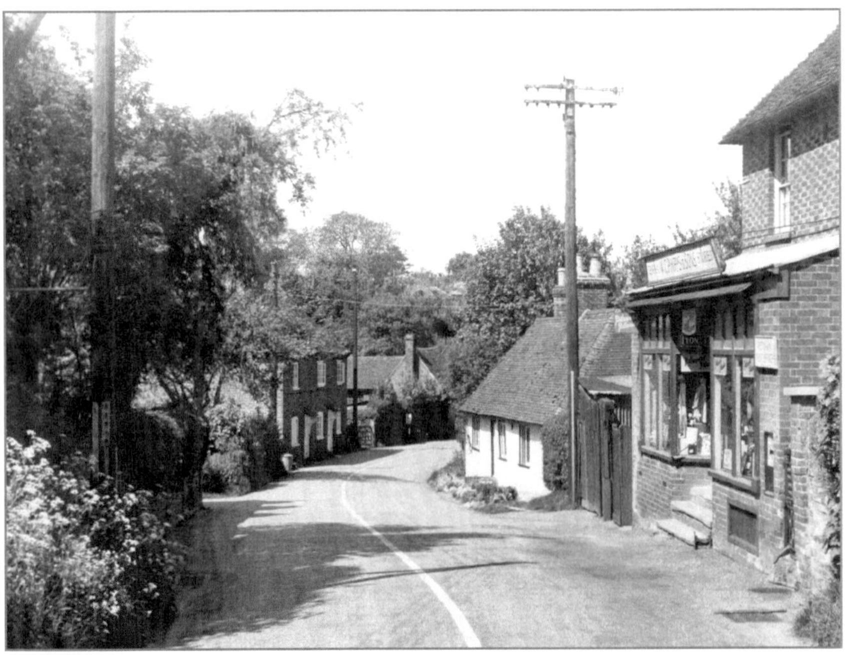

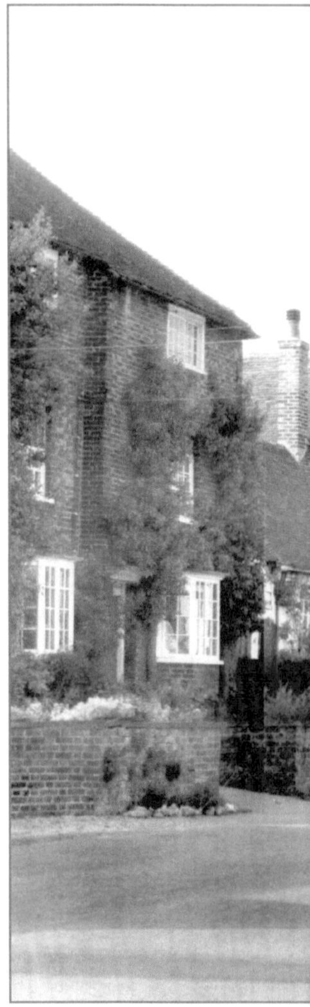

▲ **Elham, The High Street c1960** E156007
Elham, pronounced 'Eel-am', dates from Saxon times, and stands six miles north-east of Hythe. Along the nearby valley floor runs an intermittent stream, known as the Nailborne. For years its course will be dry; then suddenly it will come to life. Legend has it that the Nailbourne was brought into being by St Augustine to alleviate the effects of local droughts.

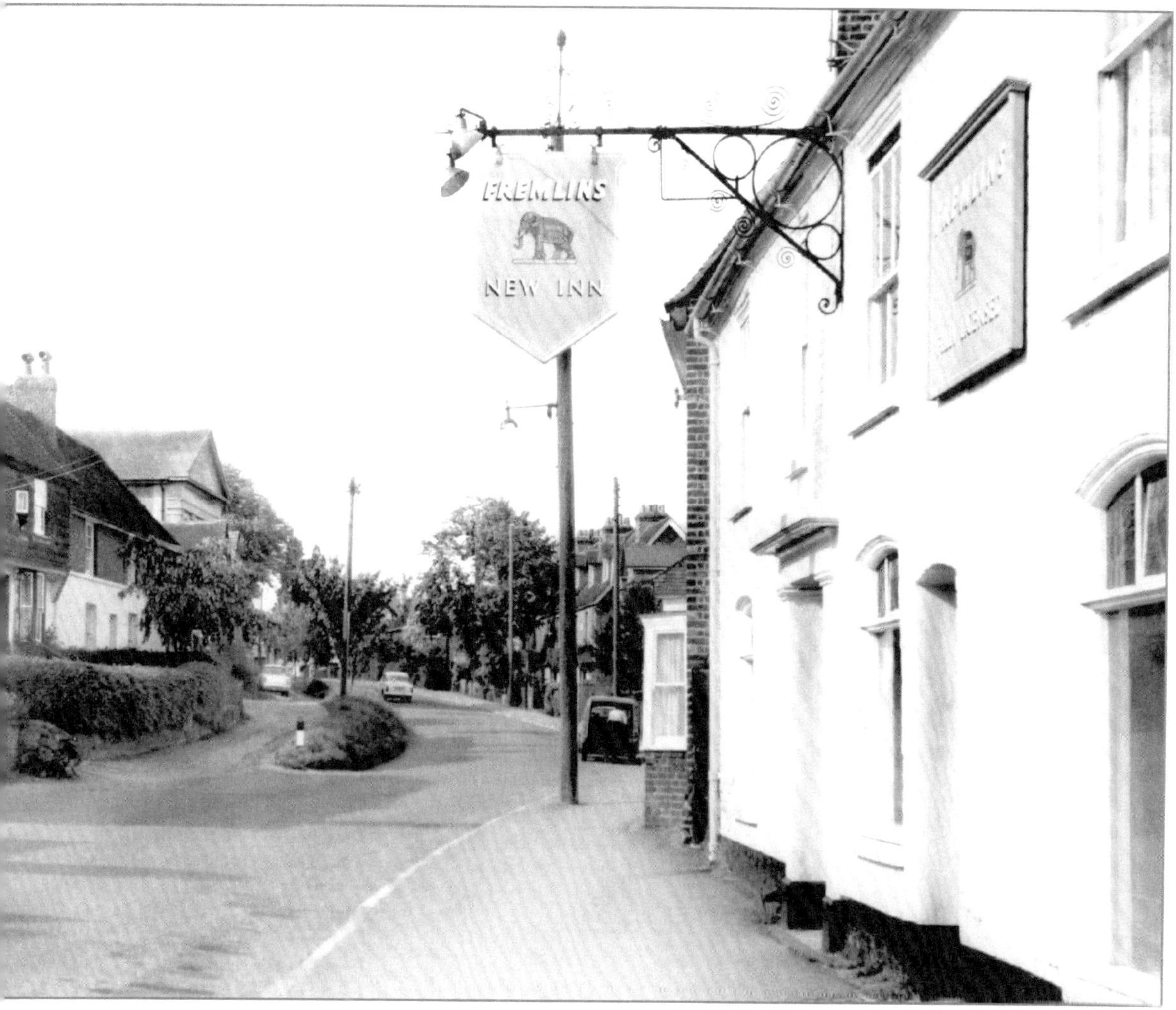

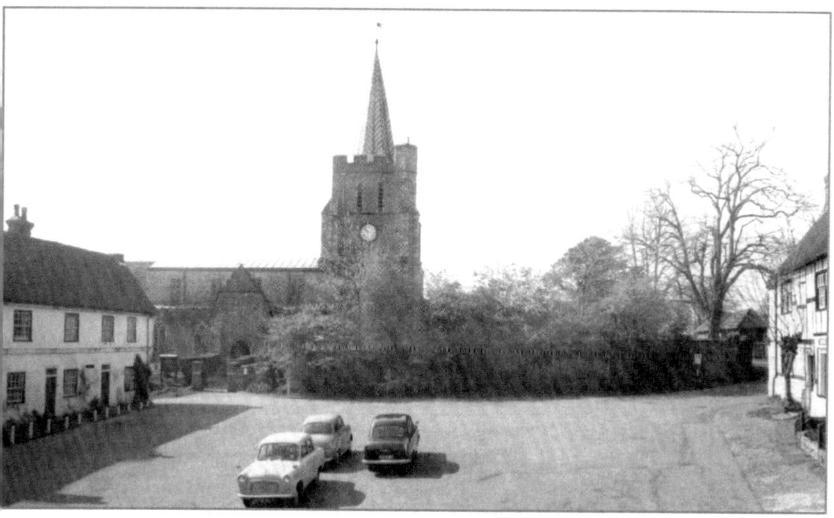

◄ **Elham, The Square c1960** E156020
Set off the main road, this square accommodates considerably more parked cars today. The Square or old Market Place of Elham adjoins the church yard on the north side, and a weekly market was held here until the 18th century. The old market booths, which backed on to the churchyard, were later converted into cottages and demolished in the 1940s. The church is built of flint, and is known as 'the capital church of the Elham Valley'.

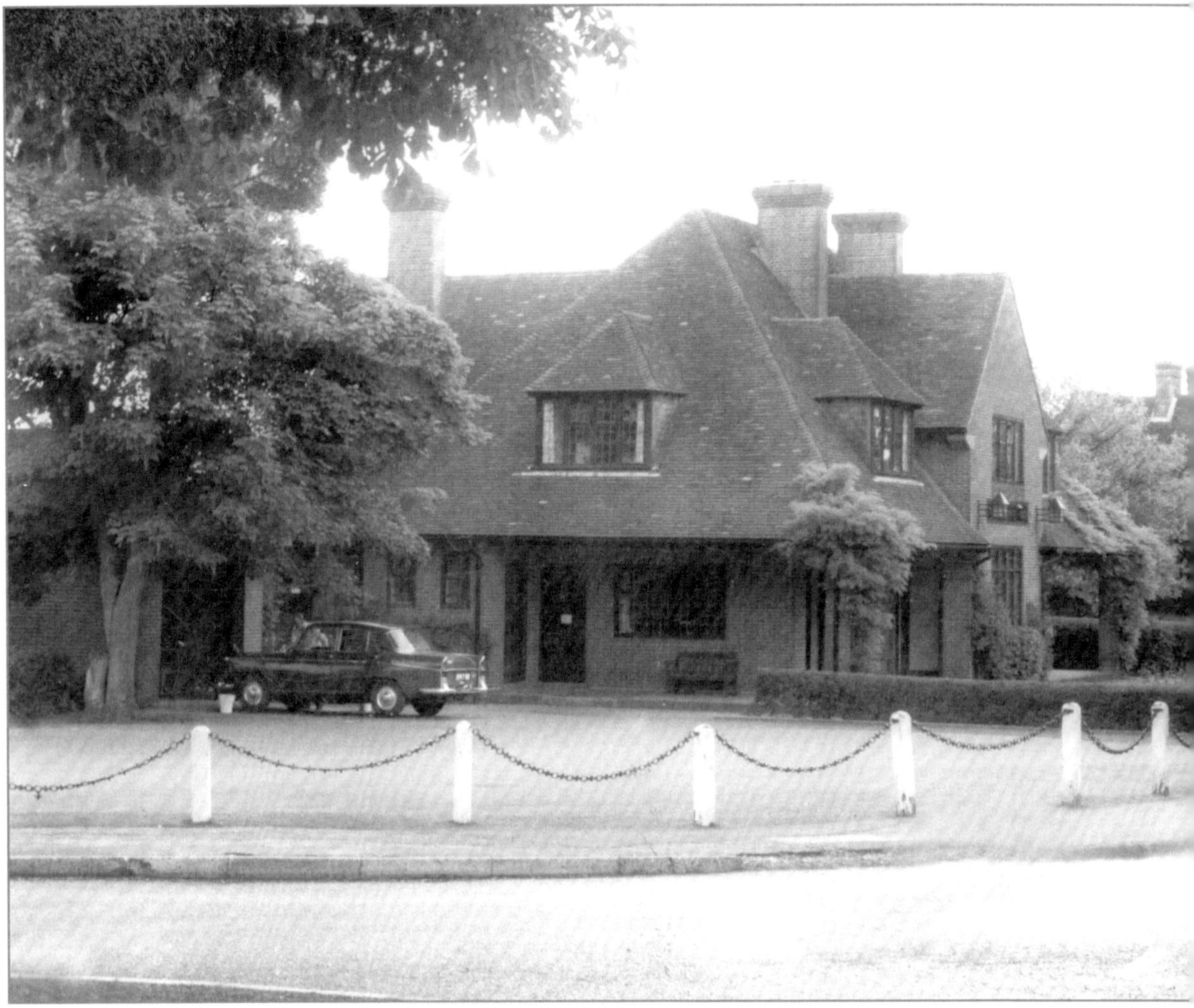

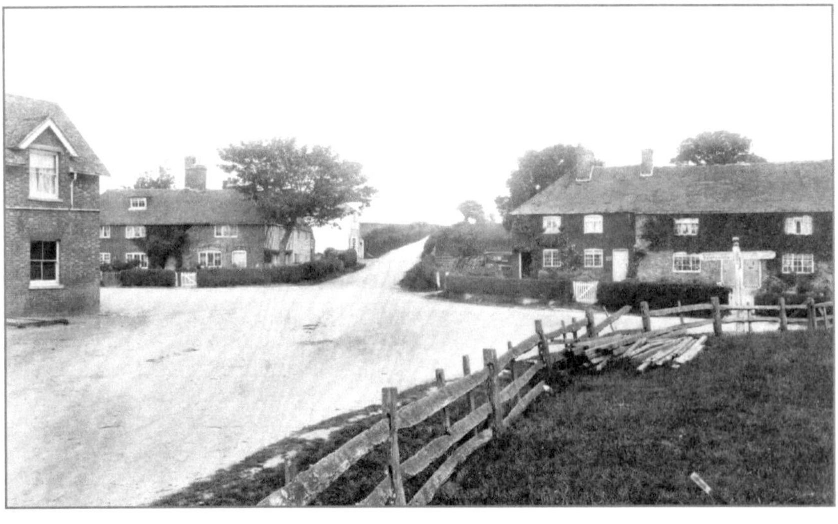

◄ **Bilsington, The Village 1909** 61577
Bilsington is a small village on the main Hythe to Tenterden road. Once near the sea, it is now several miles inland. Near this cross-roads stands a jagged finger of brickwork pointing to the sky. This obelisk was put up to Sir William Cosway, who owned the Priory nearby. He died after falling out of a stage coach in 1835. The obelisk has been fully restored following a recent lightning strike.

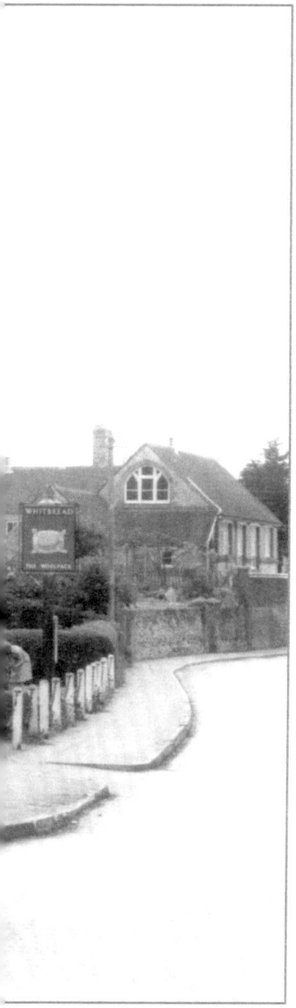

Smeeth, The Woolpack Inn c1960 S534010
The large attractive Woolpack Inn is very popular with those en route between Ashford and Folkestone, though it is possibly less busy than it was years ago - the M20 has taken most of the through traffic away from the old A20. The village name Smeeth means 'smooth clearing'.

Bilsington The Village 1909 61578
Bislington looks over Romney Marsh, a region both low and flat, which was reclaimed from the sea in ancient times. The Romans farmed here and constructed massive dykes that still perform a role in safeguarding the region's interests. They also founded the port of Romney.

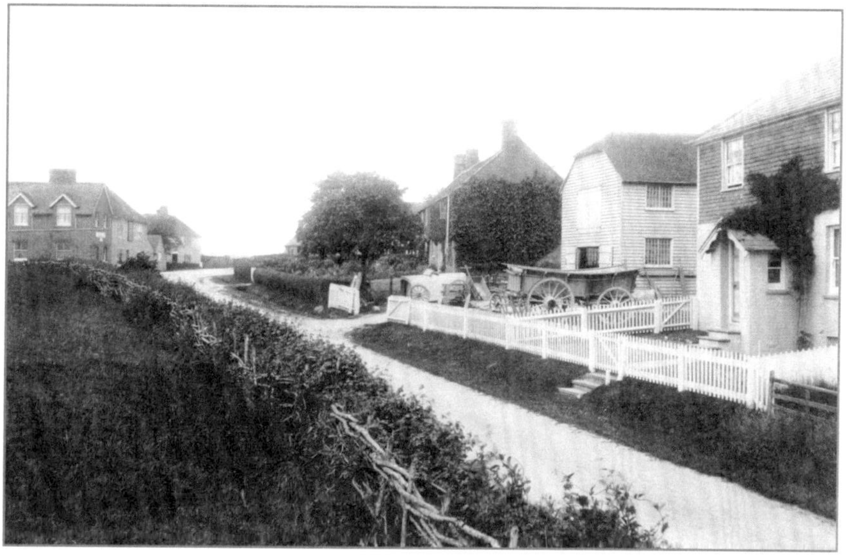

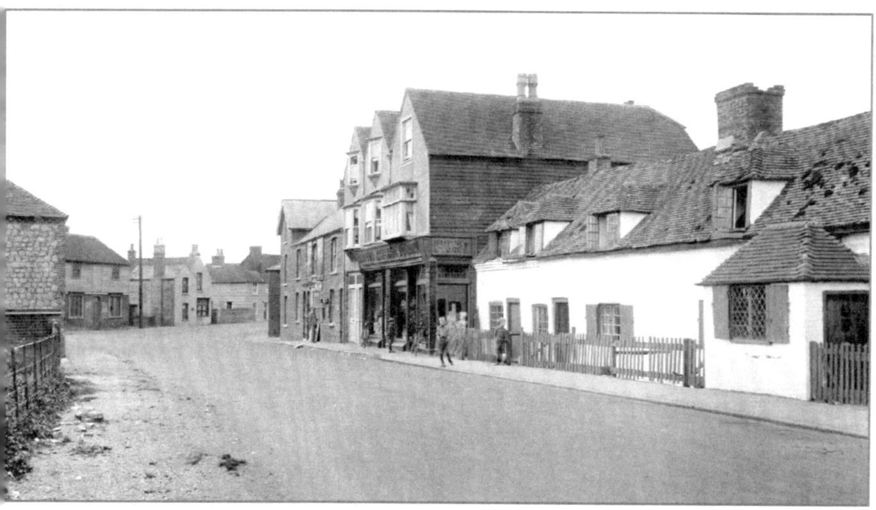

Dymchurch The Village 1921
71107
At this time, Dymchurch was a tranquil place; it attracted the author Edith Nesbit, who wrote 'The Railway Children'. She lived in one of the two-storey terraced cottages on the right of the picture. Dymchurch's other literary son was Russell Thorndike; he penned the 'Dr Syn' series of novels, concerning the activities of Romney Marsh smugglers.

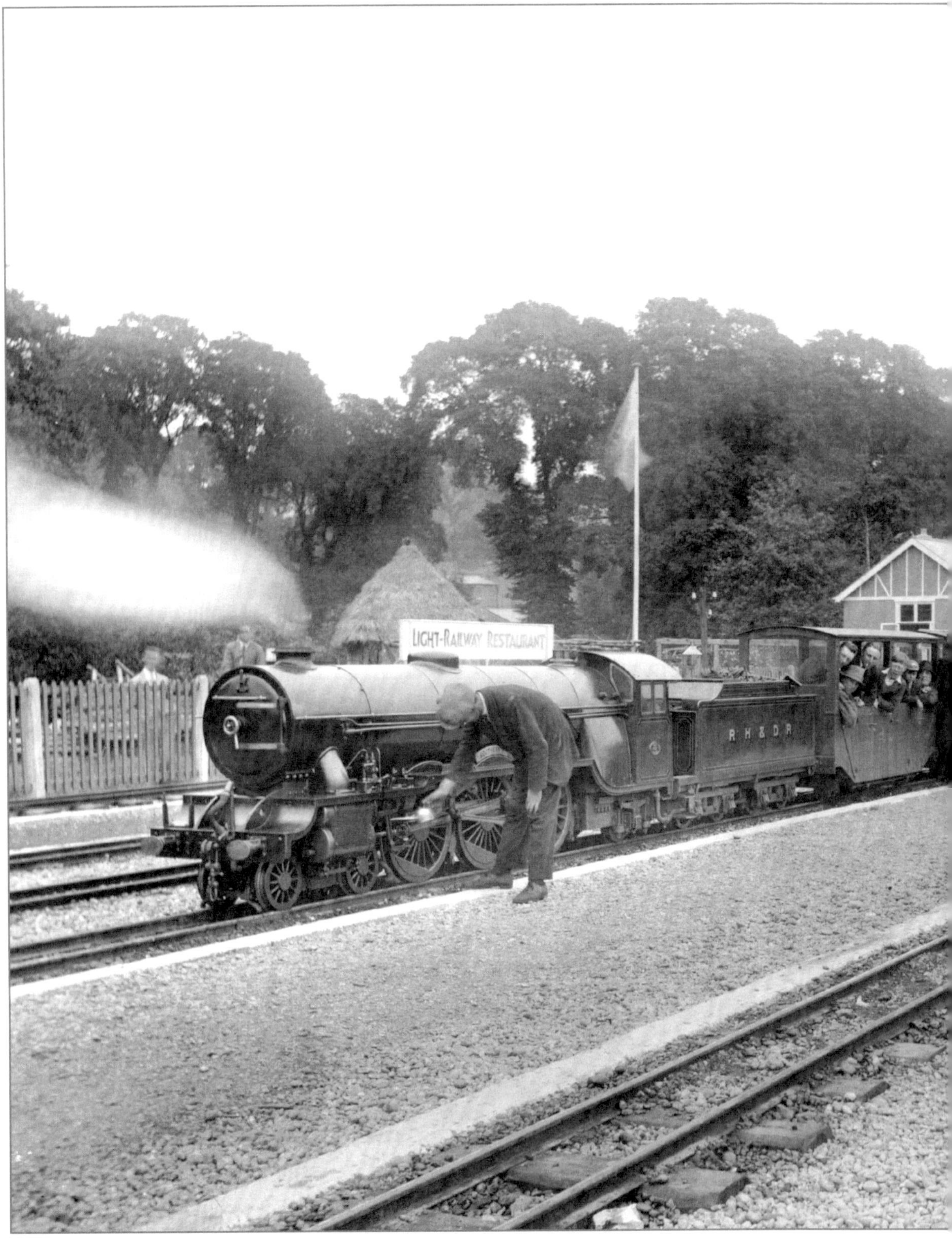
LIGHT-RAILWAY RESTAURANT
R H & D R

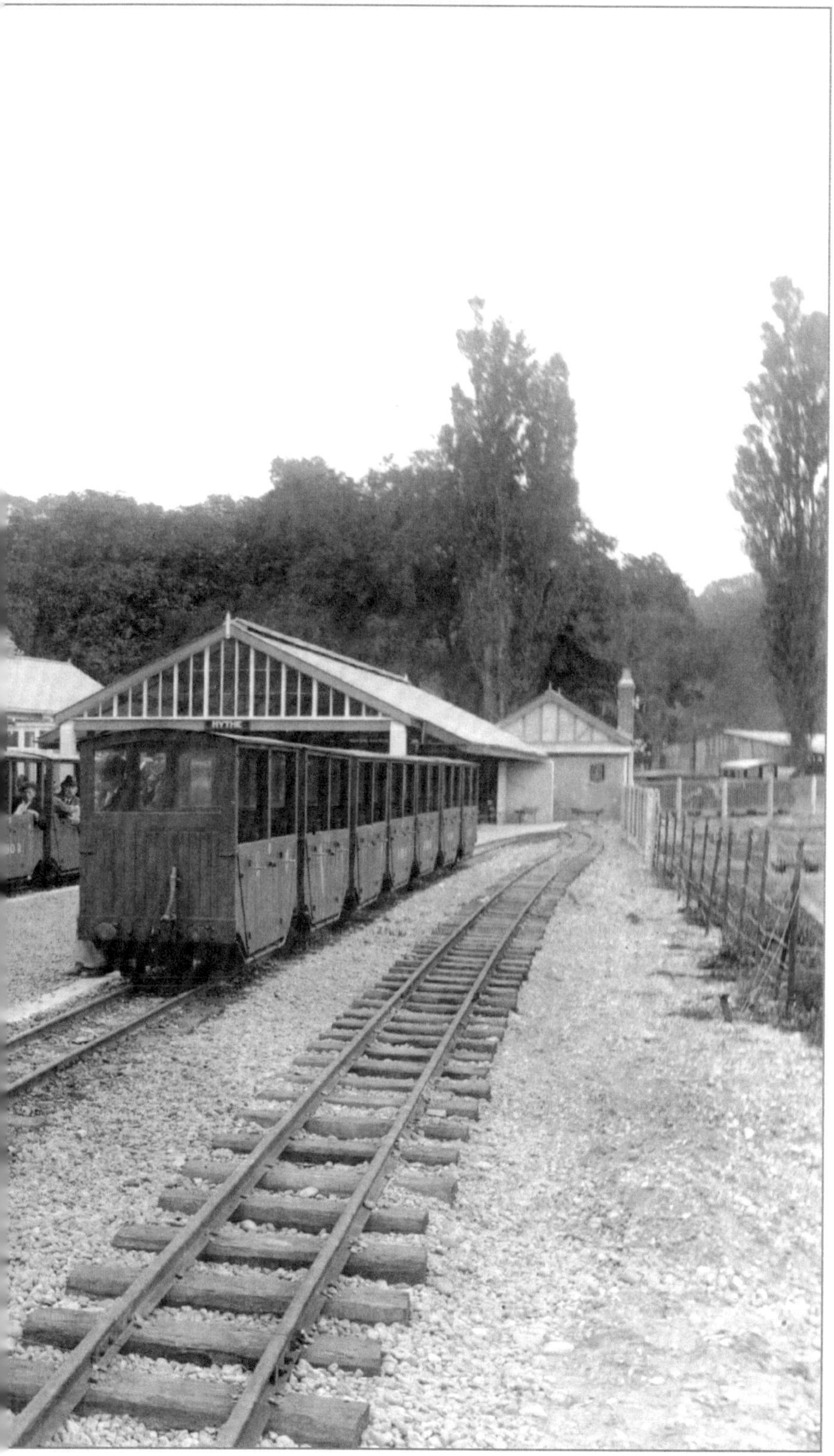

Dymchurch
The Light Railway
1927 80395

The Romney, Hythe and Dymchurch Railway is said to be the world's smallest public railway service. The 15 inch gauge line opened in 1927, and was the brainchild of Henry Greenly, Captain J E P Howey and Louis Zborowski. From Hythe to New Romney the line is double tracked, so trains travelling in the opposite directions can pass each other. However, beyond New Romney the line is a single track to Dungeness with a passing place at Romney Sands. It is still running today, and serves both as a novelty for holidaymakers and as a commuter train for local schoolchildren.

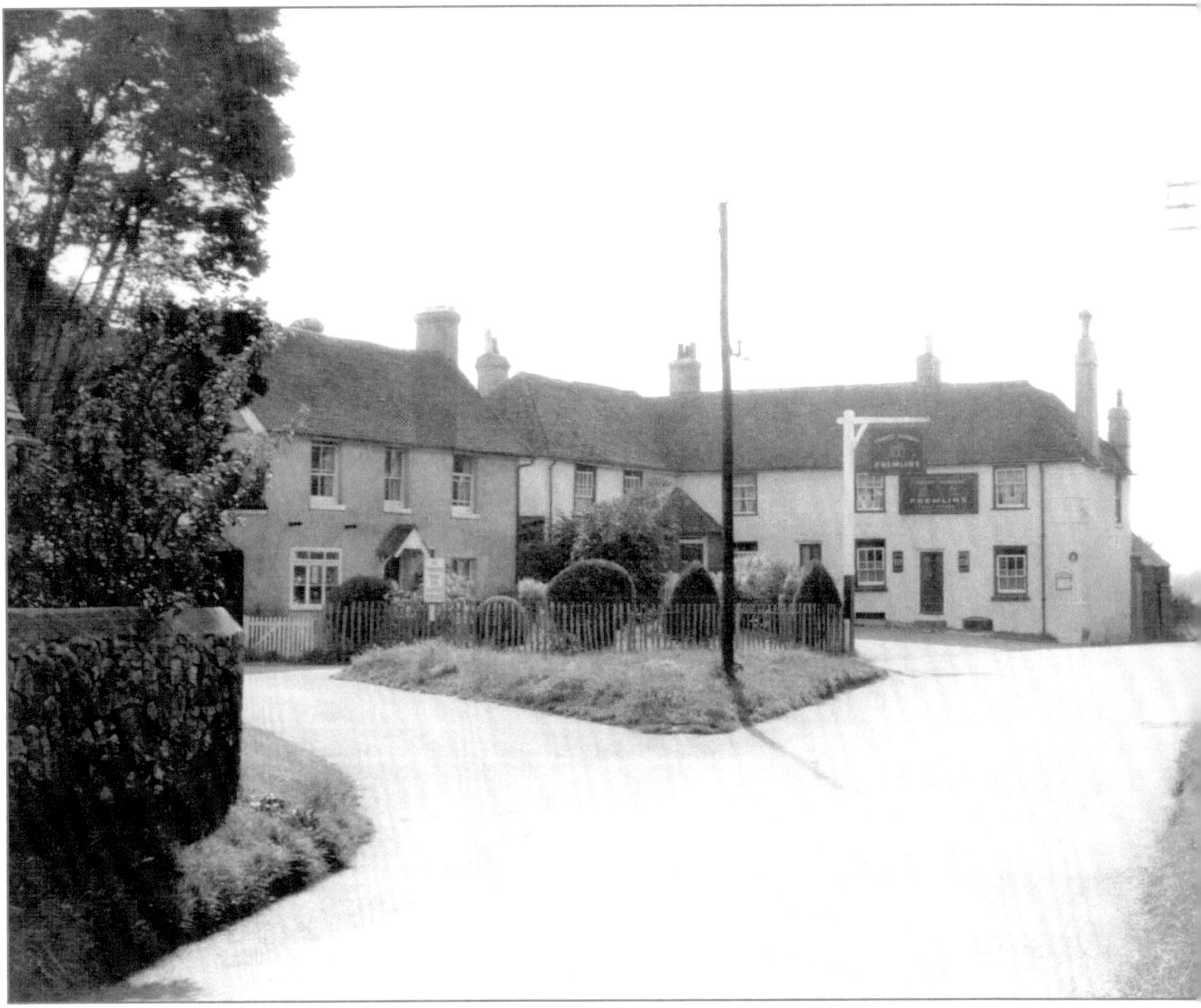

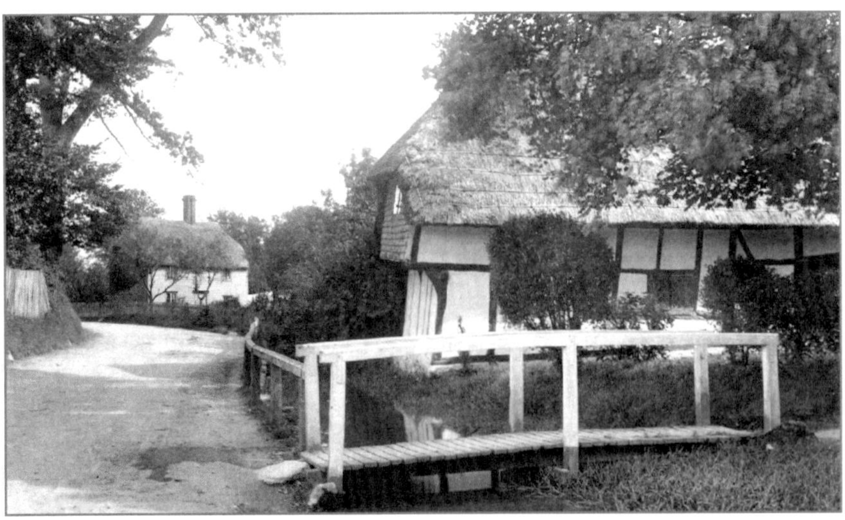

◄ **Newington, Cottages at Frogholt 1903** 50394
We may be thankful that this beautiful cottage in the tiny hamlet of Frogholt near Newington (just outside Folkestone) remains unchanged today. Just a few hundred yards from here, Channel Tunnel trains whistle past on their way to and from the continent.

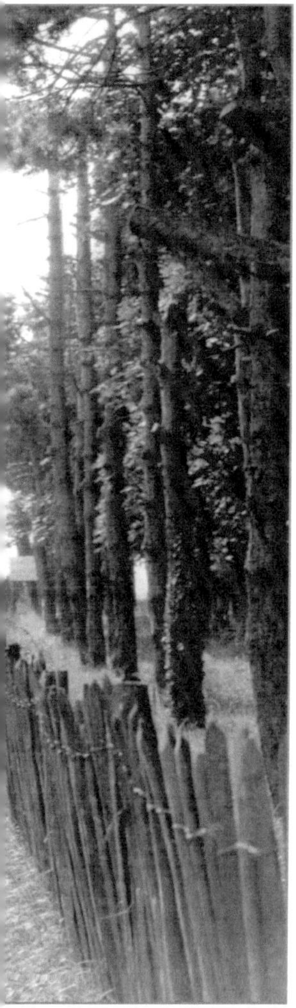

Lympne, The Village c1955 L335011

Lympne is a very ancient place indeed, and stands on a hilly scarp overlooking Romney Marsh. The Victorian art critic John Ruskin loved to walk the breezy heights here. Nearby are the ruins of a Roman fort, a medieval castle and a church, and there is a still-extant Roman road. The Roman fort once enclosed several acres of coastal land and must have been a powerful stronghold for the occupying army. The pub seen here was, and still is, much-used on this busy but pleasant route. H G Wells set part of his story 'The First Men in the Moon' in Lympne.

Cheriton, St Martin's Church 1903 50391

Cheriton's original parish church is of considerable antiquity – it contains some stonework dating from the Norman conquest. In the graveyard lies buried Samuel Plimsoll, who invented the Plimsoll Line. Modern housing now occupies most of the area between the church and the photographer, and the rural aspect is much diminished.

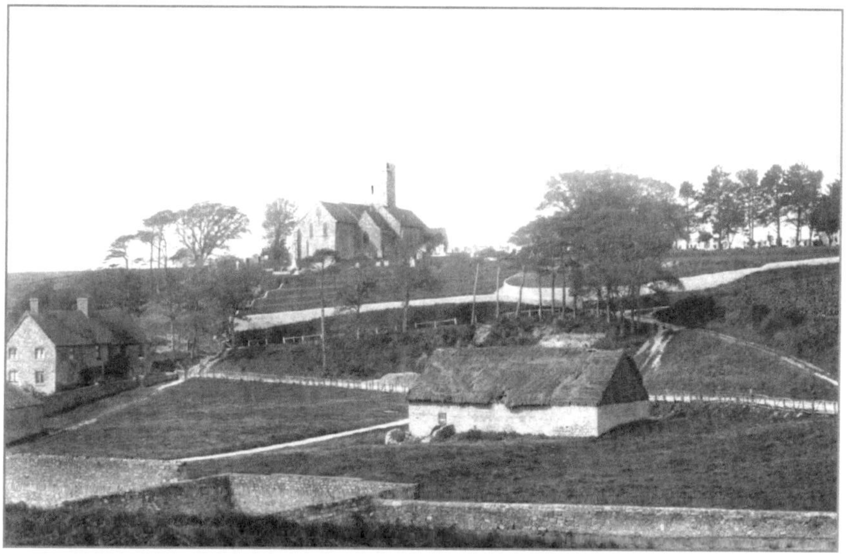

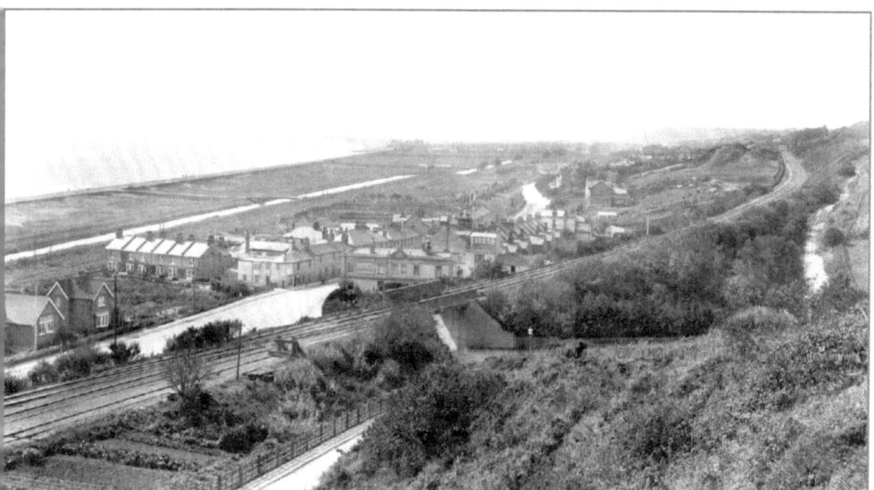

Seabrook, General View 1903 50372

The village of Seabrook has now merged with the town of Hythe, but at the time of this photograph was quite separate. The railway we can see here once ran from Sandgate to Sandling, but it was discontinued in 1931. Beyond is the old Fountain Hotel, which today is still welcoming visitors. The broad sweep of coastline stretches out towards Dungeness.

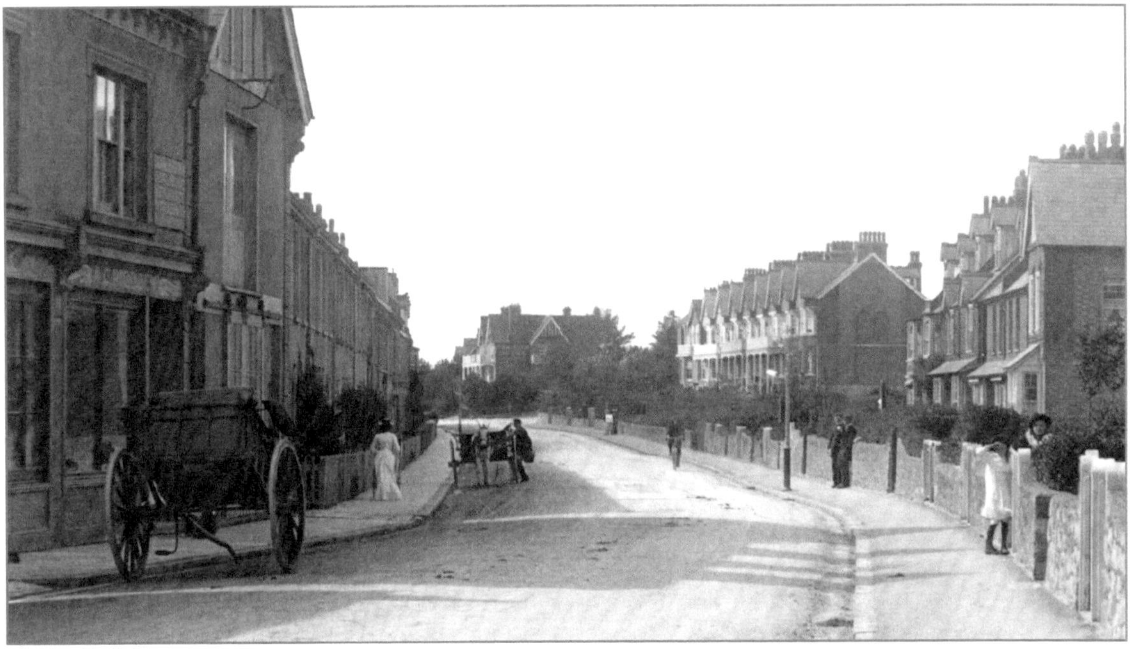

Seabrook, The Village 1903 50373
We are looking along the gently curving road towards Hythe. On the left are two small shops owned by Mr Bushell and Mr Ruddock and, in the distance, the Seaview Hotel. New terraces have been built to accommodate the large numbers of tourists who were flocking to enjoy the delights of a seaside holiday on the Channel coast.

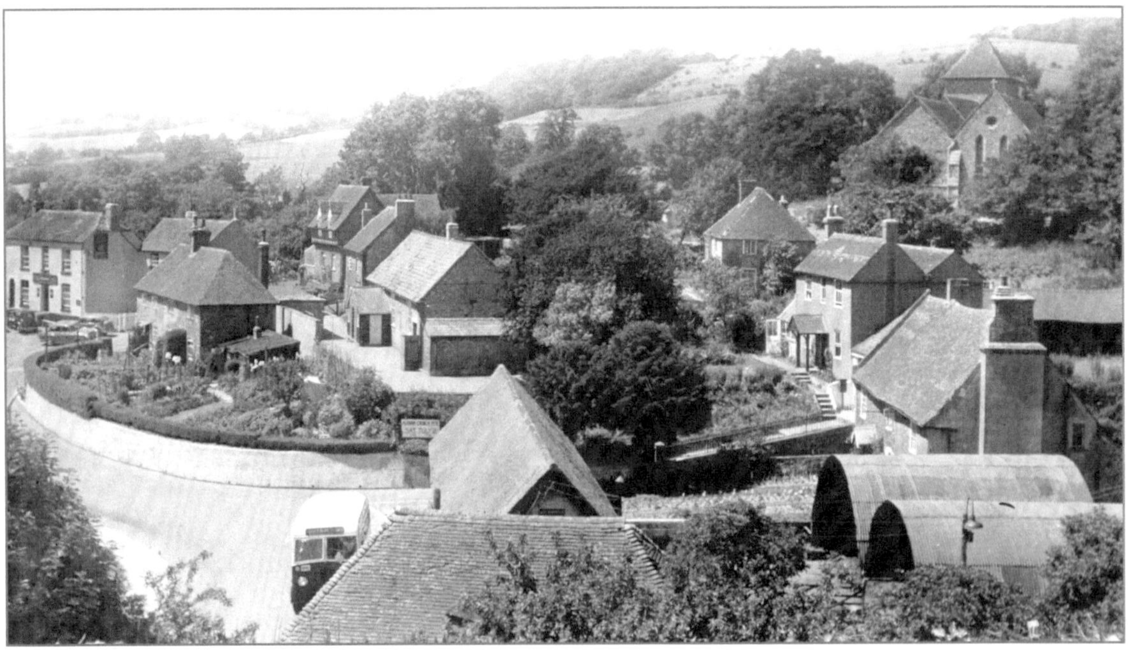

Alkham, The Village c1960 A22801
Alkham is an attractive little village nestling in the valley of the river Dour between Folkestone and Dover. The church seen behind the village is 13th-century; it was largely built of flint by the monks from nearby Radegund's Abbey, itself now just a ruin.

Coast to Coast

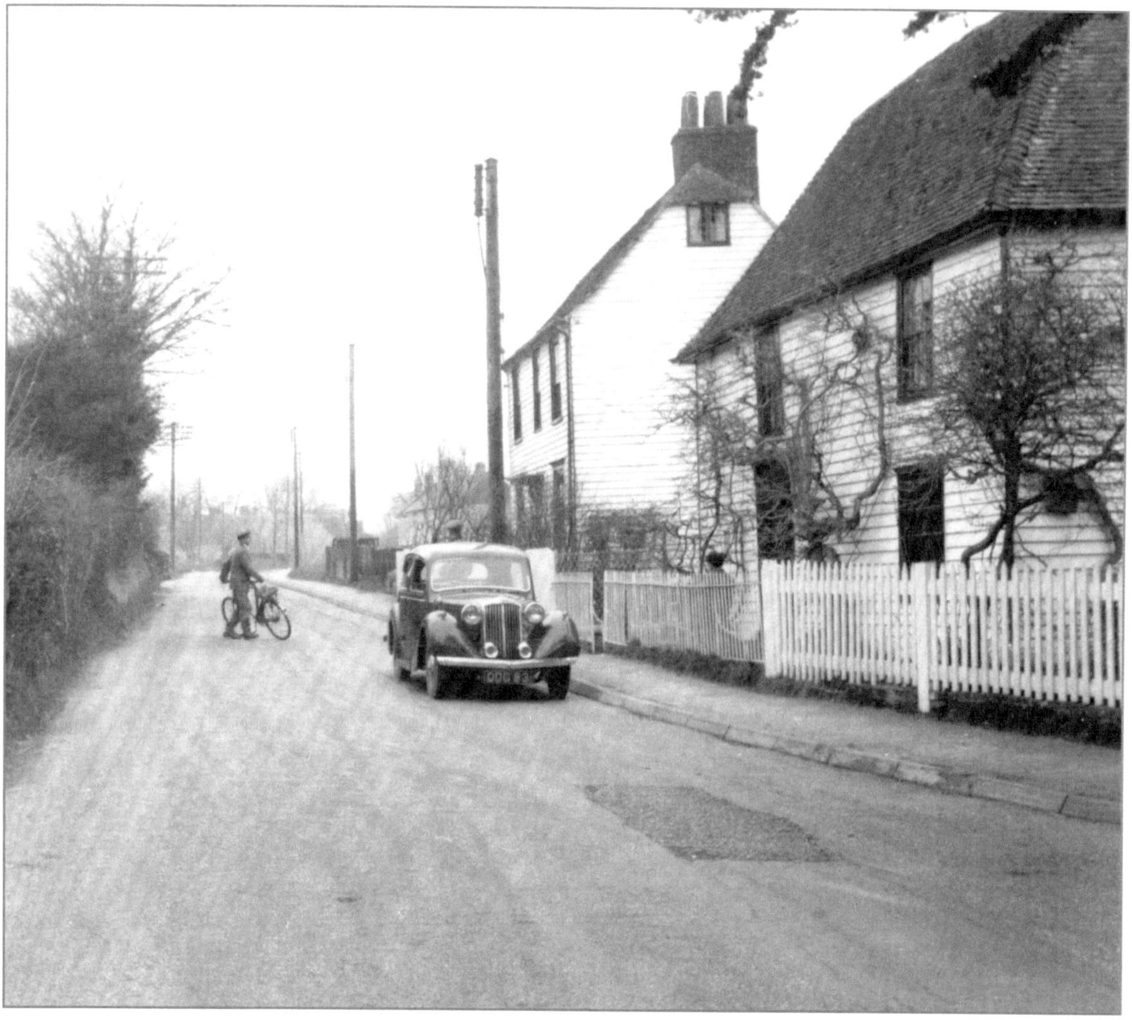

Borden, The Village c1950 B574005
This village is situated just outside Sittingbourne, but has avoided being swallowed up so far. We see a view of the main street here; this was probably as busy as it got in those days! The name Borden means 'woodland pasture by the hill'. A number of Roman coins and the foundations of two Roman buildings were dug up at Sutton-Barn here in 1846. The church has a Norman tower and west door, and traces of Roman brickwork have been discovered in its walls. It was restored in 1865.

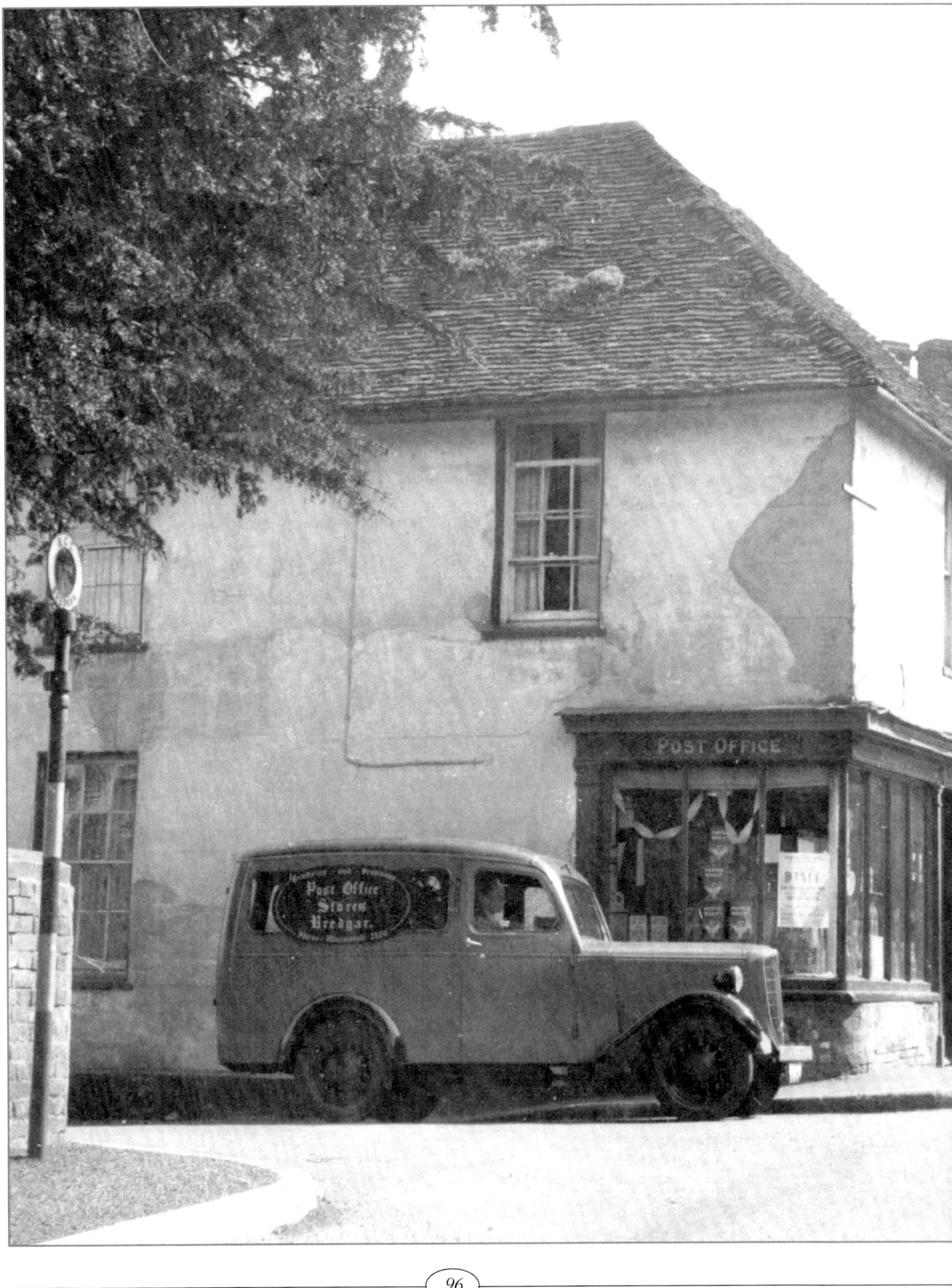
POST OFFICE
Post Office
Stores
Bredgar.

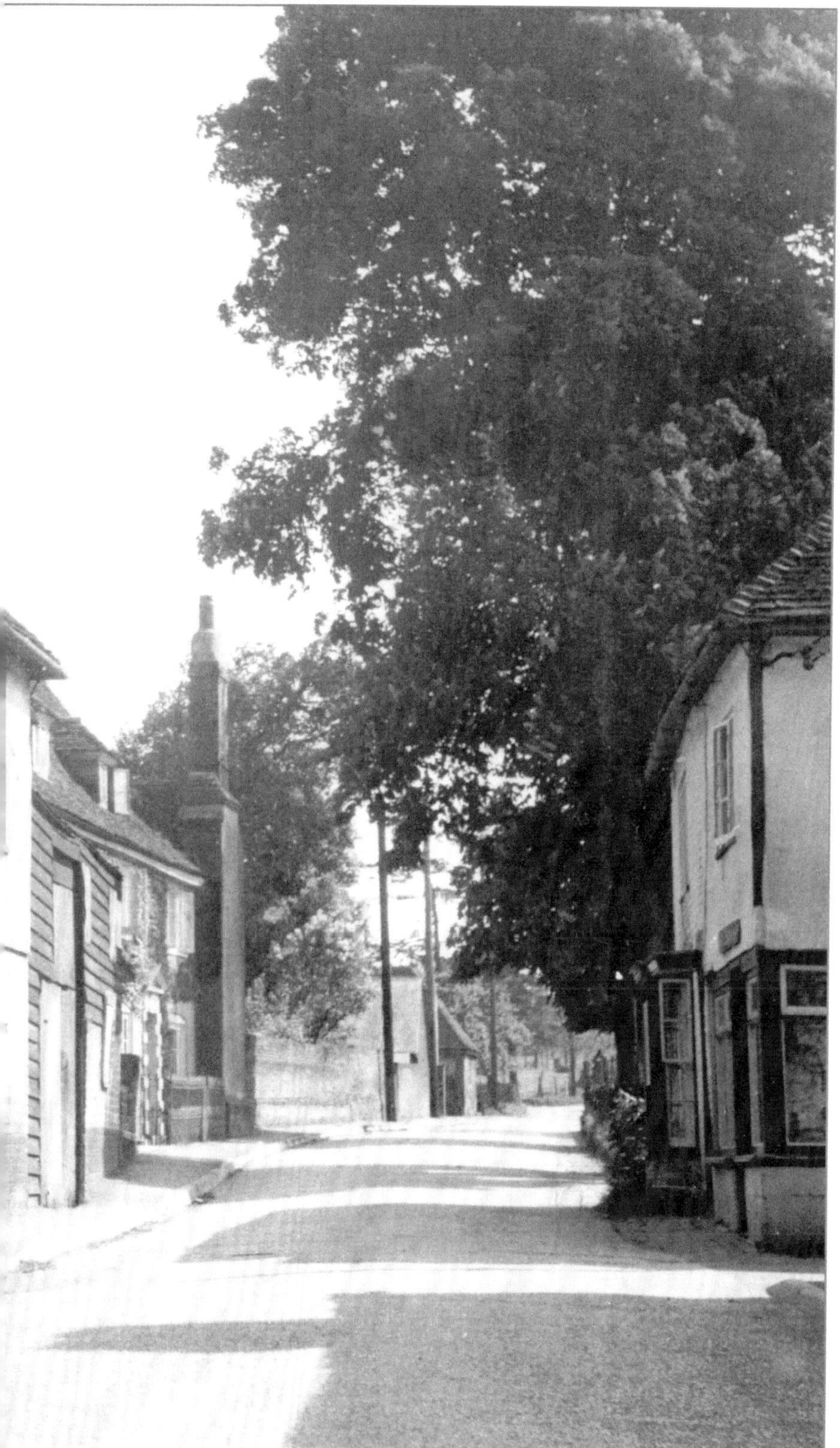

Bredgar, The Street c1955 B581011
This lovely old picture of the village centre shows the Post Office and a Post Office van outside. Francis Frith and his successors seemed to take some interest in Post Offices as photographic subjects, as I am sure you will have noticed; after all, it was the village post office and stores that usually sold Frith postcards.

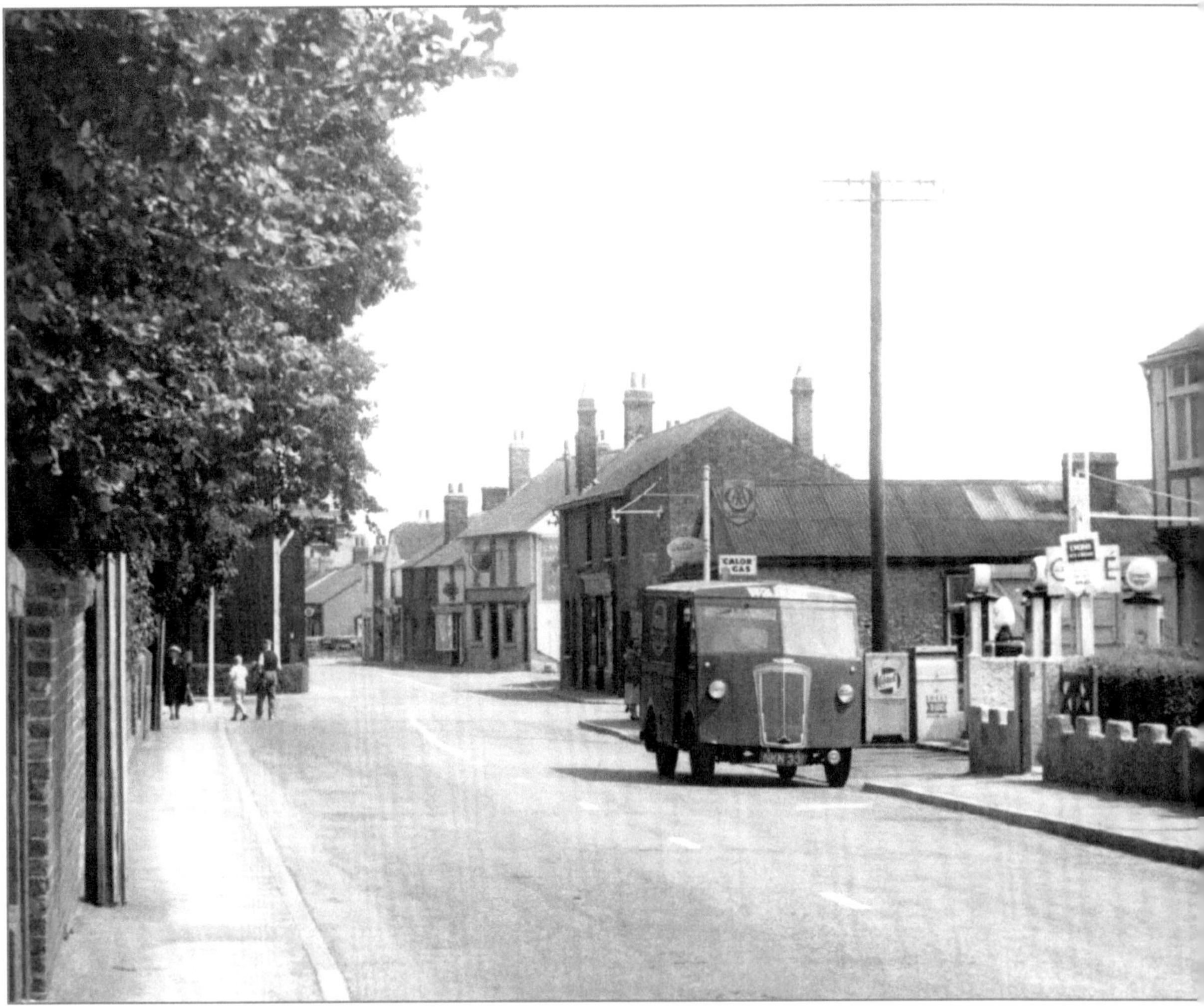

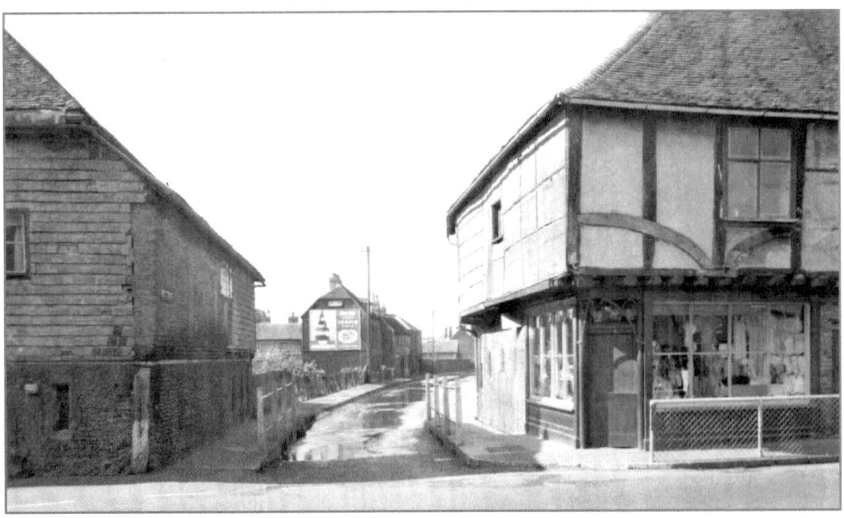

◄ **Ospringe, Water Lane c1955** 025010
Here we see the appropriately named Water Lane in the village, which was named after the spring that arises here. Ospringe was once a pilgrims' stop on the way to Canterbury. The half-timbered house stands on the site of a hospital founded by Henry III in 1234. Roman relics have been found here and authorities in the past believed Ospringe to be the site of the Roman Durolevum.

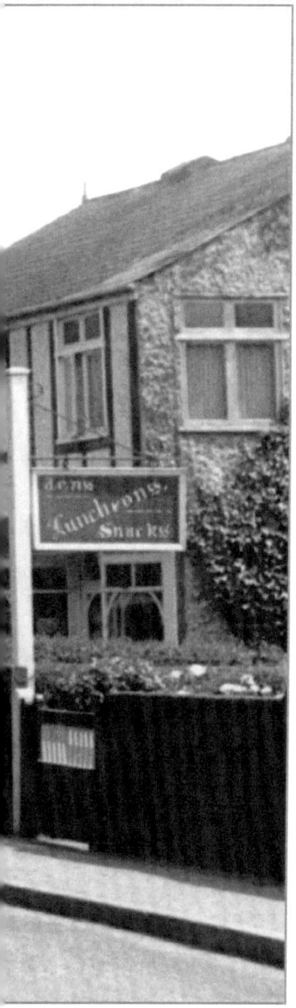

Eastchurch, High Street c1955 E153014
Known today for the nearby open prison situated on an old RAF camp, Eastchurch's claim to fame in earlier days was that it was the site of the first British airfield. The village lies on the north side of the Isle of Sheppey. In 1895 it comprised over 7,000 acres of land and 950 of tidal water and foreshore. The population was 854.

Davington, The Priory 1892 31479
The Priory, and what is left of the Priory church, has an ancient history. Two nuns from here were shipwrecked at Reculver on their way to Minster in Thanet. To give thanks for the saving of their lives, they instituted the construction of the twin church towers that once existed at Davington. Thereafter the Reculver towers were called the 'two sisters'. What was left of the Priory was severely damaged in 1781 when a Faversham gunpowder mill exploded. Since then the Priory has undergone extensive restoration and modernisation, and is now a private house.

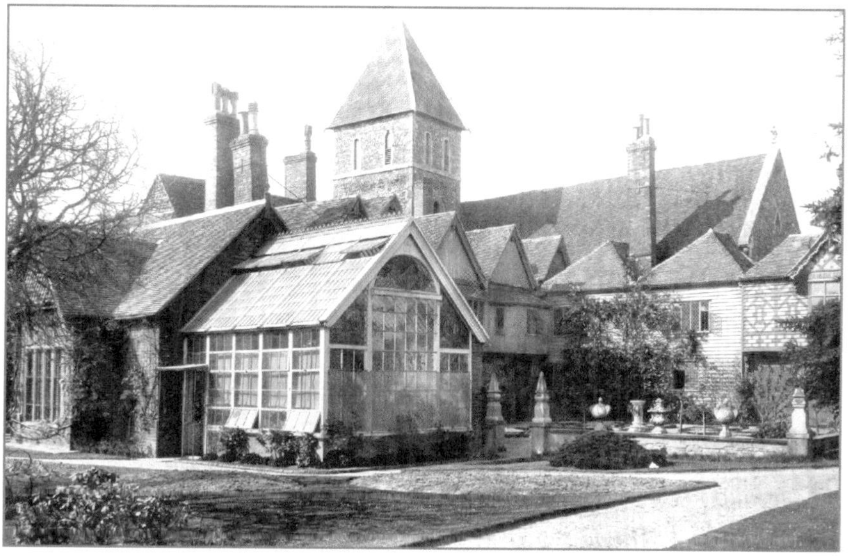

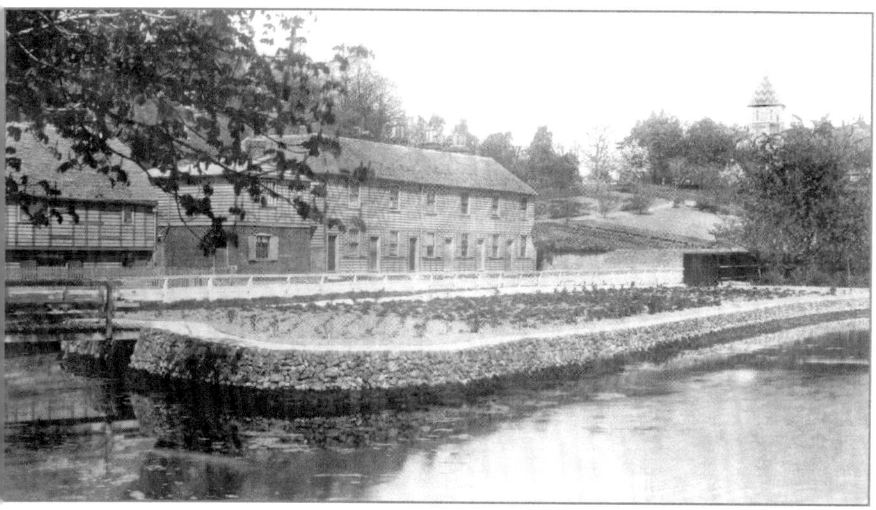

Davington, The Priory 1892 31480
The single remaining tower of the Priory church can be seen across the creek and parkland in this turn-of-the-century view. The church was restored and rededicated in 1932. It is said to be haunted by the ghostly figure of a nun.

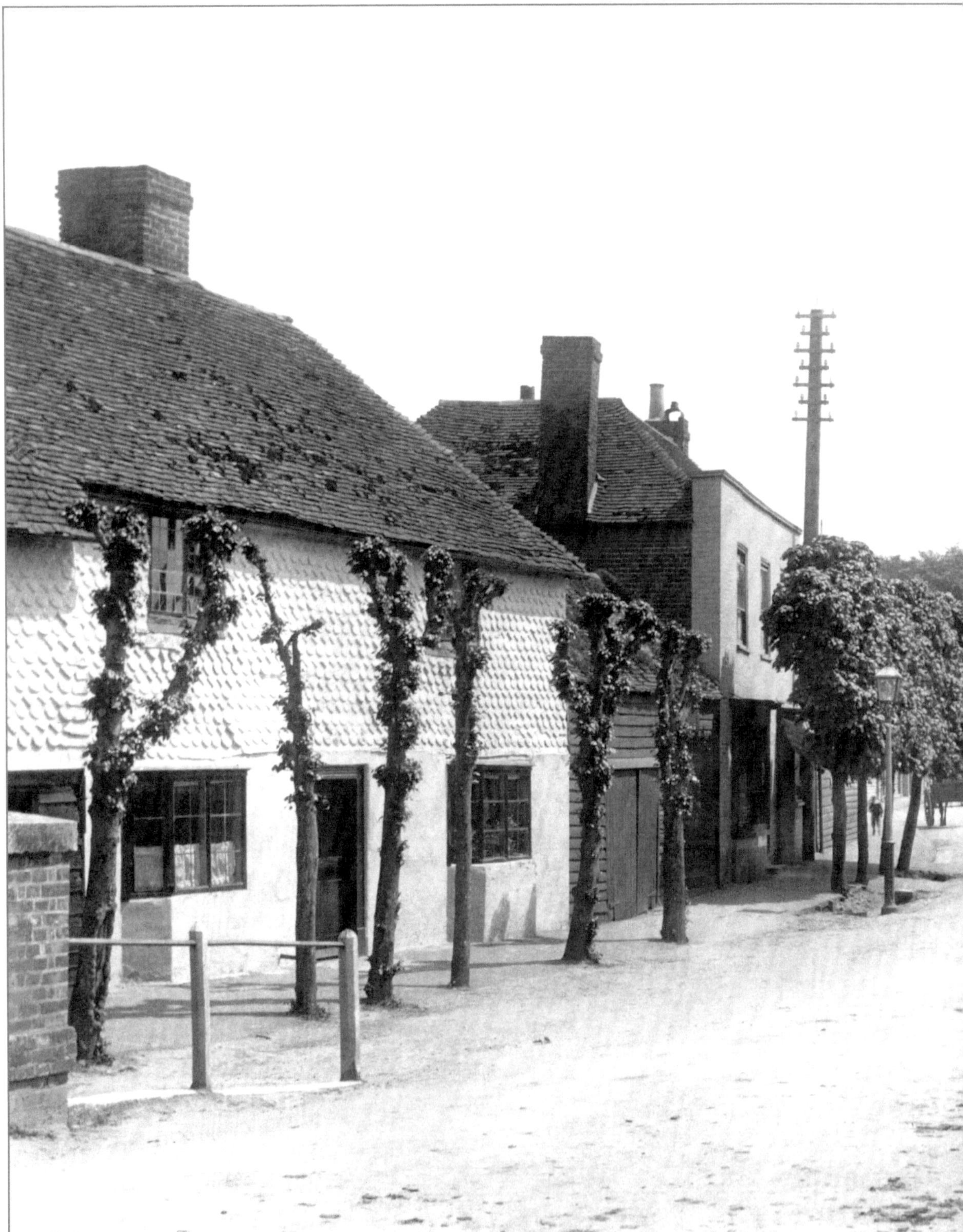

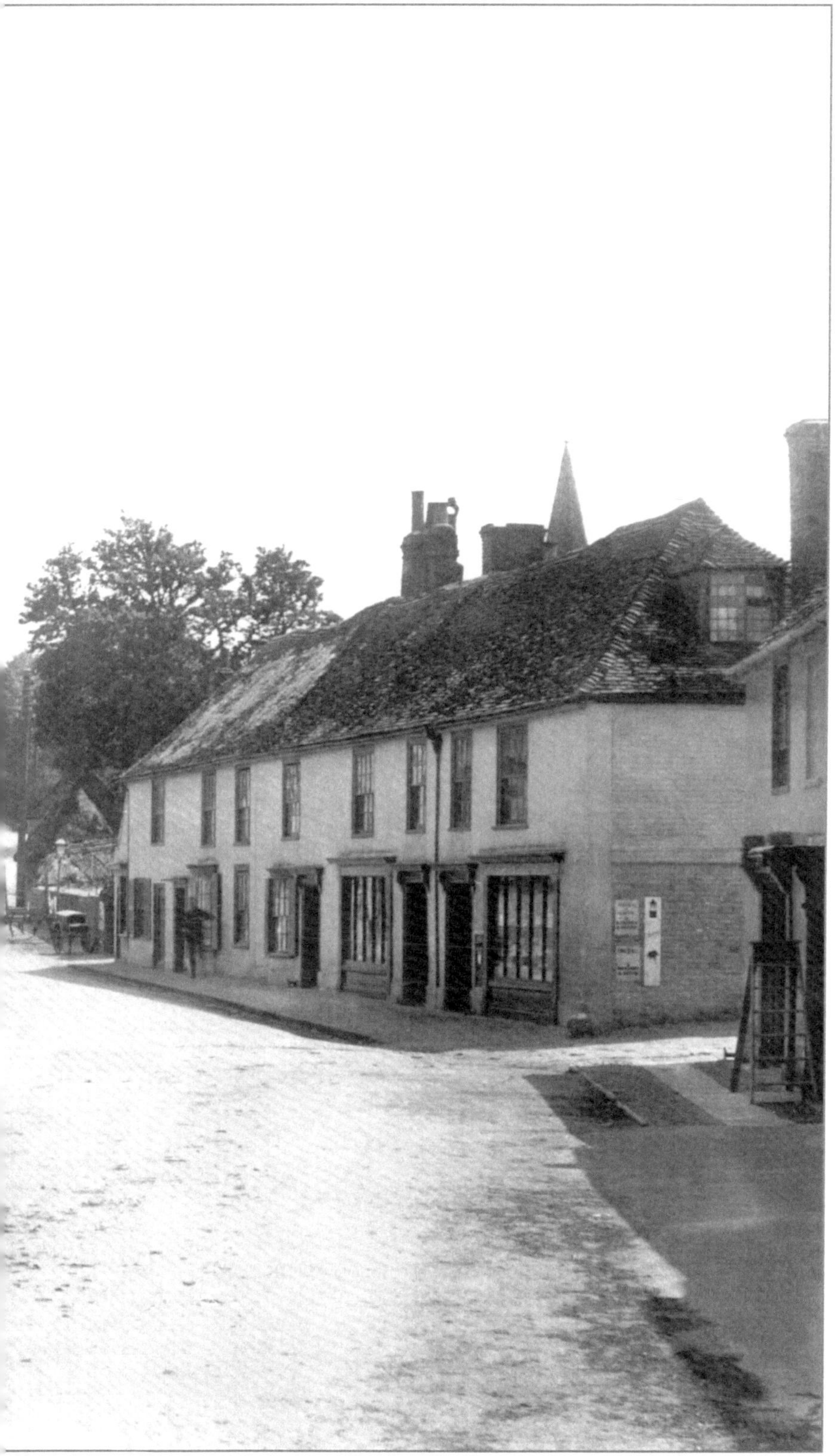

Bridge, High Street 1903 49400

This village stands on Watling Street close by the Little Stour. Years after this photograph was taken, traffic passing through the long, winding main street with its pollarded trees made life unbearable for residents; after a long protest campaign, a bypass was opened in the late 1970s. Nearby Higham Park was once the home of Count Zborowski, whose racing exploits were the inspiration for the book 'Chitty Chitty Bang Bang' by Ian Fleming. The artist Jansen lived here for some time, the painter of the popular portrait of a lady 'The Star in the East'.

▼ **Selling, Oast Houses c1955** S526010
Selling is a pretty village of orchards, oasts and timbered houses set amongst hills. It summons up the essence of the old county of Kent with its hop gardens and orchards. The church is nicely situated amongst cedars and yews, and has a particularly fine 13th-century east window.

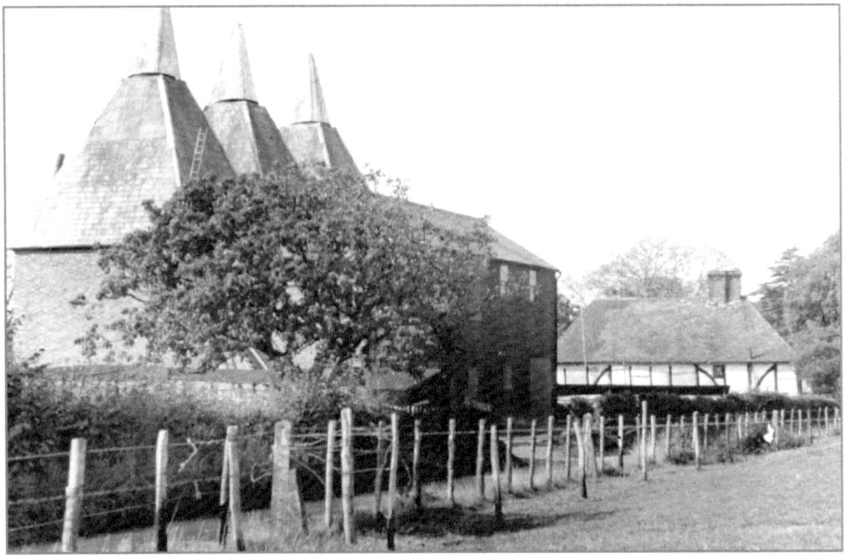

▼ **Bishopsbourne, The Church 1903** 51059
The church occupies a particularly idyllic location. It is of 14th-century origin, and has some 16th-century and Victorian restoration work. Bishopsbourne is next to the Nailbourne, which runs along the Elham Valley eventually to become the Little Stour. Joseph Conrad, author of 'Heart of Darkness' and 'The Secret Agent', spent his final years in Bishopsbourne, and was buried in Canterbury.

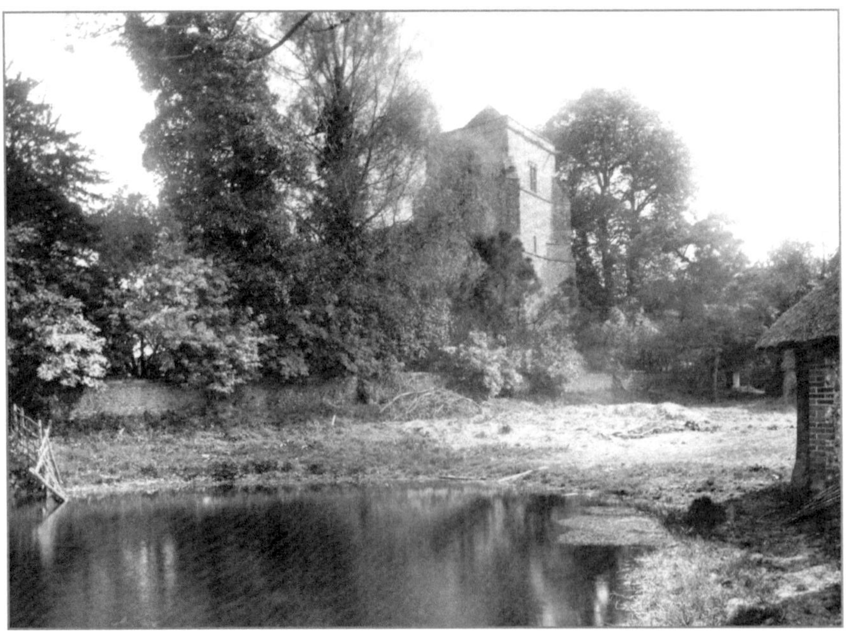

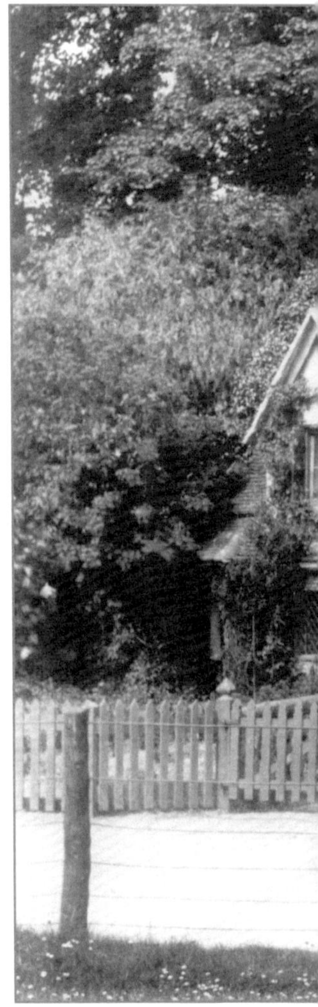

▲ **Patrixbourne, Cottages 1903** 49414
This 'Tudor' house may not be all it seems, as many houses in this pretty village were built in this style as recently as 1860. There is a very good example of a Norman church here, built around 1160. The Nailbourne passes through in the form of a small stream, flowing intermittently; however, in February 2001 it was a raging torrent, swamping many of the properties hereabouts.

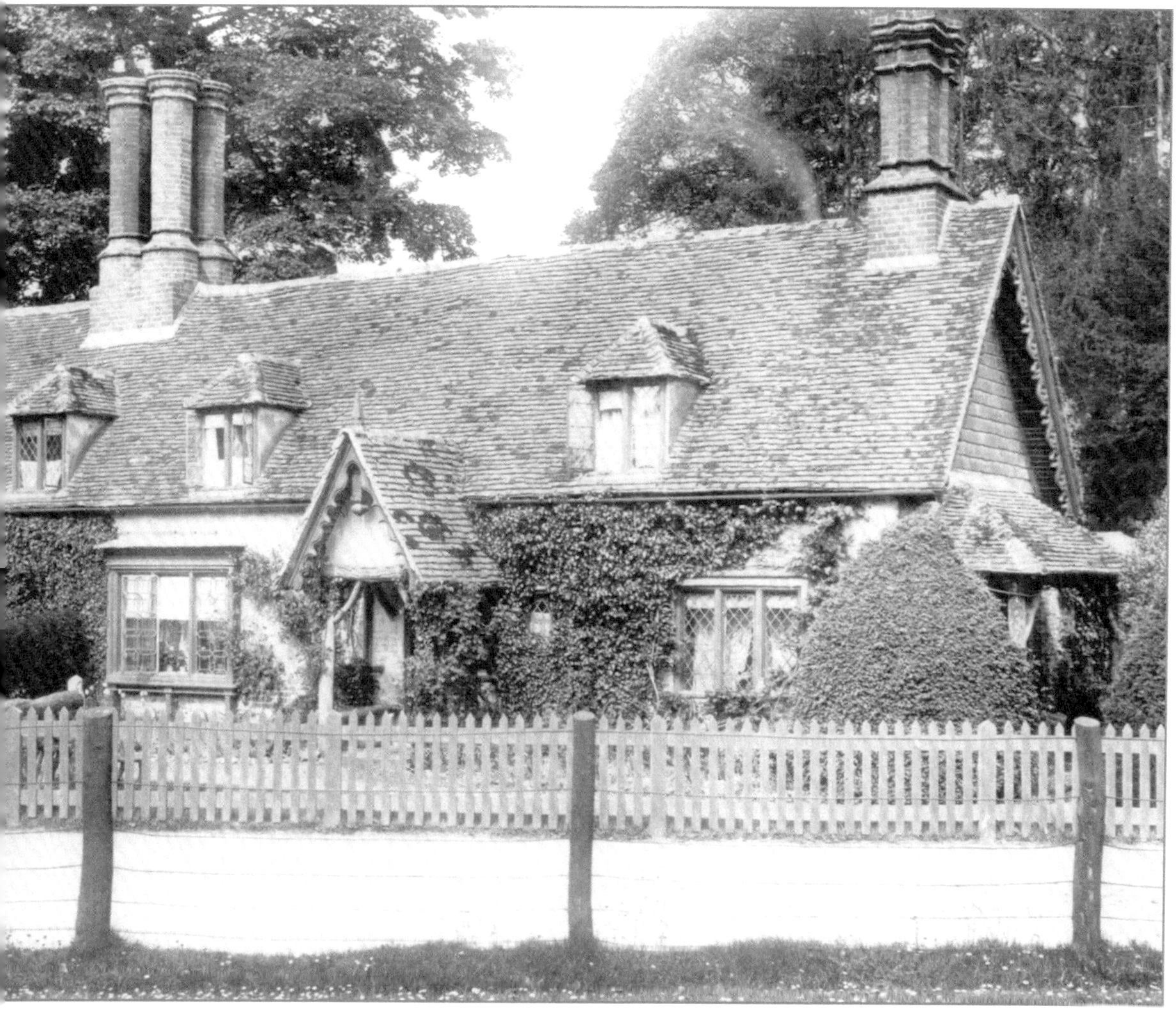

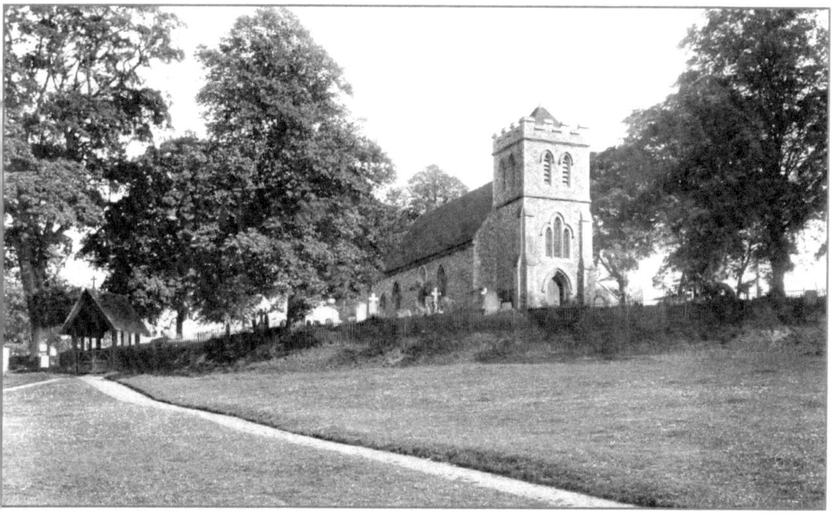

Bekesbourne
The Church and Lychgate
1903 49415

Here we see another church in an attractive location near the small village of Bekesbourne, which contains 18th-century cottages and some modern housing. The church has been much renovated over the centuries, and shows little early work. Remains of a Tudor palace razed in the Civil War have been found nearby. Bekesbourne is one of the three 'bournes'; the others are Bishopsbourne and Littlebourne.

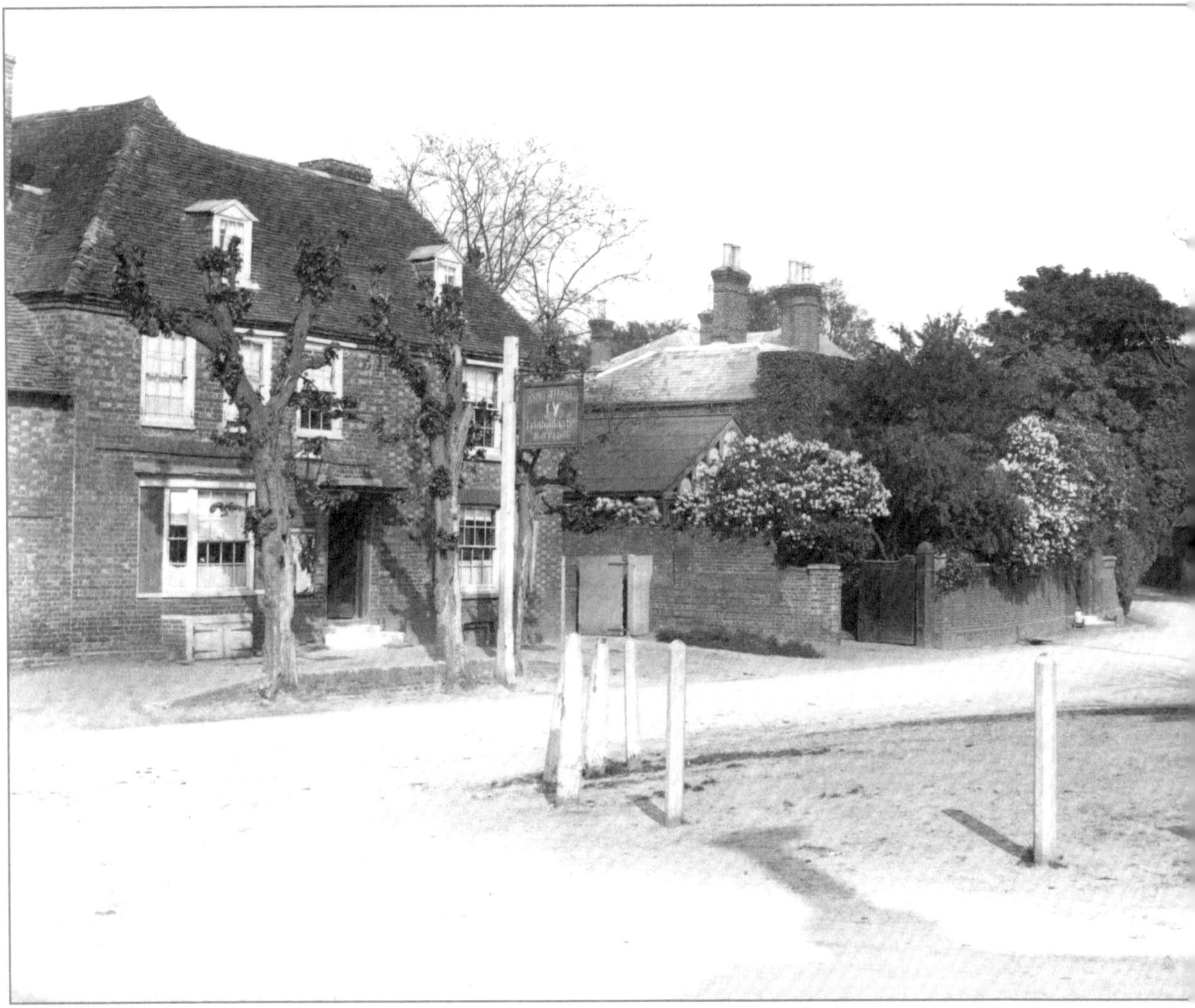

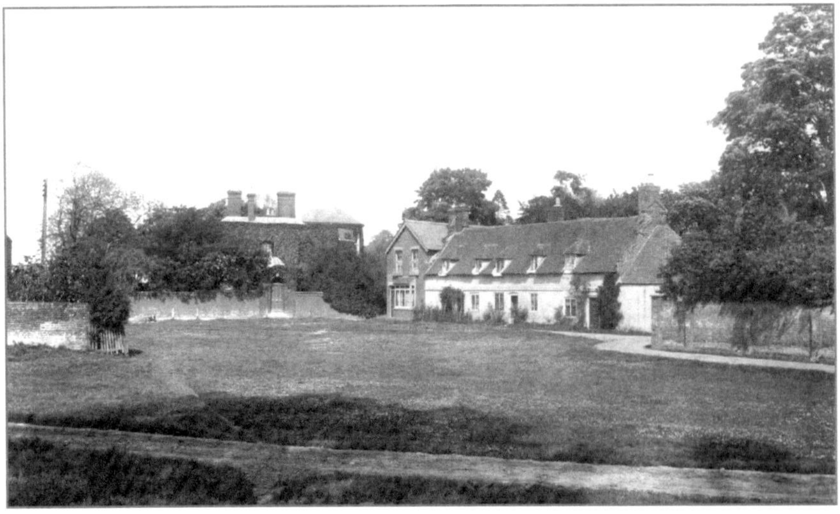

◄ **Littlebourne**
The Green 1903 51054
Here we see a lovely view of the wide flower-flecked green on what looks like a warm evening. Littlebourne has a long history, and had a closely-knit community in those days. The existence of the village is first mentioned in the Domesday Book of 1086. The manor belonged to the abbey of St Augustine and to an Italian monastery.

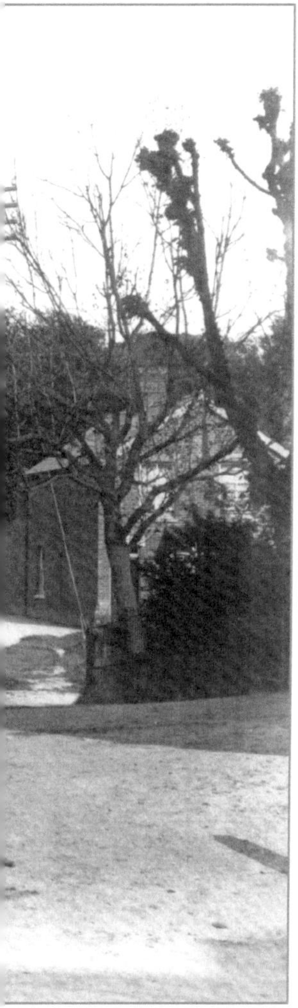

◄ **Littlebourne, The Village 1903**
49428
A view of the King William IV public house, one of the four that existed in the village at this time. There were also two butchers, four grocers, a hardware store, a post office, a newsagent, a saddler, a laddermaker, shoe menders, a plumber, a builder/decorator, a forge, a blacksmith, malthouses, hop kilns and breweries. The village was virtually self-sufficient, as were many during the first half of the 20th century.

▼ **Ickham, The Old Rectory c1960** 11021
The 17th-century scholar Meric Casaubon lived in this rectory. This fine building shows a pleasing mix of different styles. On the left we can see medieval stonework and windows, whilst a Flemish influence seems apparent on the right of the building. Ickham itself is another of the villages of the Little Stour; it consists of a pleasant mixture of weatherboard, brick and tile faced dwellings. There was once a mill on the stream here.

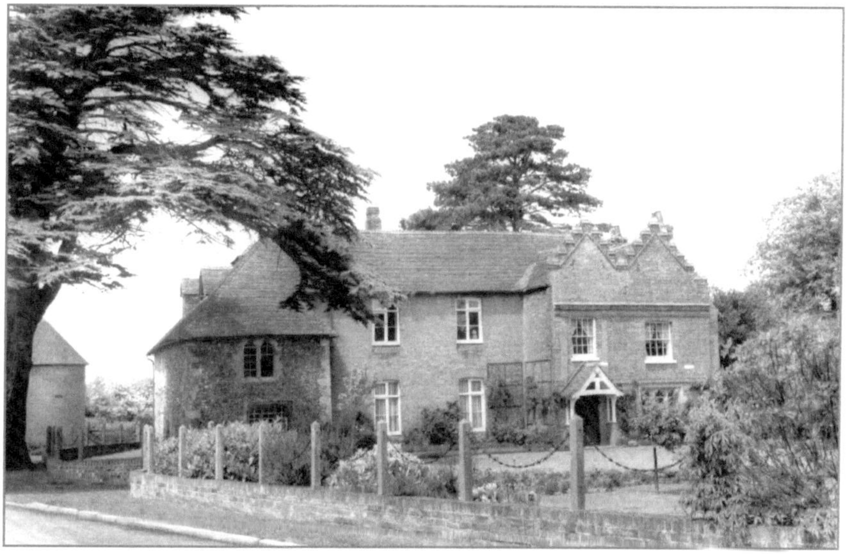

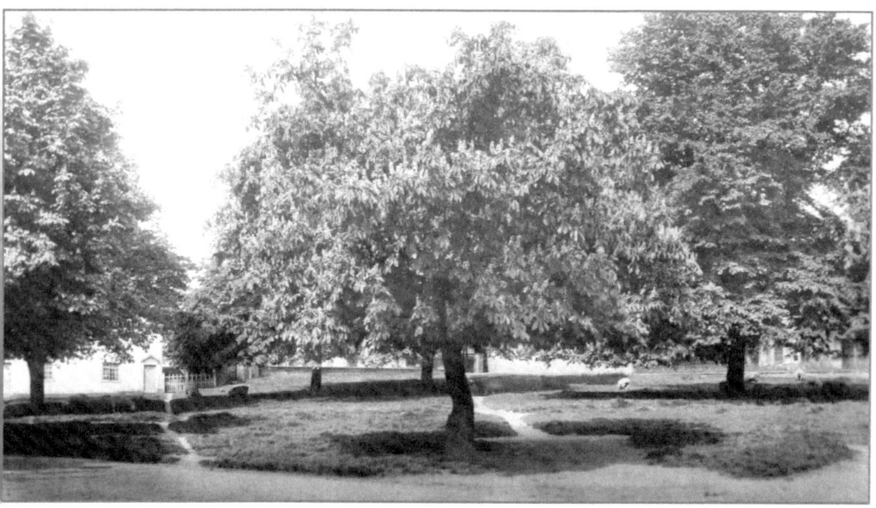

◄ **Wickhambreux The Green 1903** 49420
This pretty old Kentish village of Saxon vintage has a lovely green (alas, not now as rural as it looks here) surrounded by lime and chestnut trees, some grand Georgian houses and simpler homes. There is a pleasant rushing stream, swans, and a watermill.

▼ **Wickhambreux, The Old Bell House 1903** 49421
This attractive Tudor building is known as The Bell House because in 1525 the then owner decreed that upon his decease the money raised from renting out the building should be used to pay for the ringing of the curfew bell.

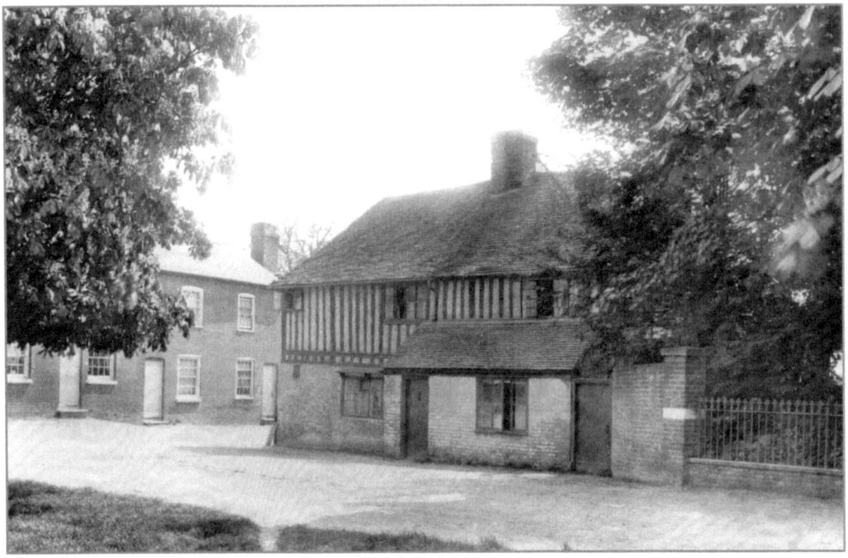

▼ **Fordwich, The Village c1950** F38002
Once the port for Canterbury, Fordwich was a town when Domesday was compiled. Now it is now just an attractive riverside village. The church is 14th-century, though there are some traces of Saxon work, and is dedicated to St Mary. The Caen stone used in the construction of Canterbury Cathedral was landed here.

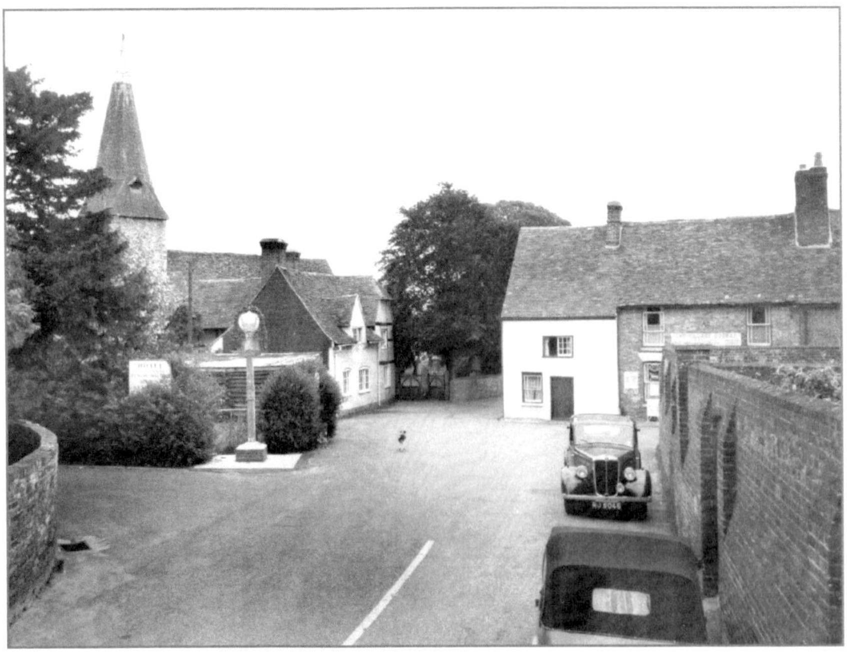

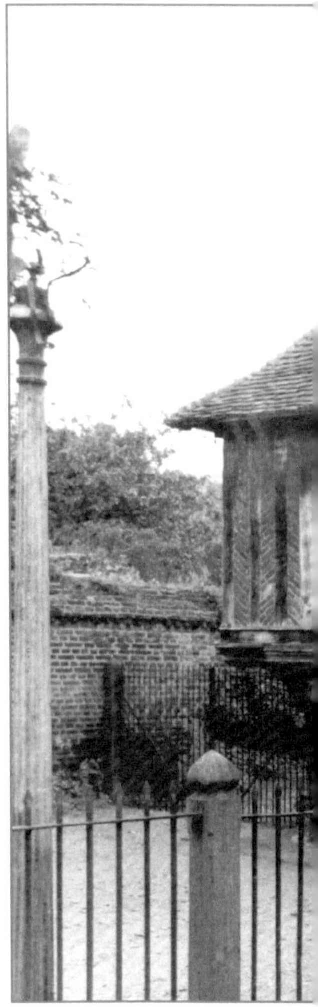

▲ **Fordwich, The Town Hall c1955** F38017
Now a National Trust property and open as a museum, this stone, brick and timber building is said to be the smallest town hall in Britain. It is an ancient structure and needed repairs as early as 1474! Nearby is a ducking stool once used for the punishment of those accused of witchcraft.

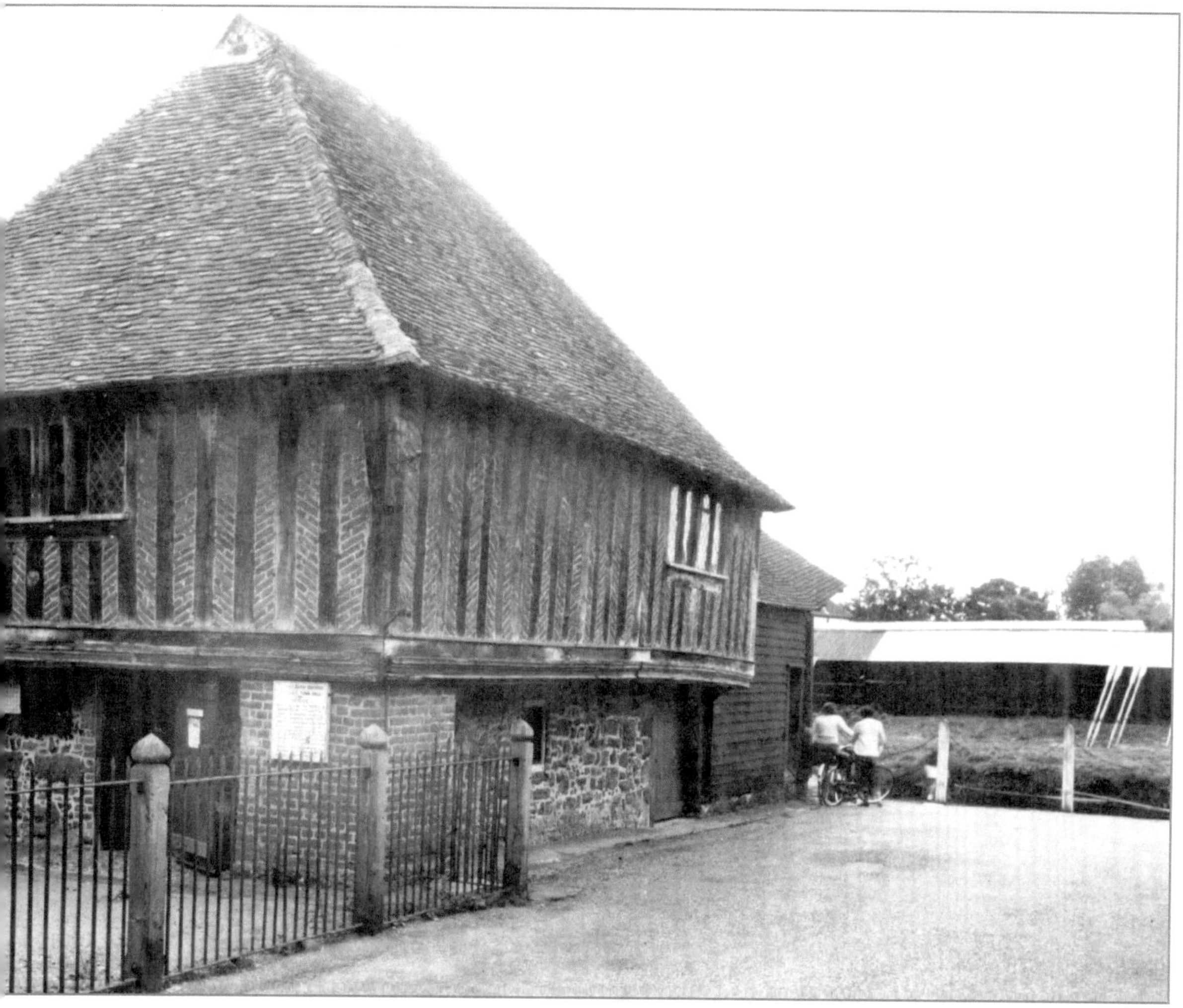

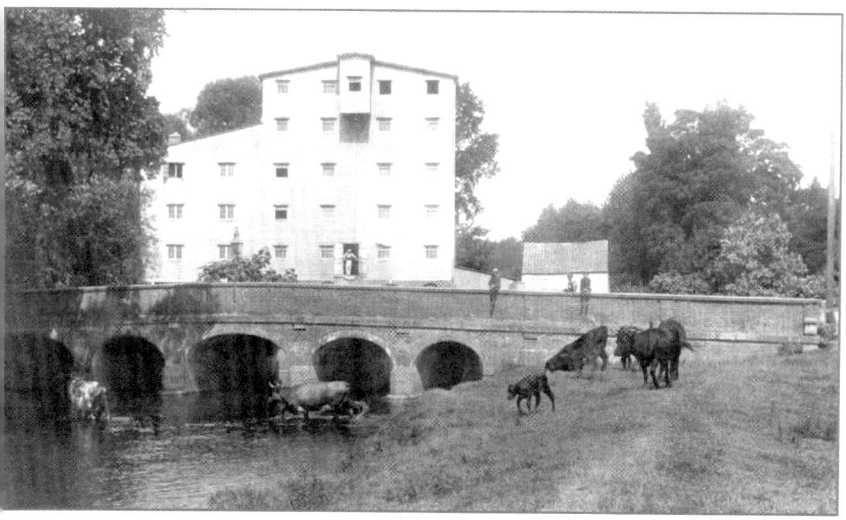

Sturry, The Village 1899
44226
This is a wonderful old view of bygone years, with the old mill, the bridge and longhorn cattle crossing the river. The name Sturry means 'Stour-y', on or by the Stour. The settlement may date back to the earliest Saxon arrivals in Britain.

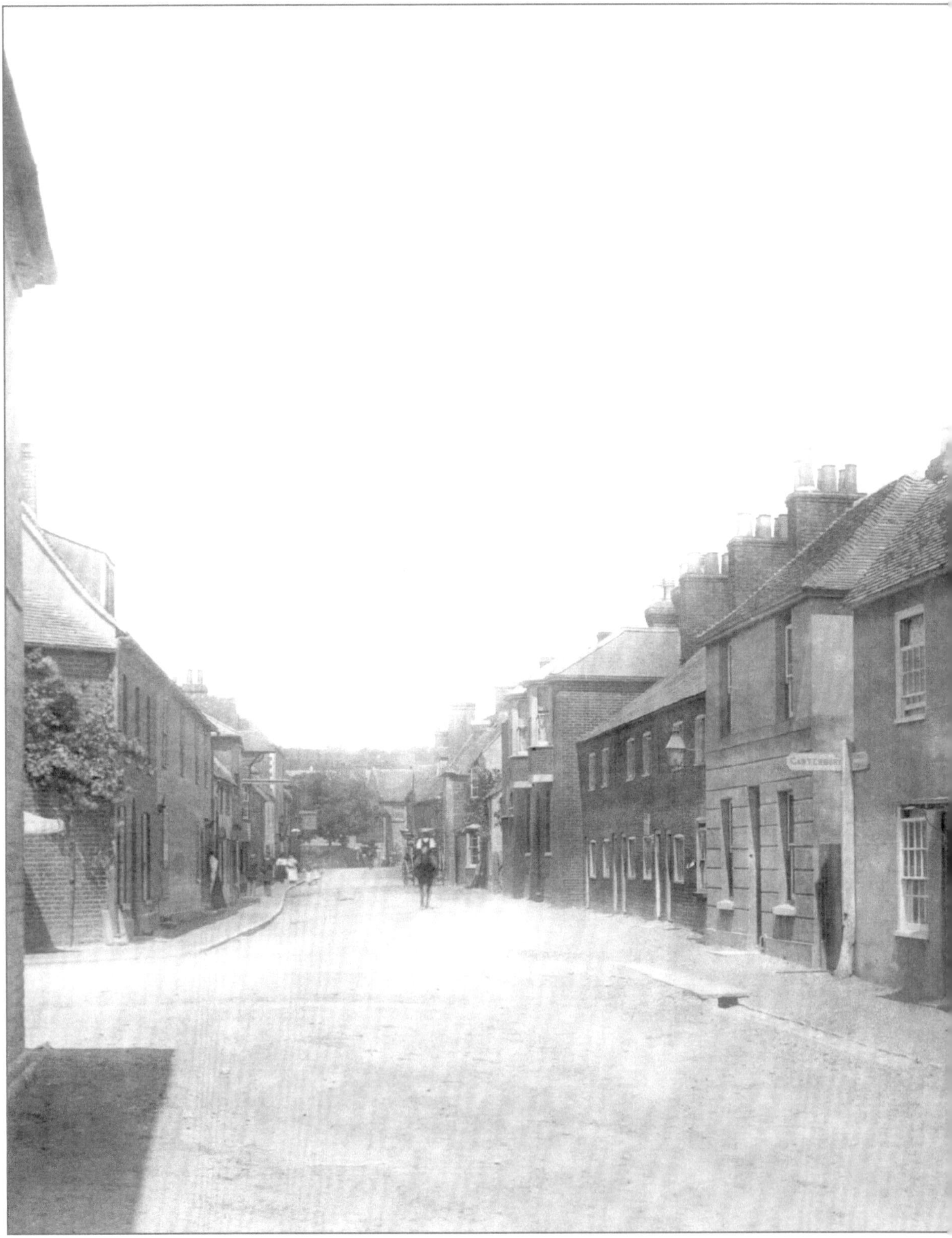

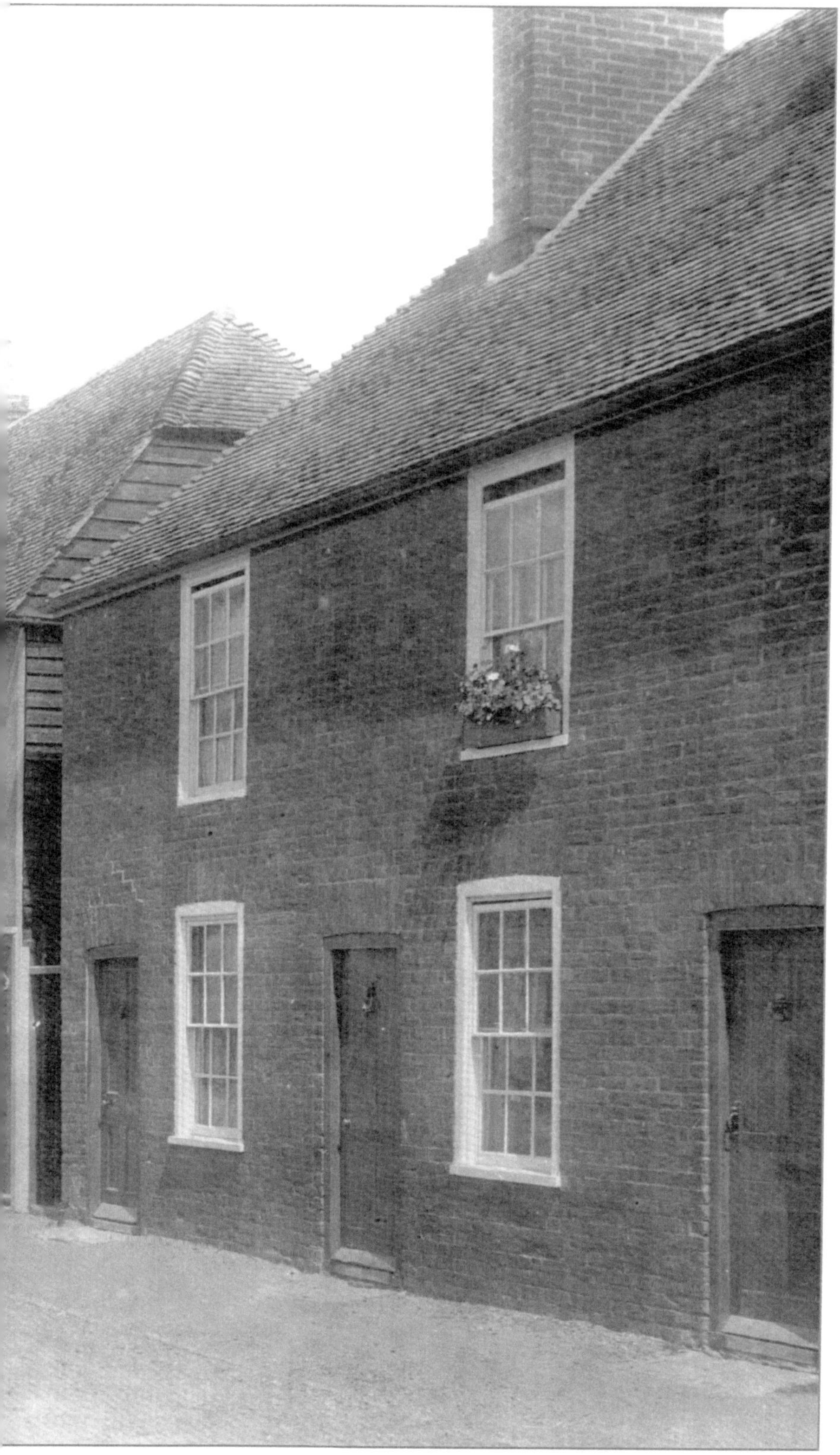

Sturry, The Village 1899 44221

Now on the main road to the North Sea seaside resorts from Canterbury, Sturry was, along with Canterbury itself, bombed heavily during the Second World War. Much rebuilding has occurred since. This is definitely a picture where there have been some changes since the photograph was taken.

▼ **Reculver, The Tower c1950** R14005

Reculver is a popular little seaside town on the coast between the Thanet resorts and Herne Bay. There was once a Roman Saxon Shore Fort here. Its bricks were later used to build the towers we see here, known locally as the 'two sisters' (see Davington). The towers are open to the public, and there is a small interpretation centre about the history and natural history of the area. The pub is the King Ethelbert; it is still there today, though it is now surrounded by amusement arcades, tea and burger vans and a car park.

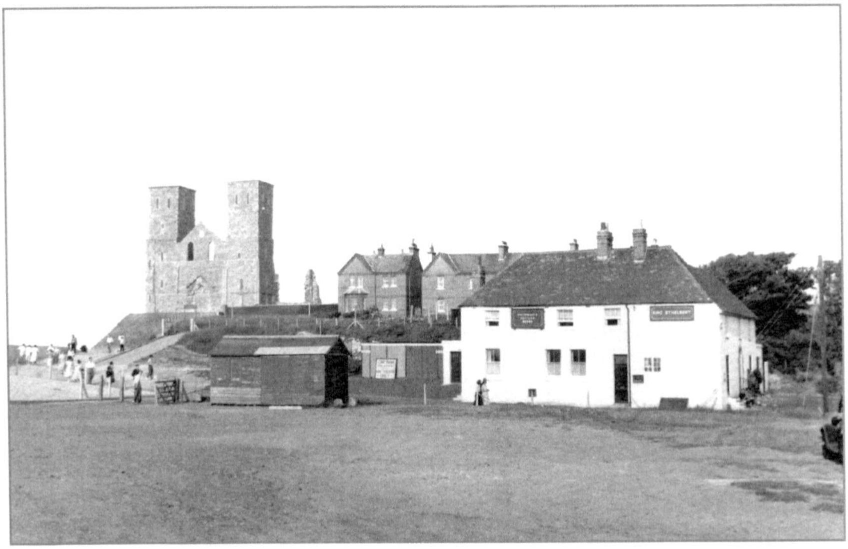

▼ **Ash, The Village c1955** A232014

There are two villages called Ash in Kent. This one lies about three miles from Sandwich. This scene has not changed much since the picture was taken; we may be thankful that a bypass routes most traffic past the village. Ash has a very striking tall-spired church which can be seen for many miles around.

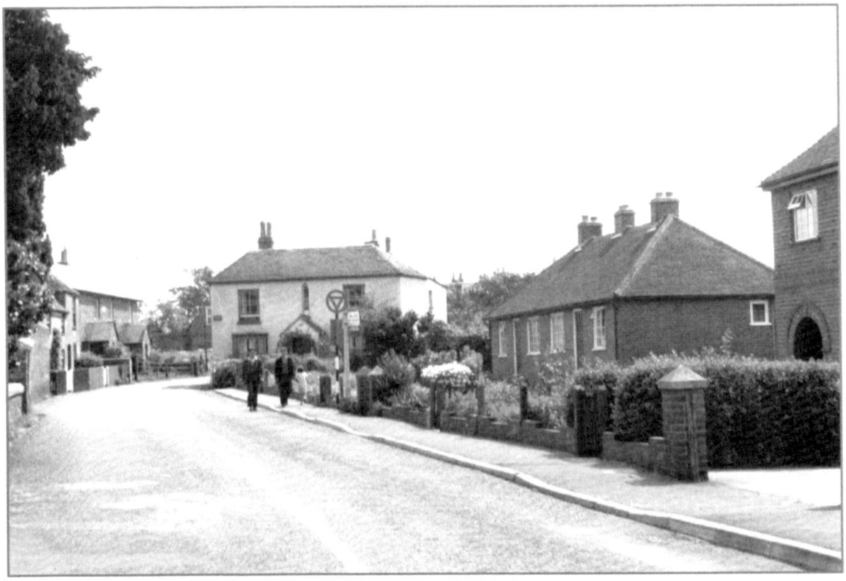

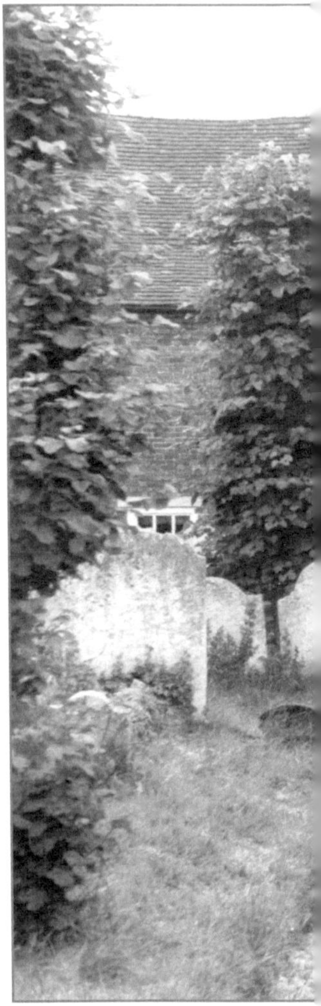

▲ **Ash, The Village c1955** A232031

We are close to the centre of the village. The Ship Inn can be seen on the left. Ash is one of the places in Kent rumoured somewhere to conceal a four-feet-tall effigy of a man in solid gold, a treasure that had belonged to one of the early Saxon Kings, according to legend.

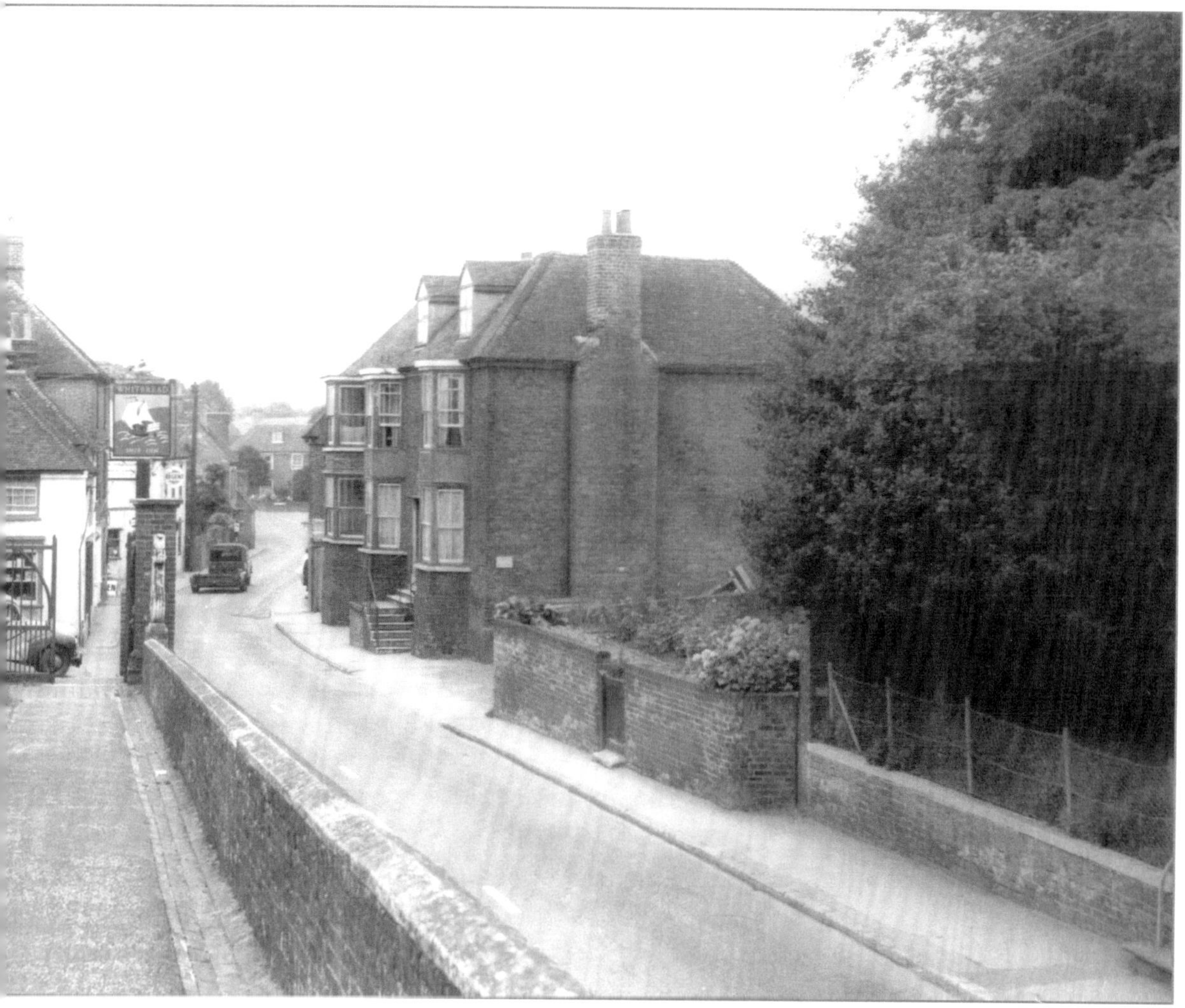

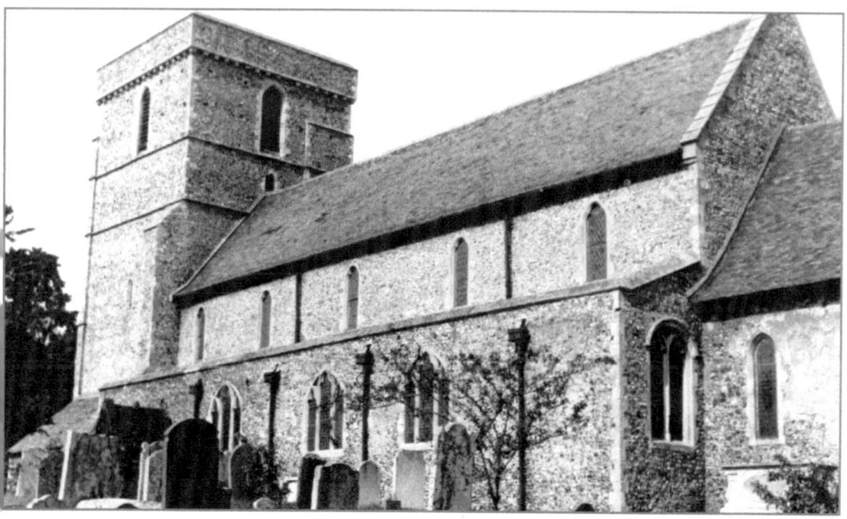

◄ **Eastry, The Church c1965** E154014

This is a large solid church of Early English design with a Norman tower. Nearby was once the royal palace of the early Saxon kings of Kent. There is also an underground labyrinth of caves. Some say these were dug for lime, others that they were excavations by those searching for the legendary 'golden man'. Thomas Becket was said to have hidden in them whilst awaiting a crossing from Sandwich to the continent.

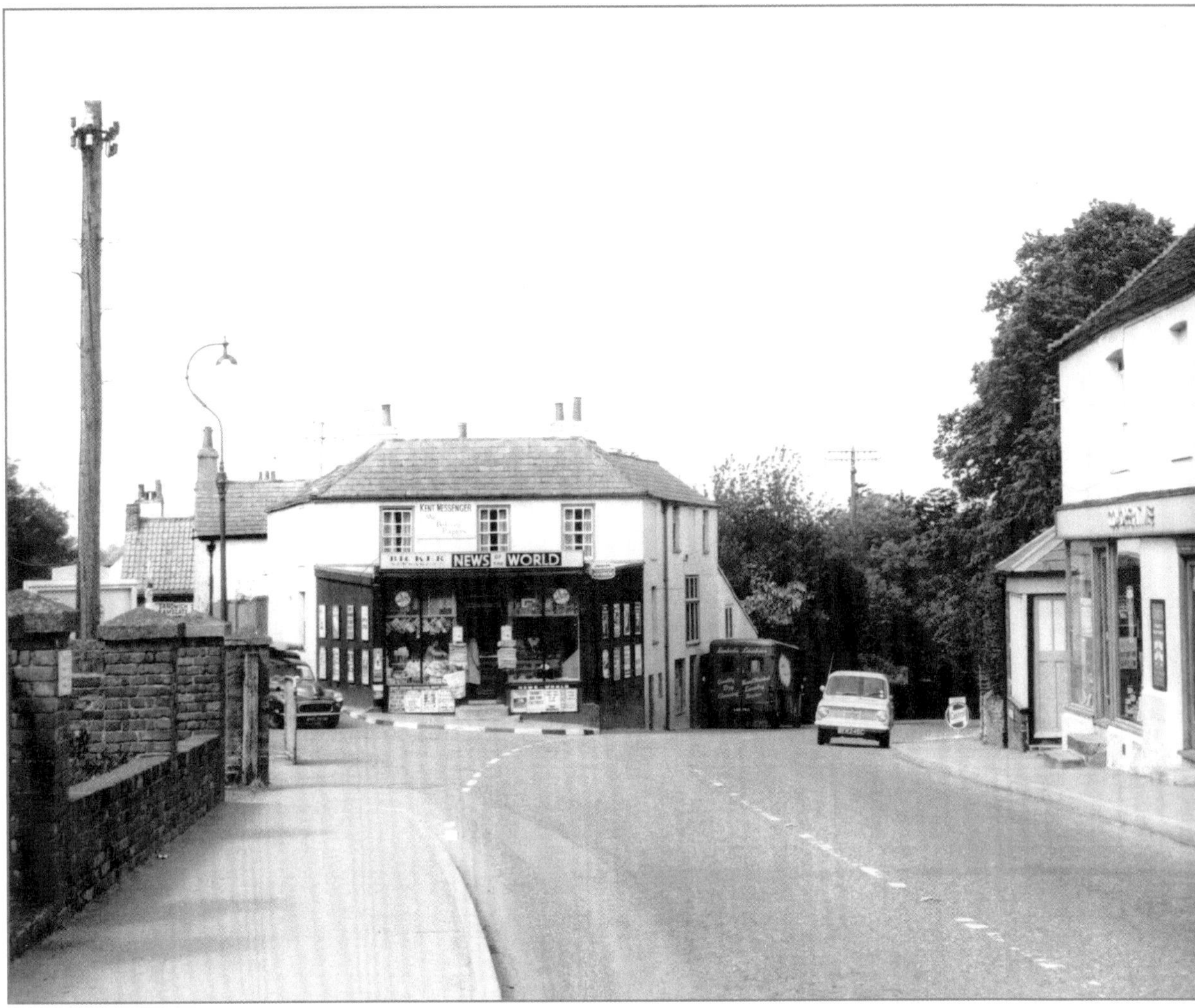

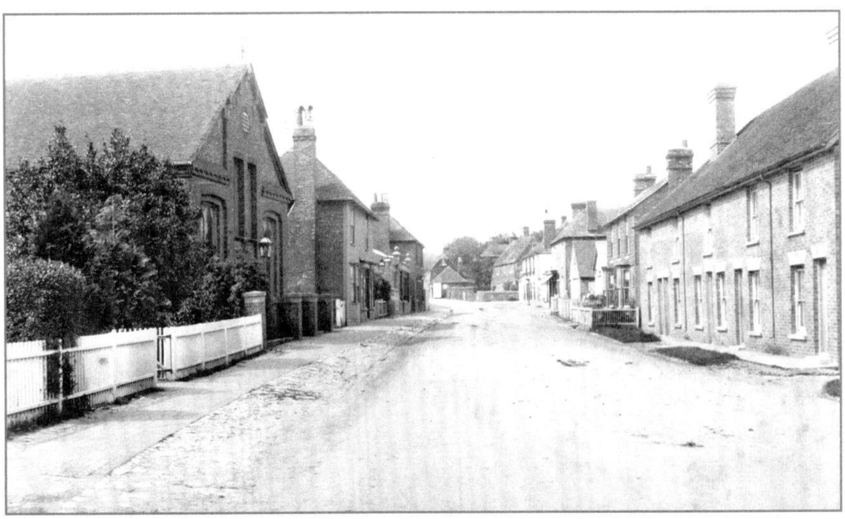

Ham Street
The Village 1909 61575
This village name has caused some amusement locally: a road sign indicates the distance first to Ham, then underneath to Sandwich. Naturally, at first sight the sign just reads Ham Sandwich!

◄ **Eastry, The Village c1965** E154032

We are on the main road to Sandwich. On the right can be seen the Co-operative Store, and on the left Bicker the newsagents. The road off to the left leads to the very ancient village of Woodnesborough ('Woden's barrow'), said to be where the Scandinavian god Woden was buried.

▼ **Frogham, Cottages c1955** F225002

On the high ground between Dover and Canterbury are a number of one-time mining villages; amidst them is the surprisingly attractive hamlet of Frogham, a collection of pretty cottages. It is not even marked on the standard road maps, with the exception of Ordnance Survey of course.

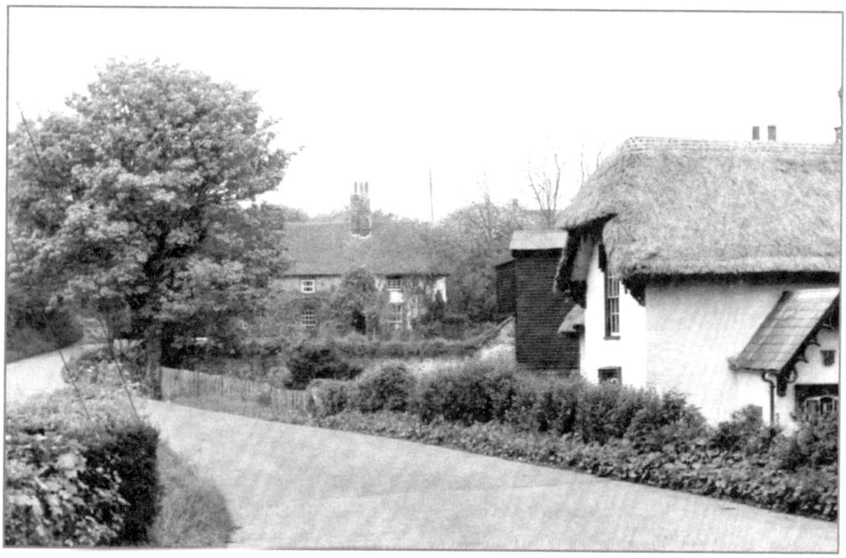

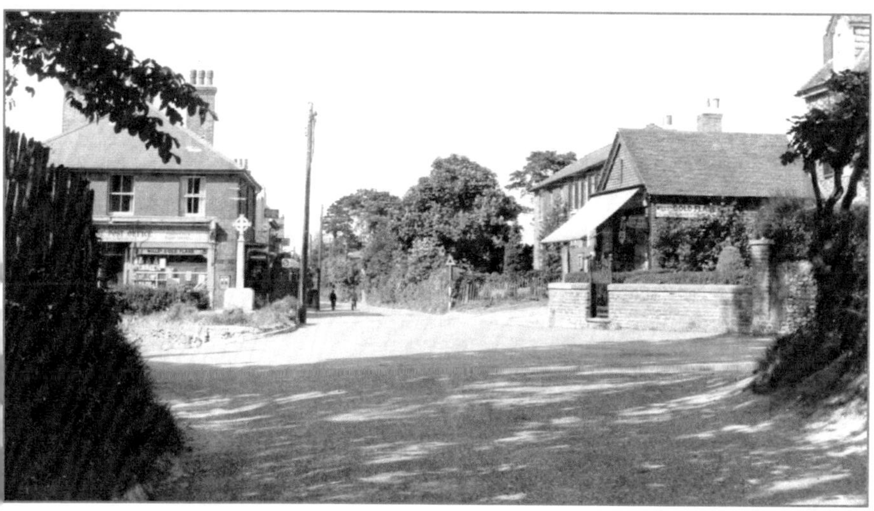

◄ **Eythorne, The Village c1960** E158012

At the time of this photograph, Eythorne was primarily a dormitory for the local coal mines. These have long since been closed, and the village is a rural backwater again. In this picture we can see, the local Post Office on the left; it also carried out electrical and radio servicing.

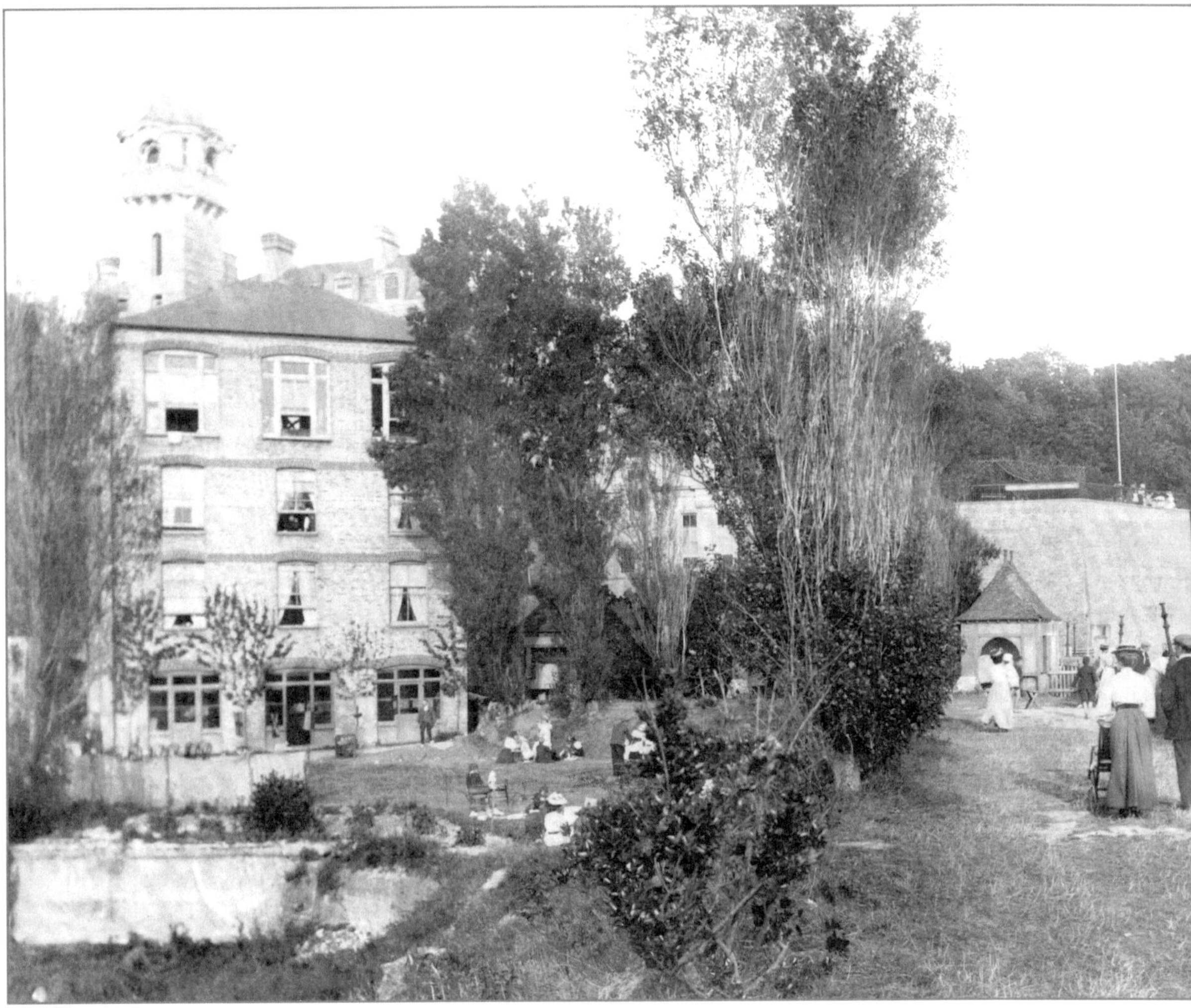

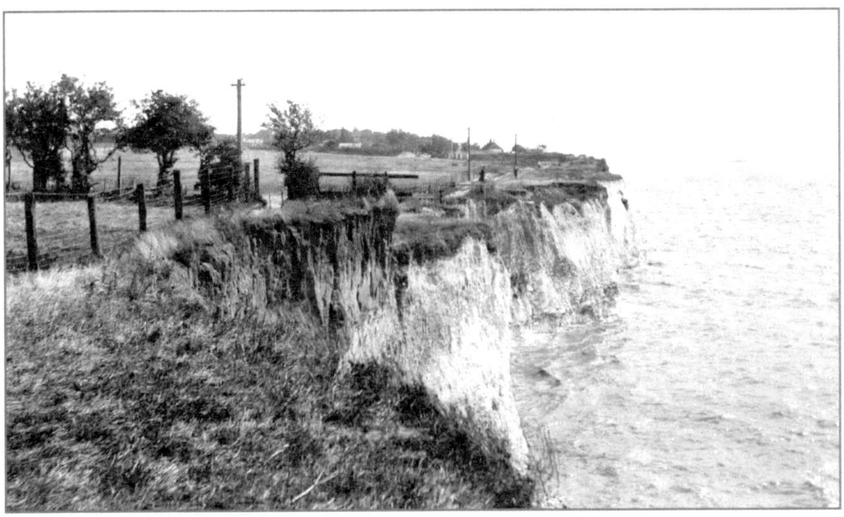

Pegwell, The Cliffs 1918
68476
Here, nearer to Ramsgate, the cliffs become higher and make pleasant walking, though they have become more built-up in recent years. The coast near Pegwell has seen some history. It is said that in 449AD Hengist and Horsa brought the first Saxon settlers to nearby Ebbsfleet. A couple of decades later, according to Geoffrey of Monmouth writing in 1136, King Arthur fought his adversary Modred on this shore.

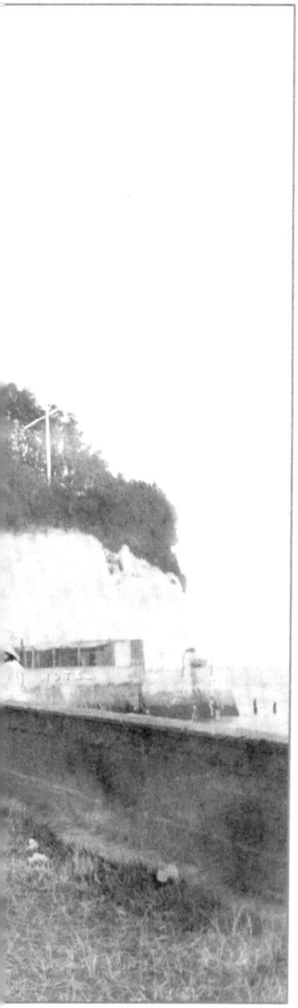

Pegwell Bay 1907 58295

Here we have a wonderful picture of this peaceful seaside resort; the distinctive large hotel on the left is still there. Otherwise, Pegwell Bay has seen some changes. In 1968 it became a hoverport with a cross-channel service. With the demise of the hovercraft service, a noisy go-kart circuit was established. The bay itself, an expanse of salt marsh and sand, has become the domain of ornithologists and bait diggers. The coastline of cliff, estuary, dune and marsh is now a nature reserve.

Ripple, Cottages and the Post Office c1955

R318001

Ripple is only a hamlet, but in the 1950s it still warranted its own Post Office. As we can see, cigarettes, ice creams and cakes were sold as well. No doubt the signs for Lyons and Senior Service will be familiar to many.

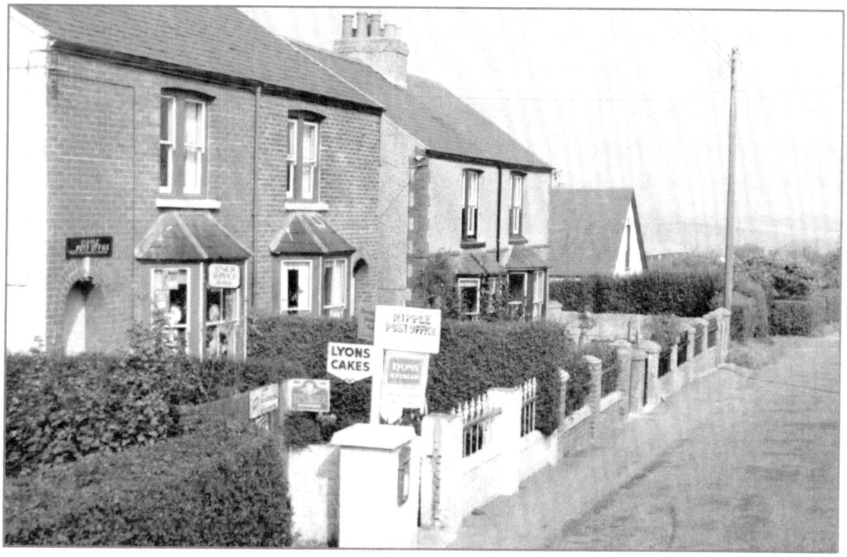

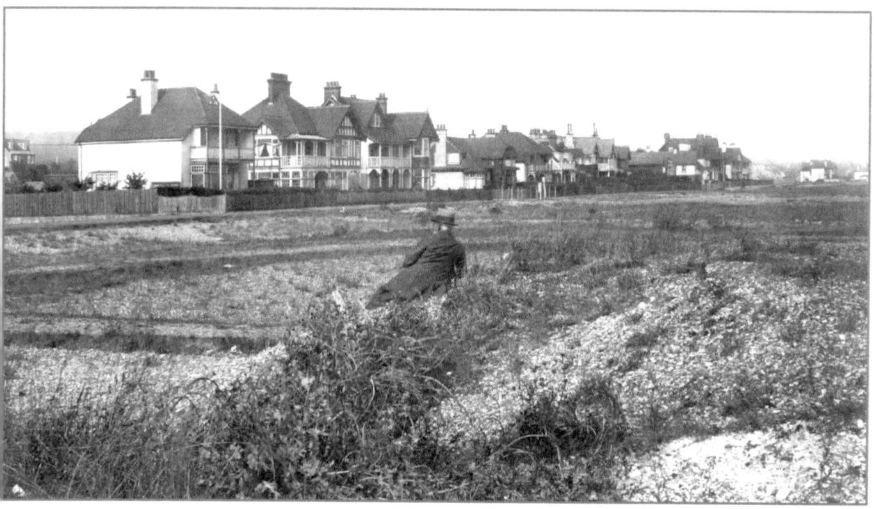

Kingsdown
The Bungalows 1918

68508

Kingsdown stands on the coast where the white cliffs of Dover give way to the extensive shingle beach that runs eastwards to Walmer & Deal. Caesar is said to have landed in this vicinity in 55BC. This view shows the newer part of Kingsdown. A variety of houses and bungalows - some with verandas and balconies - are serviced by a rough shingle track. A gentleman is sheltering from the wind on the shingle bank.

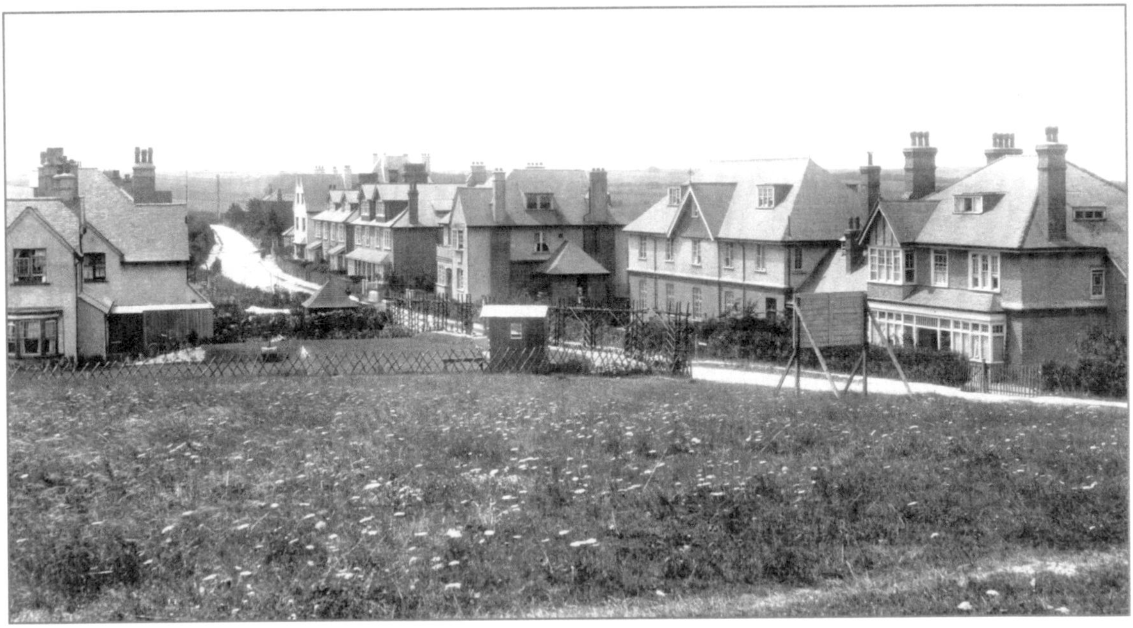

St Margaret's at Cliffe, The Droveway 1908 60346
These large houses stand in an idyllic situation on the cliffs above the Channel overlooking St Margaret's Bay. Since this picture was taken, trees have grown up around the houses, giving shade and an atmosphere of seclusion. An obelisk has also been erected at the end of the road to commemorate the sacrifices of the Dover Patrol during both World Wars.

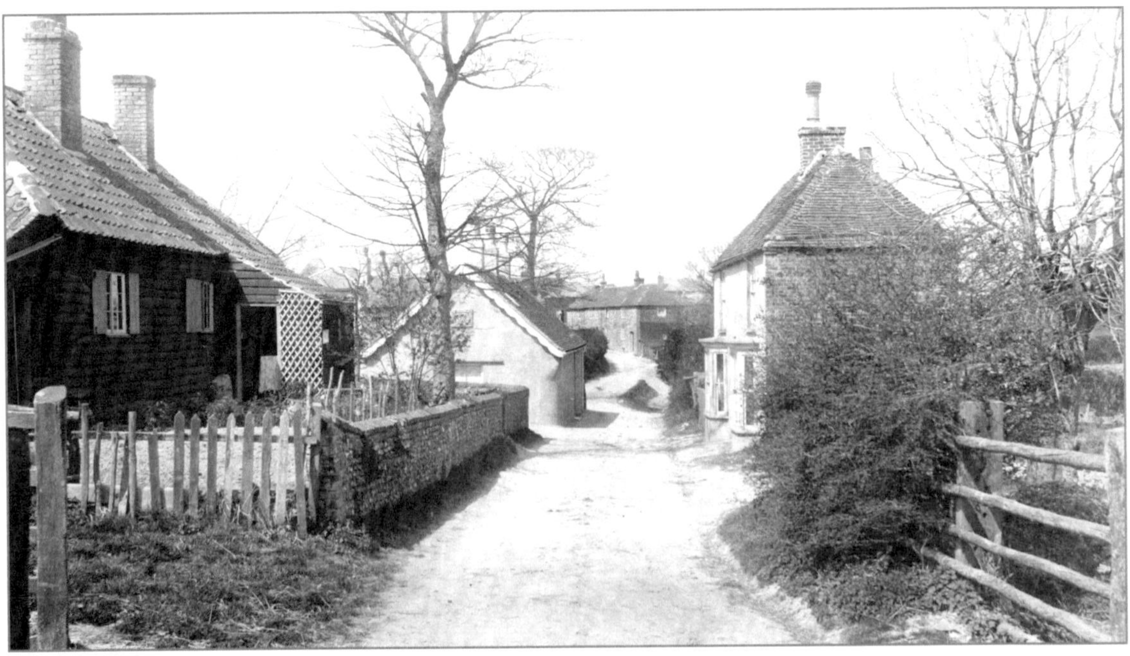

St Margaret's at Cliffe, The Village 1898 40817
A little back from the shore in the older part of the village, we see a rural-looking scene along a dusty, unmetalled road. More recently, St Margaret's was the home of two literary giants, Noel Coward and later Ian Fleming, who rented a house from Coward. It was here that Fleming wrote some of his James Bond novels.

Index

FRITH PRODUCTS & SERVICES

Francis Frith would doubtless be pleased to know that the pioneering publishing venture he started in 1860 still continues today. Over a hundred and forty years later, The Francis Frith Collection continues in the same innovative tradition and is now one of the foremost publishers of vintage photographs in the world. Some of the current activities include:

INTERIOR DECORATION

Today Frith's photographs can be seen framed and as giant wall murals in thousands of pubs, restaurants, hotels, banks, retail stores and other public buildings throughout the country. In every case they enhance the unique local atmosphere of the places they depict and provide reminders of gentler days in an increasingly busy and frenetic world.

PRODUCT PROMOTIONS

Frith products are used by many major companies to promote the sales of their own products or to reinforce their own history and heritage. Frith promotions have been used by Hovis bread, Courage beers, Scots Porage Oats, Colman's mustard, Cadbury's foods, Mellow Birds coffee, Dunhill pipe tobacco, Guinness, and Bulmer's Cider.

GENEALOGY AND FAMILY HISTORY

As the interest in family history and roots grows world-wide, more and more people are turning to Frith's photographs of Great Britain for images of the towns, villages and streets where their ancestors lived; and, of course, photographs of the churches and chapels where their ancestors were christened, married and buried are an essential part of every genealogy tree and family album.

FRITH PRODUCTS

All Frith photographs are available Framed or just as Mounted Prints and Posters (size 23 x 16 inches). These may be ordered from the address below. Other products available are - Address Books, Calendars, Jigsaws, Canvas Prints, Postcards and local and prestige books.

THE INTERNET

Already ninety thousand Frith photographs can be viewed and purchased on the internet through the Frith websites and a myriad of partner sites.

For more detailed information on Frith products, look at this site:
www.francisfrith.com

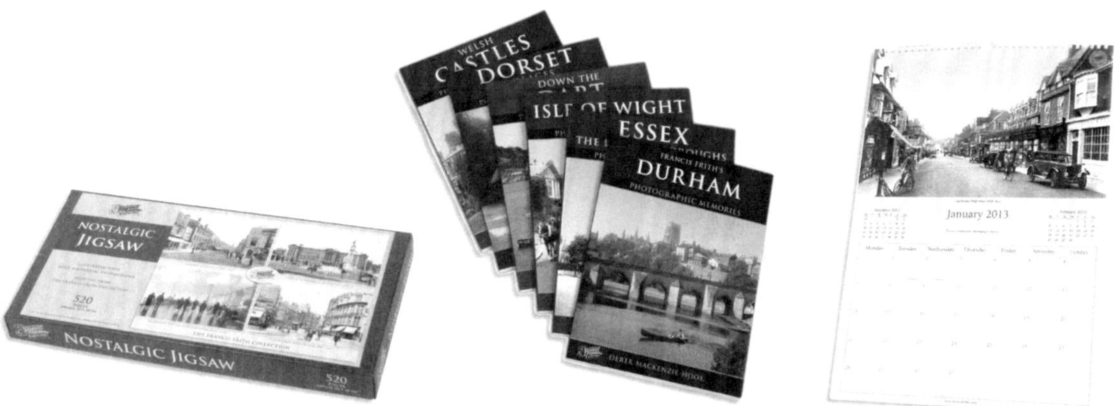

See the complete list of Frith Books at: www.francisfrith.com
This web site is regularly updated with the latest list of publications from The Francis Frith Collection. If you wish to buy books relating to another part of the country that your local bookshop does not stock, you may purchase on-line.

For further information, trade, or author enquiries please contact us at the address below:
The Francis Frith Collection, Unit 6, Oakley Business Park, Wylye Road, Dinton, Wiltshire SP3 5EU.
Tel: +44 (0)1722 716 376 Fax: +44 (0)1722 716 881 Email: sales@francisfrith.co.uk

See Frith products on the internet at www.francisfrith.com

FREE PRINT OF YOUR CHOICE

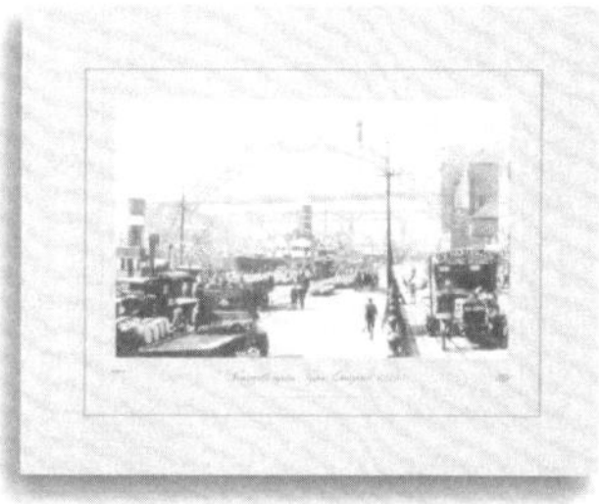

Mounted Print
Overall size 14 x 11 inches (355 x 280mm)

Choose any Frith photograph in this book. Simply complete the Voucher opposite and return it with your remittance for £3.50 (to cover postage and handling) and we will print the photograph of your choice in SEPIA (size 11 x 8 inches) and supply it in a cream mount with a burgundy rule line (overall size 14 x 11 inches). **Please note: aerial photographs and photographs with a reference number starting with a "Z" are not Frith photographs and cannot be supplied under this offer. Offer valid for delivery to one UK address only.**

***PLUS:* Order additional Mounted Prints at HALF PRICE - £9.50 each** (normally £19.00)
If you would like to order more Frith prints from this book, possibly as gifts for friends and family, you can buy them at half price (with no additional postage and handling costs).

***PLUS:* Have your Mounted Prints framed**
For an extra £18.00 per print you can have your mounted print(s) framed in an elegant polished wood and gilt moulding, overall size 16 x 13 inches (no additional postage and handling required).

IMPORTANT!

These special prices are only available if you use this form to order. You must use the ORIGINAL VOUCHER on this page (no copies permitted). We can only despatch to one UK address. This offer cannot be combined with any other offer.

Send completed Voucher form to:
The Francis Frith Collection, Unit 6, Oakley Business Park, Wylye Road, Dinton, Wiltshire SP3 5EU

CHOOSE A PHOTOGRAPH FROM THIS BOOK

Voucher *for **FREE** and Reduced Price Frith Prints*

Please do not photocopy this voucher. Only the original is valid, so please fill it in, cut it out and return it to us with your order.

Picture ref no	Page no	Qty	Mounted @ £9.50	Framed + £18.00	Total Cost £
		1	Free of charge*	£	£
			£9.50	£	£
			£9.50	£	£
			£9.50	£	£
			£9.50	£	£
			£9.50	£	£
Please allow 28 days for delivery.			* Post & handling		£3.50
Offer available to one UK address only			Total Order Cost		£

Title of this book ....
I enclose a cheque/postal order for £ ....
made payable to 'The Francis Frith Collection'

OR please debit my Mastercard / Visa / Maestro card, details below

Card Number:

Issue No (Maestro only): Valid from (Maestro):

Card Security Number: Expires:

Signature:

Name Mr/Mrs/Ms ....

Address ....

....

....

.... Postcode ....

Daytime Tel No ....

Email ....

Valid to 31/12/12

Free Print - see overleaf

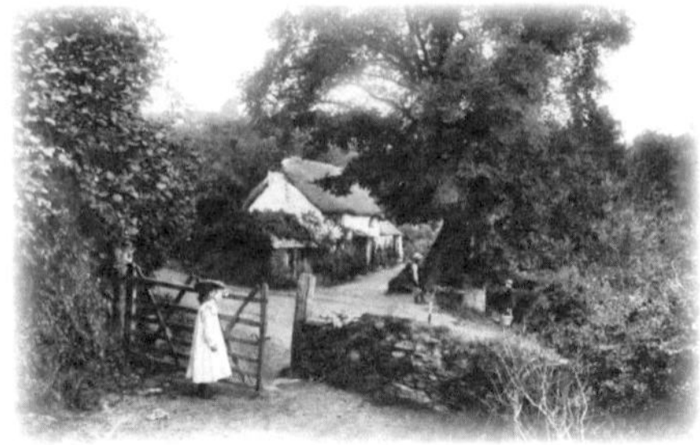

Can you help us with information about any of the Frith photographs in this book?

We are gradually compiling an historical record for each of the photographs in the Frith archive. It is always fascinating to find out the names of the people shown in the pictures, as well as insights into the shops, buildings and other features depicted.

If you recognize anyone in the photographs in this book, or if you have information not already included in the author's caption, do let us know. We would love to hear from you, and will try to publish it in future books or articles.

An Invitation from The Francis Frith Collection to Share Your Memories

The 'Share Your Memories' feature of our website allows members of the public to add personal memories relating to the places featured in our photographs, or comment on others already added. Seeing a place from your past can rekindle forgotten or long held memories. Why not visit the website, find photographs of places you know well and add YOUR story for others to read and enjoy? We would love to hear from you!

www.francisfrith.com/memories

Our production team

Frith books are produced by a small dedicated team at offices near Salisbury. Most have worked with the Frith Collection for many years. All have in common one quality: they have a passion for the Frith Collection.

Frith Books and Gifts

We have a wide range of books and gifts available on our website utilising our photographic archive, many of which can be individually personalised.

www.francisfrith.com

FF006484